More praise for *The Architecture of the Soul:*

"Like an Old Testament prophet in blue jeans, Dr. LaChance speaks in our own language the words we are too busy to hear but urgently need to embrace: that our continuing neglect of the contribution of Nature to the wheel of life is destroying our inner guidance mechanisms. Or as Albert puts it, 'when a species goes extinct, there is a de-structuring of *our own* psyches.' Thus, we slumber on toward individual and collective disintegration. Read this book. Its message is one insightful man's powerful glimpse of two possible futures—one a hell, the other a heaven on earth. We still have time to choose."

—J. PHILLIP JONES, Life Wheel Institute,
Golden Volcano Sanctuary, Hawaii

"*The Architecture of the Soul* is not unlike the healing artworks of the Navajo shamans: A sand painting 'made in beauty' has the power to restore one who has fallen away from a state of beauty to his or her proper, beautiful existence. As such, Dr. LaChance comes to us as a modern day shaman."

—ANGELA MANNO, visual artist and iconographer

THE
Architecture
OF THE
Soul

A Unitive Model
of the Human Person

Albert J. LaChance, Ph.D.

FOREWORD BY PAUL WEISS

North Atlantic Books
Berkeley, California

Published by
North Atlantic Books
P.O. Box 12327
Berkeley, California 94712
www.northatlanticbooks.com

Cover and book design by Susan Quasha
Cover photo by Barbara Leon
Printed in the United States of America
Distributed to the book trade by Publishers Group West

The Architecture of the Soul: A Unitive Model of the Human Person is sponsored by the Society for the Study of Native Arts and Sciences, a nonprofit educational corporation whose goals are to develop an educational and crosscultural perspective linking various scientific, social, and artistic fields; to nurture a holistic view of arts, sciences, humanities, and healing; and to publish and distribute literature on the relationship of mind, body, and nature.

Library of Congress Cataloging-in-Publication Data
LaChance, Albert J.
  The architecture of the soul : a unitive model of the human person / by Albert J. LaChance.
       p. cm.
  Summary: "Presents a comprehensive model for viewing the human person based on integral psychology, which draws upon a wide range of philosophies and disciplines. The model provides a new clinical lens for treating dysfunctions on the individual, community, and planetary levels"—Provided by the publisher.
  Includes bibliographical references (p.   ).
  ISBN 1-55643-602-5 (pbk.)
  1. Psychology—Philosophy. 2. Soul. 3. Human beings. I. Title.
  BF38.L22 2005
  150.19'8—dc22

2005020556

1 2 3 4 5 6 7 UNITED 10 09 08 07 06

This book is dedicated to
Shirley and Brian Wallas,
two of the most generous and decent people
I have been privileged to know.

Permissions

Excerpts from *Human Feelings* by Steven L. Albon, et al, reprinted with the permission of the Analytic Press. Excerpts from *Twelve Steps and Twelve Traditions of Alcoholics Anonymous* reprinted with the permission of Alcoholics Anonymous World Services, Inc. Excerpts from *Dance Therapy and Depth Psychology* by Joan Chodorow reprinted with the permission of the Taylor & Francis Group. Excerpts from *Dawn After Dark* by René Huyghe and Daisaku Ikeda reprinted with the permission of Mrs. René Huyghe and Soka Gakkai. Excerpts from *Life: An Enigma, a Precious Jewel* by Daisaku Ikeda reprinted with the permission of Soka Gakkai, Tokyo. Jung, C. G.; *The Structure and Dynamics of the Psyche,* Vol. 8 of *The Collected Works* © 1960 by Bollingen Foundation, New York, NY. Second edition © 1969 by Princeton University Press. Reprinted by permission of Princeton University Press. Excerpts from *Horse Sense and the Human Heart* by Adele McCormick and Marlena Deborah McCormick reprinted with the permission of Health Communications, Inc. Copyright © 1997 Adele von Rüst McCormick, Ph.D. and Marlena Deborah McCormick, Ph.D. Excerpts from *What Is Life?* by Lynn Margulis, Ph.D. and Dorion Sagan reprinted with permission of Simon & Schuster Adult Publishing Group. Copyright © 1995 by Lynn Margulis and Dorion Sagan. Excerpts from pp. xii, 127, 211–212, 267 of *Care of the Soul* by Thomas Moore reprinted by permission of HarperCollins Publishers. Copyright © 1992 by Thomas Moore. Excerpts from "Space-time: The Final Frontier" by Sten Odenwald, *Sky & Telescope,* February 1996, reproduced with permission of Sky Publishing Corp. Excerpts from *Visions of Caliban* by Dale Peterson and Jane Goodall reprinted by permission of SLL/Sterling Lord Listeristic, Inc. Copyright © 1993 by Dale Peterson and Jane Goodall. Excerpts from *The Voice of the Earth* by Theodore Roszak reprinted by permission of International Creative Management, Inc. Copyright © 1992 by Theodore Roszak. Excerpts and charts from *The Lemur's Legacy* by Robert Jay Russell, copyright © 1993 by Robert Jay Russell. Used by permission of Jeremy P. Tarcher, an imprint of Penguin Group (USA) Inc. Excerpts from *The Rebirth of Nature* by Rupert Sheldrake, copyright © 1991 by Rupert Sheldrake. Used by permission of Bantam Books, a division of Random House, Inc. Excerpts from *Almost Human* by Shirley C. Strum reprinted with the permission of the author. Copyright © 1987 by Shirley C. Strum. Excerpts from *Origins of the Sacred* by Dudley Young, copyright © 1991 by the author and reprinted by permission of St. Martin's Press, LLC.

The author has made every effort to trace the copyright holder of *The Chimpanzees of Gombe* by Jane Goodall. If you have such information, please contact North Atlantic Books.

Contents

Foreword

ALBERT LACHANCE SPEAKS WITH A VOICE that is at once strongly conservative and traditional while also broadly visionary and synthesizing. It is a voice that speaks urgently for the web of life on this planet in a way that seeks to transcend the narrow dualities and frequent hypocrisy on both sides of the moral discourse of our times. In *The Architecture of the Soul* he calls us to an investigative journey that weaves the threads of science, psychology, philosophy, religion, and meta-poetic inspiration into a picture of a living universe—a picture that integrates the "tao of human conduct" with the "tao of evolution" with the "tao of origins." In so doing he seeks to address and awaken in us an awareness of every part of the multi-layered psyche of which he speaks. And he ventures a singular prophetic warning: When we allow the dismantling and the destruction of habitat, ecosystems, and living species, we are actually dismantling or undermining our own psyche.

Buddhism speaks of the interpenetrating net of reality: that all things reflect and include everything else. And as such all things nourish everything else. For us as conscious beings to see the world as alive, and our responsibility for feeding and nourishing it as primary, is the mark of human maturity. What are the consequences of the modern infantile notion that we can deaden the world and then freely feed off its plate? Or that the prevailing impulse of our economic activity, which dominates our political and cultural activity, and colonizes our own psyche, is one of exploitation and degradation rather than of caring and sustenance and the promotion of the diversities of life?

Buddhism aside, our most indigenous earth wisdom teaches us that he who hunts the deer is also within the deer, is made of the deer, and also must restore the deer. How many ways are there to say it: The whole creation is the body of the Mother, the body of Christ, the body of the Deer. And our psyche—our soul—is not other than that. Albert spells it out.

Paul Weiss
Mount Desert Island
Union River Watershed

Acknowledgments

I would like first of all to acknowledge the patience and support I have received throughout this project from my wife Carol and my daughters Rebecca and Kateri. There were seven years during which the research and writing of this book made demands on me which limited my presence emotionally and spiritually to them. Throughout those years they remained faithful and supportive, encouraging me day by day. I thank them from the bottom of my heart.

I want to thank Paul Weiss and Richard Grossinger for their openness and willingness to believe in the importance of this model of the human person. I want also to thank Kevin Sharp and the other members of my faculty during the doctoral program that resulted in this book. I want to thank Phillip Jones and the laughter that is his soul. I would be remiss if I didn't thank my brother-in-law Andrew Wallas for his financial help and friendship during the years I spent studying with Thomas Berry. That foundation in the mid-eighties enabled this later work to be accomplished. And of course I thank my great teachers Thomas Berry and Brian Swimme. So too, I thank Matthew Fox for the early inspiration that supported my journey of exploration into this work.

But there is still one person for whom a very special note of gratitude must be made. Carl Golden showed up in my life at a time when I needed one person who could help me with the research and writing of this book. Carl's contribution to this book has in fact made this book possible. During the time that this model of the human person was being constructed, it was Carl who carried the burden of the research with me. He had the cosmological, geological, theological, and psychological vocabulary necessary to fully grasp the intent of this project. He insisted that I spend a year reading Ken Wilber.

He found this project to be as exciting as I did. And then, when the prospect for publishing this project was in jeopardy because of its enormous size as a doctoral thesis, Carl was able, with incredible language skills, to edit the manuscript down to one-third its original size. Without Carl Golden, this book would not be in your hands at this moment. While it doesn't feel adequate, I nonetheless feel the need to say "Thank you."

Introduction

"WE'RE LOST!" Those two words are the most important we can utter to ourselves if we are ever to be found. They are the true prerequisites to being found. We must begin by admitting that we are lost. We must admit that, for whatever reasons, our maps have been inadequate, our judgments mistaken, our assumptions flawed. It doesn't help to blame each other. Each of us has had our share in the present confusion, as have most of those who have preceded us. In any case we're lost, and as I see it, we've been in denial of being lost for a very long time. While I understand that it is the human condition to live in some fear, doubt, and insecurity, it really does seem that the problems we are facing are different by orders of magnitude than those faced in the past. At the same time, the very supports that we would have used in the past in order to cope with these feelings—the family, religion, an intrinsic relationship to the created order—are themselves threatening to disintegrate altogether.

We seem to lack satisfying answers to our individual dilemmas. The number of suicides continues to rise. The number of us who are becoming addicts of one sort or another continues to rise as well. In the end, suicide and addiction are the same phenomenon; addiction is simply destroying oneself more slowly. Divorce rates are above 50 percent and have been there, or higher, for decades. Divorce has become an institution. Because we are so accustomed to divorce, we tend to forget that our children are torn in half by our failure each and every time we divorce. You ask, "Do I need another book about the pathological nature of life in the western world?" My answer to you is "No," if that book is just another catalogue of woes. We are all woeful enough. If, however, you were given a whole new way to frame reality, ourselves, the plants and animals, the planet, the cosmos, and God, frame them in a unitive vision that could be used by all healing disciplines to lead us from being lost to being found, would you read on?

Eliade wrote "Life cannot be repaired, it can only be recreated" (Chodorow, 1991, p. 107). When we're lost we become dependent on someone who might not be lost, who might be looking for the way home for us. If Eliade is correct in saying that life must be recreated—and I believe he is—then we must allow the Creator to find and recreate us, the other life forms, Earth, and cosmos, and even our way of understanding the Creator! But two things are required of us. The first has already been mentioned: we must clearly admit to ourselves and to each other that we are lost and that if we depend on our own resources—whether personal, cultural, or biological—we cannot and will not find our way. Second, we must attain a yielded will, individually and collectively.

A Yielded Will

It is precisely our own thinking and will that have brought us into addiction. Surely, unchanged thinking and an unyielded will would not be the best tools to lead us out. Similarly, it has been our own confusion that has brought us to whatever this unhappy impasse is that we are presently experiencing. Will we continue to depend on the same confusion? They will bring us to madness and death if we do. What we need, what is called for, is a yielded will and a new Mind with which to think. The latter is born of the former. It is the Mind of the Creator.

A yielded will is a will that experiences its contingency upon a much larger, much wiser, and more elegant Will—the Will of the Creator. A yielded will is empty of a selfish agenda; consequently, it is empty of deluded arrogance. Arrogance is premised upon the delusion that one is self-existing, which is absurd. This is like a flea jumping up and down on an elephant's back denying the existence of elephants! A yielded will, on the other hand, is able to feel and intuit a much larger intelligence, the Mind of its Source or Creator. As one becomes more adept at feeling and intuiting this Source, one is eventually able to think by means of that Source. One's brain thus becomes the receiving instrument for this much more profound level of thought, which I have named Sourcepsyche.

Information vs. Transformation

Sourcepsyche is the presence of the Mind of the Creator. Evolution is the history of the Creator's being. While Sourcepsyche, or God, exists independently of space/time, space/time does not exist independently of Sourcepsyche. Space/time is the emanation and presence of Sourcepsyche. The galaxies, the planets, life, human culture, and our own "interiority," along with the interiority of every being, can trace their very existence to Sourcepsyche. The existence of Sourcepsyche cannot be proven; it can only be felt and intuited. It cannot be proven if the very existence of a cosmos, an Earth, a life community, and ourselves are not sufficient proof. None of these are proof enough to an unyielded will. Thus, deluded arrogance. As the will is yielded, on the other hand, we begin to understand that the whole cosmos, Earth, the whole living community and culture clearly exhibit the presence of Mind. Every major religious system known witnesses to the presence of that Mind by one name or another. But what if the cosmos, Earth, and culture are also the actual presuppositions upon which human instinct, feeling, and thought rest? Put another way, what if the whole cosmic process—its order, its creativity, and its Source—are the deeper layers of the human psyche, both individually and culturally? I don't mean this symbolically in the way C. G. Jung meant it in his theory of the archetypes as representations of earlier life forms inherited by us in the fabric of our psyches. What I suggest (and cannot ultimately prove) is that the actual living community of beings, i.e., the evolving Earth and the expanding cosmos, *are* the living and dynamic deeper layers of all humans' psyches. If this is so, then when a species goes extinct there is a destructuring of our own psyches. If we allow the same species to evolve, we are allowing the ongoing restructuring and evolution of the human psyche.

If we stop to think about it, we realize that it is the actual sea and the living community of the seas that support all life within the seas. When the actual sea is polluted, when the actual sea loses keystone species, it is then that the seas themselves suffer devolution. It is the actual community of the forests that supports the emergence of new species as well as new individuals within them. It is the actual pond that supports aquatic wildlife, the actual community of the air and the actual air itself that supports that community of life.

So it is with us humans. The combined contributions of the communities of soil, water, and air support us physically and mentally. When we disassemble those communities, we do so at our own peril. When we allow them their creativity, all of us benefit. How can we expect to repair human consciousness and its collective dimension—culture— when we continue to disassemble the deeper layers of our psyches? In that question lies, I believe, the key to healing a large portion of our collective suffering, the "socially shared hallucinations … our collusive madness" that, according to Laing, is "what we call sanity" (Roszak, 1992, p. 55).

Ours is a very scary time. Sometimes the present seems to be too much for us. Most of us feel overwhelmed and experience alternatively symptoms of both anxiety and depression. We can temporarily cool the anxiety with alcohol or with benzodiazepines such as Librium and Valium and we can lift some symptoms of depression with mood elevators such as Prozac or Zoloft. But to ease symptoms is not to cure. If the problem lies in the disassembling of the deeper layers of our psyches, then treating symptoms only prevents us from hearing what the symptoms are trying to tell us. We must face the reality we've created if we are to find our way through to something better. We can run to prescription, chemical, behavioral, consumer, or religious addictions, but all of these only rob us of creativity and ultimately deepen our dilemma, our despair, and our anxiety. If—and I grant you that it's a large *if*—nature is a deeper layer of our psyche, living, functional, dynamic nature, then to disassemble it is to condemn ourselves to epidemic madness. Many of us believe that we are already there. The question is: How much further shall we proceed? To quote Anthony Stevens: "The unconscious is nature, but we have to confront its contents if we are to become conscious of them" (Stevens, 1993, p. 34). The question becomes: How do we do that?

Our awareness is assaulted over and over again each day with horrors, such as the incident at Columbine High School and ethnic cleansing in Kosovo. Every newscast brings the madness to us until we finally stop watching the news. Women and children butchered by their husbands or boyfriends. Sexual crimes leave us stunned and breathless, though not without engendering a certain fascination with the gore. Another public servant is caught peddling the big lie. Those interrogating him will become tomorrow's headlines for similar crimes. A person nominated to sit upon the supreme bench of justice blatantly lies to us in order to get into office. We are left knowing that our final appeal for justice might be presided over by liars. Our representatives sell us out. Multi-millionaire sports figures charge children for an autograph! Another huckster is dragged kicking and screaming, lying and denying, from office, to be replaced by yet another. Tankers split open and pristine areas of the planet are smeared with oil. Wildlife perishes. The courses of rivers are altered. Forests are uprooted. Frogs die around the world and no one knows why. All amphibians represent the link between terrestrial and aquatic life forms. What does it mean to lose that link? No one knows. Could amphibians represent the linkage between the right and left hemispheres of the human brain, or between some crucial phases in ontogenesis? The atmosphere frays, and ozone holes appear. Families fray. Children who survive their parents' "choices" are moved from relationship to relationship like suitcases. There are genocides, bombings, rapes, and starvation in the midst of gluttony. Millions of abortions are performed, while rhetoric on the "religious" right is polarized with rhetoric on the "feminist" and liberal left. The fraying legal establishment cannot long contain the multiple tumors of our pathologies. When we come out of our denial, we know that something is dreadfully wrong. We know that we cannot "fix" it, so we collude with the insanity. Daily life makes this necessary. We continue to try to address the problem in consciousness while we disassemble the deeper layers of the unconscious. We need a personality model that includes the cognitive cortex and all that goes into creating and supporting it. *The Architecture of the Soul* is my attempt at that model.

A Fraying Culture on a Fraying Planet

"The asphyxiation faced by our civilization is one of morality, sensitivity, and the spirit" (Huyghe and Ikeda, 1991, p. 96). If Huyghe and Ikeda are correct in stating that our problems are moral, and have to do with sensitivity and spirit, then it must follow that our answers must address the questions of morality, sensitivity, and spirituality. Some physicists are scandalized by any talk of God as Source of the universe. They make it clear that "they have no need for that hypothesis." They prefer to assert that the universe popped into being by accident, by mistake, by what Ken Wilber humorously calls "oops." As Wilber points out, there are those who would like us to think that they have some special insight into this incomprehensible beginning out of nothing. If true, then they occupy the seat of God. But do they understand any more than we do? If the universe came into being by accident, then who had the accident?

I like to remember that even Jean Paul Sartre, after a life dedicated to atheism, recanted to his girlfriend on his deathbed. There has to be an intelligent and creative Source. We know it and cannot avoid it because that very Sourcepsyche is the depth of our own. To deny it, we must deny the depths of our own psyches. I will suggest in this book that this is exactly what is happening in us.

Sourcepsyche has three phases. The first is its transcendent or pre-existent phase. The second is its existent phase, and the third is its emergent phase. Out of pre-existence came the fireball. Out of the fireball, the existent phase, came the first atoms, galaxies, and stars. Out of the

Milky Way galaxy came the sun and planets and among these, our Earth. From Earth came early life forms, and then the reptiles, the mammals, and primates. We, being the self-reflexive tip of the whole process, represent the emergent phase. From us, culture has emerged with its major phases, the tribal, the Neolithic, the great religious cultures, and, if we are to survive, the present emerging ecological age. All around us in what consists of the present age, the air, water, soil, microbes, insects, animals, plants, humans, and our cultures, we can observe the emergent phase of Sourcepsyche. In Christ, in Krishna, and perhaps in many others, the pre-existent phase of Sourcepsyche became incarnate, or existent, as the emergent phase of Sourcepsyche in order to remind us of who we really are! In its emergent phase, Sourcepsyche wants to heal the planet.

Murdering the Biosphere

> Sick souls may indeed be the fruit of sick families and sick societies; but what, in turn, is the measure of sickness for society as a whole? While many criteria might be nominated, there surely ranks above all others the species that destroys its own habitat in pursuit of false values, in willful ignorance of what it does, is "mad" if the word means anything. (Roszak, 1992, p. 68)

Imagine this: I go to a doctor because I slipped with a linoleum knife and cut a nasty gash in my thumb. But even as the doctor is stitching my thumb, I produce the knife from my pocket and slice my forearm open! The good doctor is dismayed, but as he rushes to close the cut in my forearm, I scream, "A ha ha!" and cut open my abdomen! The nurses are frantic now, trying to keep my intestines from falling out. As they're doing so I scream, "Long live Vincent!" as I cut my ear off! Then I slice my thigh in half, and, finally, I cut my throat. The doctors and nurses begin to see that they are helpless. I am in need of something more than medical care! Clearly I am delusional and if I remain in my delusional state I'll win! I'll kill myself! In the same way that the science of medicine cannot save me if I am suffering from a deeper suicidal delusion, so the science of ecology cannot save our species if we don't treat our deeper problem. I suggest that we will continue in the creation of the Culture of Death as long as we refuse to allow Sourcepsyche to heal us. As the planet frays, so will the culture.

The pre-existent God gave birth to a cosmos, which then evolved from galaxy, to planet, to life, to Mind. As we disassemble planet and life, we disassemble the supports for Mind. We are finding ourselves collectively and epidemically mad, but seem unable to hear the advice of the emergent God speaking in those who have yielded their wills. That advice can be found in all scriptural traditions from the tribal to the present emergent religions, such as B'ahai. If we continue to ignore the advice, we may be forced to watch as the natural community of life continues to unravel, and with it, our own sanity. Neither psychology nor ecopsychology will heal us either. We must be in conscious contact with our Source. We need a unitive psychology if we are to heal the architecture of our souls. We need a psychology unitive to matter, mind, and mystery.

When I say "myself," of whom am I speaking? Am I the fifty-year-old gent who is writing these words? Am I the father of these two girls? Am I the husband of this woman? Am I the master of these two dogs wrestling in those autumn leaves? Am I an expression of New Hampshire, her beautiful hills and forests? Her proud, stubborn libertarian bent? Am I an expression of New England, her air, water, soils, and her elegant subculture, embryo of the United States? Am I the Northeast bioregion, shared with southeastern Canada? Am I Canada with a name like LaChance? Am I North America? The Earth? The Sun? The Milky Way? The universe? The Source? I am all of these, and I'd do well to remember that. My story is the story of time and time's eternal and infinite Source. My story is the story of matter and its timeless and infinite Source. This is the architecture of my soul.

A Layered Brain and a Layered Self

We need a model of who we are if we are ever to understand and become who we are. *The Architecture of the Soul* provides that model. The ocean is layered. Soils are layered. Rocks are layered. The atmosphere is layered. Rainbows are layered. Gravitational fields are layered. Skin is layered. When a rocket leaves Earth's field it will pass through discernible zones of attraction that will lessen as the rocket's distance from Earth's center of gravity increases. When we fly through the atmosphere in a plane, we go through successive layers or envelopes of air until we reach the thinnest layers toward the ozone. We feel no barriers between these atmospheric or gravitational layers because there are none. Still, there are layers. If we dive in a submarine, we encounter no barriers between oceanic layers, because there are none. Still, there are layers. We dive through different layers of pond water when swimming, reaching colder layers as we go down. No barriers, but layers. The same is true with rocks and soils. Like the rest of Earth, I am holding that our selves are layered. Who knows how many subtle layers there are in the human mind? The brain with which I speak about this is itself layered! There's the outer cognitive cortex, the older mammal brain or limbic system, and the oldest or reptilian brain, the seat of primary life functions. These ideas are not new. As Anthony Stevens confirms, Carl Jung was investigating this phenomenon of the triune brain even before it was proposed:

> … although Paul MacLean proposed his concept of the triune brain several years after Jung's death, Jung had already anticipated it, maintaining that dreams about mammals or reptiles related to phylogenetically ancient mammalian and reptilian structures in the brain and were expressions of the deepest intentions of nature itself. "The evolutionary stratification of the psyche," wrote Jung, "is clearly more discernible in the dream than in the conscious mind. In the dream, the psyche speaks in images, and gives expression

to instincts, which derive from the most primitive levels of nature." (Stevens, 1993, p. 41)

Julian Jaynes emphatically states the need for naming a layered psyche:

> What we need is a paleontology of consciousness, in which we can discern stratum by stratum how this metaphored world we call subjective consciousness was built up and under what particular social pressures. (Jaynes, 1976)

In the following model, I have articulated what I believe to be the major zones of the psyche and their major sub-layers:

Zone One: Primary Awareness

Layer 1: The Cognitive Subpsyche
Layer 2: The Affective Subpsyche
Layer 3: The Instinctual Subpsyche

Zone Two: Secondary Awareness

Layer 1: The Personal Subpsyche
Layer 2: The Familial Subpsyche
Layer 3: The Cultural Subpsyche

Zone Three: Tertiary Awareness

Layer 1: The Trans-Primate Psyche
Layer 2: The Trans-Mammalian Psyche
Layer 3: The Trans-Organic Psyche
Layer 4: The Pre-Organic Psyche
Layer 5: The Temporal Cosmological Psyche
Layer 6: The Pre-Temporal Cosmological Psyche

Consciousness: Primary Awareness

The three layers of Zone One, Primary Awareness, are held loosely, without hard and fast boundaries. They fit within and reflect the three major layers in the triune brain model. That is, what I am calling the Cognitive Subpsyche, the first layer, has as its major seat or center the neo-mammalian or outer cortex of the brain. The main feature of this psychic layer is self-reflexive thought. Again, the layer is permeable in that other animals clearly think and there is much evidence that chimpanzees can think self-reflexively. That is, they can hold themselves as an object of thought. Animals do not think in the way and to the depth and complexity of humans. Not only are we able to think about ourselves, we are able to think about thinking itself. No other living being that we are aware of has created a philosophy or a psychology.

Humans also think about feelings. It is clear that other animals feel emotions. Primates and mammals certainly, but there are rudiments of affect in other animals as well. Bees seem to have the ability to "love" certain keepers and to sting others. Behaviorists will have difficulty with the word *love,* but it really does seem to me from what I've read that, like us, they seem to "warm up" to some and feel cool toward others. Why should not completely different animals sharing a common biosphere share the energy of love that permeates that biosphere? No one can convince me that my golden retriever worshipping at my feet does not love me. Nature does seem to conserve and use the same things and energies for vastly different purposes. It is the level and complexity of human feelings that seem to be what separates us from other species. Only humans write sonnets. Only humans can detest entire classes of other people and animals. Only humans could write a *Mein Kampf.* In the human brain, as with the other mammals, these feelings are experienced in the paleomammalian cortex, the second cortex of the brain in from the skull. I have called the equivalent psychic layer the Affective Subpsyche. In the first layer, the layer of the Cognitive Subpsyche, we are aware of thought. In the Affective Subpsyche we are aware of feeling and emotion.

Still deeper within our brains lies the brain stem. The equivalent psychic layer is the Instinctual Subpsyche. In this layer we become aware of instincts that come to us not only from primate mammalian evolution generally, but from even earlier life forms such as the amphibians, reptiles, fish—indeed, all chordates to some extent. We experience instincts through intuition. We have a feeling experience of them in the affective layer and think about them in the cognitive layer. We have powerful instinctual experiences when we experience sexual jealousy, when others violate our children, when thieves invade our territory or home, when we are envious, when we are threatened in war, or on the street, or by hunger. They are primitive wisdoms we have received from the whole evolutionary event. We are armed with them from conception.

The longing for mystical union, which is the only valid reason for religious practice, is a product of instinct. The ancients had a feel for this mysticism and a feel for the mind of all beings, animate and inanimate. As Carsun Chang, writing about sixteenth-century Chinese idealist philosopher Wang Yang-Ming, herself says:

> Wang Yang-Ming's premise is the intelligibility of the world. Intuitive knowledge is not restricted to mankind but extends to all animate beings and even to inanimate beings. "Man's intuitive knowledge," Wang said, "is shared by grass and trees, stones and tiles. Grass and trees, stones and tiles could not function if they did not possess the capacity to know. The universe itself would be incapable of 'running' or operating, if it were not for man's intuitive knowledge." (Chang, 1962, p. 14)

We ritualize our instincts in religious symbolism and practice. Because these psychic energies are deeper than language, we dance them, we paint them, we make music with them and ultimately, they bring us to our knees before mysteries too profound to comprehend. Religion is the cultural equivalent of instinctual behavior in animals. Just as insects and birds as well as mammals ritualize their instinctive drives in mating rituals, humans create religious rituals through which to marry. The animals seem to be almost completely involuntarily coded to these behaviors. Our own behaviors around sex and marriage are equally coded to emerge in the evolution of cultural-religious systems. They are not free! We can choose to override them through the use of cognitive consciousness, wherein we can override the deeper signals coming to us from the organism. But when we do so, we do so at our own peril. To deny our religions is to deny our own governing mechanisms. At the point that we practice that denial, we can speak of moral or instinctual disorders. For now, we need to say this: The voice of the Cognitive Subpsyche is thought. The voice of the Affective Subpsyche is feeling. The voice of the Instinctual Subpsyche is intuition. But where do they come from?

Going Deeper: Secondary Awareness

We think about things the way we do because we have thought about them that way before. A sudden change in our thinking represents growth, enlightenment—a "paradigm shift" or conversion. Behavior, thought, feeling, and instinct can all be habitual. As we think, feel, and intuit day after day, year after year, we begin at some point to find certain of our thoughts and feelings to be painful, or incompatible with our view of ourselves as a person. Or we might begin to think and feel in ways that are not sanctioned by our family or culture. When this happens, we often begin a process known as repression. To repress is to push out of Primary Awareness. The contents thus pushed from Primary Awareness into the lower layer of consciousness form a semiconscious layer called the Personal Subpsyche. This is the storehouse of memories where layer after layer of our individual life experience is recorded. Not only events are stored here, but the pain, love, joy, and sorrow associated with these events are stored as well. Thus, if I remember something pleasant, pleasant feelings float into my awareness and experience. If, on the other hand, I remember something painful, pain will accompany the memory.

Before we even have a choice, we think in ways that our families have thought. Born and raised in a Ku Klux Klan family, we will have certain feelings about blacks, will think certain thoughts about them before we can even articulate those thoughts and feelings. Being born and raised in the family of Martin Luther King, Jr., will presuppose a very different set of feelings, thoughts, and behaviors. Our thinking is to a great extent shaped by our families. The paradigm of our thought is the paradigm of our family's thought life, and it was formed before we were conceived. As we grow into feeling and thought, both will move down the "canals" of that formatting.

Families are embedded in cultures, and cultures are coded systems of thought, feeling, and behavior that provide a basic shape to the family. Cultures provide us with stories that create guidelines around the "right" and "wrong" ways to think and do things. They are the underlying assumptions that mold our instincts, feelings, thoughts, and behaviors. Ask any native people why they do the rituals they do, and they'll answer that it has been done this way throughout time since the gods gave these insights to their ancestors.

In a sense, our families are "scripted" with the cultural story; then, in their turn, our families script our instinctual, affective, and cognitive voices. To have no family story is to be missing a layer in the architecture of our souls. To have no cultural story is to be without the scripting that enables us to have a successful family. Families are subplots in the cultural story and we are subplots in our family story.

These three layers then—the Personal Subpsyche, the Familial Subpsyche, and the Cultural Sub-Psyche—together comprise the zone of Secondary Awareness. I shall repeat again and again that while we are talking "as if" these zones and their sub-layers are discrete, they are not. There are no barriers between them. So to be "below" Primary Awareness does not mean "unavailable to" Primary Awareness. Secondary Awareness is available to Primary Awareness through feeling. Once we feel the content present in the Secondary Zone, we can then reflect upon or think about that feeling. When this happens, we remember! In doing so, we can "get a handle" on contents that might not have presented themselves to Primary Awareness for years, decades, and, some would say, lifetimes. When we have brought content from Secondary to Primary Awareness we can examine it and integrate it into our primary reality or dismiss it, provided we have felt the whole feeling charge it contains. Painful feelings left in Secondary Awareness can again create another neurotic state.

So, let me review what I am proposing thus far. The zone of Primary Awareness comprises three layers: the Cognitive Subpsyche, the Affective Subpsyche, and the Instinctual Subpsyche. They contain present experience of thought, feeling, and instinct. The longer the gap is between thinking a certain thought or performing a certain behavior, the more likely that thought or feeling or behavior will "sink" out of Primary Awareness and into Secondary Awareness. Thus, we speak of being "rusty" at a certain job skill. Being "rusty" is the experience of losing content from Primary to Secondary Awareness. Primary Awareness contents are affected by the contents present in my Secondary Awareness. This zone comprises my Personal Subpsyche, my Familial Subpsyche, and my Cultural Subpsyche.

Contained in the Personal Subpsyche is the history of my thinking from conception to the present. My thoughts about myself, others, my culture, the world about me, and even my thoughts about God are all recorded or formatted here. Recorded also are the feelings attendant to each of the above. In the Familial Subpsyche are present the structures of my thinking received in daily interaction with my family of origin. These structures are the underlying presuppositions of my thinking, my feeling, and my instincts. From the Cultural Subpsyche I inherit the structures of thought, feeling, and instinct that have gone into the shaping of my family life. The Cultural Subpsyche might force me to live with unwinnable conflicts such as a Constitution that holds that "All are created equal" and a lived experience that includes slavery, sexism, abortion, and genocide. These conflicts create pathological states that I then feel in Primary Awareness. I must either deal with them or deny them. Denial creates still more repression.

The record of our personal growth and maturity can be measured by the extent to which we have become aware of paradigmatic assumptions in our thinking, which come from our own habituated thought processes, our familial assumptions, and our cultural assumptions. If we have allowed them to be examined and confronted by Primary Awareness, i.e., made them conscious, we have the ability to formulate our own responses to them. In other words, we can individuate or become ourselves. Until we have done so, we are slaves to the formatting, both good and bad, that has been passed onto us in the architecture of our souls. It is important to remember that the entire Secondary Awareness zone exercises a profound influence upon Primary Awareness, whether we are asleep or awake. To integrate the layers of the secondary zone into Primary Awareness is to expand consciousness to exactly that extent. Therapy or counseling has up until now worked in these two zones, helping us to examine our thinking, feeling, intuitions, repressions, families, and cultures. Presently, we must go a lot further if we wish to survive as a species and as a planet.

And Deeper Still: Tertiary Awareness

Up until now, we have not departed from the field of psychology as we know it presently. It concerns itself with cognitive, affective, and, while it doesn't name them as such, instinctual disorders. Further, it goes into how family systems work and pays some attention to cultural differences between individuals, especially where those differences affect the therapeutic experience. Now, as we enter what I am calling the zone of Tertiary Awareness, we are entering the fields of ecopsychology and transpersonal psychology. The six general layers of the tertiary zone are the Trans-Primate Psyche, the Trans-Mammalian Psyche, the Trans-Organic Psyche, the Pre-Organic Psyche, the Temporal Cosmological Psyche, and the Pre-Temporal Cosmological Psyche. The Trans-Primate Psyche is that collective psyche we receive from, and share with, our cousins the chimps and other pre-human primate types. Especially in chimps, with whom we share a nearly total common genetic code, there is even a rudimentary cognitive cortex that allows for a limited ability to self-reflect and to use language. Reason is clearly present to some degree, and many scientists are saying that chimps must be considered as early humans, or humans must be considered a very recent and highly evolved chimpanzee! Thus, some insight into ourselves, into our thoughts, feelings, and instincts can be gained by understanding these pre-human primates. Because they share in so much of the architecture of our souls, we must ask serious and sustained questions about their existence and functioning. Do they embody the supporting psychic structures of humans? Does the elimination of them by poaching and by encroachments on their habitat amputate living structures of our own minds? At first this sounds impossible in that we are accustomed to thinking about ourselves as separate and autonomous members of the life community, self-contained within our skins. But if we are not, then what are we doing when we eliminate these species of living beings?

Again, I am not only concerned with those similarities that are passed on morphogenetically, genetically, or as inherited structures of our psyches and cultures. Those are certainly important to consider and we shall. My question is more frightening. What if the actual living community of primates carries the living supports for our own psyches? What if the ape families we are eliminating embody the psychic tissue, the pre-conscious supports for our own consciousness? I cannot prove that they do. But just the question makes us all want to talk to Jane Goodall ASAP! What if they carry a concentrated point of mammalian evolution that has taken up into itself and embodied all earlier life forms back to and including the most rudimentary life forms of the planet? Even the prokaryotic forms and even the planetary matrix itself, both material and psychic, from which life arose? What if they carry in the living members of their tribes, the support for our imaginations, our fascination with the night sky, for sunrise, for other life forms? What if they carry, embody, and support our fascination with the moon? Over millions of years primates have stared at it from trees, perhaps passing on to us their dreams of going there and the psychic energy to do so. What if they are the pre-conscious source of our religious sensibilities? Could their disappearance be the deeper cause of the loss of our religious imagination or the disappearance of our cultures?

In a recent film, *Instinct*, starring Anthony Hopkins, the main character describes his sense of being watched over by the silver-back gorilla, the leader of the band of primates with whom he lived for a period of time. In describing this experience, it is clear that for him it was a supreme moment of spirituality, the feeling that he was being cared for and protected by a larger being. Later in the movie the silver-back gives his life in an attempt to protect the Hopkins character and the troop. Perhaps this sense of the primate troop has been passed to us, and gives us an inherited sense of God the Father watching over the human family. Is this powerful spiritual creature, the silver-back, something we can afford to lose? Would it be helpful for us to imagine God as a silver-back gorilla watching over the human family?

An even broader and more general layer of our minds that contains and provides the context for the primate layer is the mammalian layer, which I am calling the Trans-Mammalian Psyche. In the mammals, both aquatic as well as terrestrial, we see a mirror of our own affective psyches. All mammals share the experience of having lived in the body of another. We all know the sound of another's heart beating from within. We have all journeyed through the whole living memory of evolution, beginning as single cells and then moving through all the phases of life on earth, from aquatic and in the case of all terrestrial mammals, through the whole event of terrestrial evolution. We have all experienced the closeness of sucking and touch. We share the experience of entry or of being entered bodily for the purpose of biogenesis. We share the pleasure of fleshiness, of bodily warmth. In the mammals we can see the architecture of our own propensity for caring, compassion, tenderness, and love. We see the beginnings of our own sense of humor, clearly present in the primates but also in dolphins and dogs and many other mammals, aquatic as well as terrestrial. We see the beginnings of joy, anger, jealousy, lust, and other very human attributes.

We see trust and loyalty, tickling and petting. In the mammals we see our own shared mammalian nature!

This is not a new idea because all indigenous cultures around the world recognize the fundamental soulful and psychic relationship humans have with the animal world. However, the modern and post-modern worlds disavowed this relationship until Carl Jung, the father of depth psychology, reasserted our rich connection to the animals. So, once again, the question is begged: What if the living mammalian species provide the direct source and support for our own emotional architecture? What if the withdrawal of our own desire, even our ability, to bear and raise our young, and our ability to love our children enough to allow them to be born, is dying along with the other mammalian species? What if our ability to be fully concerned for and present to our children's needs, concerned enough to work out our marriages, is being compromised? Can we be concerned enough to forgive each other's weakness and to stop pretending that we are shocked when we see them in each other as though any of us is the great uncommon exception to the weaknesses that characterize all of us? What if our own ability to make families (I'm going to use the word *family* as a verb defined as the making of families, thus, I family, you family, we family, and so on) is disappearing with the disappearance of our mammalian psychic matrix? If the ability to breed is carried genetically and the ability to form families is not, then are we losing our ability to family? Are we forgetting how to family? Are we disassembling the very structures of our affective psyches as we disassemble the communities of mammals?

Deeper still in our Tertiary Awareness exists the Trans-Organic Psyche. This layer includes the whole evolutionary event from the amphibians and reptiles "down" to the earliest unicellular life forms. One of the goals of unitive psychology is to draw the wisdom of this Trans-Organic Psyche into the level of awareness I am calling Primary Awareness. Up until now these deeper layers have truly been unconscious, i.e., out of our awareness. For two hundred or so years, in the West at least, we have tried to live as though these simpler life forms are of no importance to us whatsoever. I suggest that our instincts and our instinctual psyches are directly dependent on the existence and functioning of these earlier forms.

From the reptiles we inherit our brain stems; reptiles inherited them from even earlier chordates. The instinctual inheritance of this layer is territoriality and even more primitive instincts, such as hunger and thirst. Similarly, our deepest, most fundamental physical functions, such as breathing and heartbeat, are similarly stored deep inside our brains. Included in the Trans-Organic Psyche are birds from whom we receive much that fires our imaginations. Ideas such as grace, nobility, flight, and other ideas that we associate with beauty are gifts of the birds. When birds disappear, so do the stimuli that evoke these feelings in our shared psyches.

As we continue to go backward in time and evolution, we arrive at the Earth's mind, her ability to bring forth life from her mineral, water, and atmospheric base in the first place. This layer of Tertiary Awareness is the Pre-Organic Psyche, the Spiritus Mundi, the creative pressure in matter itself that caused living forms to become. If there is a global formatting or shape to the Pre-Organic Psyche, a basic patterning or way in which the Earthmind brings forth life and supports its evolution, then we have to wonder what we do to our own minds, totally dependent as they are on all previous minds, when we alter, impair, or altogether impede the functioning of the Pre-Organic mind. Are the roots of cancer or schizophrenia to be found in interrupted sequences of patterning in the Pre-Organic mind? What sorts of organic, instinctual, affective, and cognitive disorders arise from our distortion of the primary planetary imagination or creativity? When we destroy or alter the planetary architecture by ruining forests, wetlands, oceans, and soil systems—the basic format for bio-creativity generally—are we setting the stage for subsequent breakdown in the physical and psychic functioning of mammals, primates, and ourselves? The truth is, we don't know what we are doing when we alter the deep dynamisms of planetary functioning! We haven't really even begun to ask these questions, let alone know what the answers are!

The source and context for the Pre-Organic Psyche is the Temporal Cosmological Psyche, the layer beneath it in Tertiary Awareness. The Temporal Cosmological Psyche is the intelligence, the creativity, and order out of which the Sun and planets emerged and evolve. It took ten billion years of creativity on the part of the cosmos for a planet so complex and beautiful to emerge. For a planet capable of life to emerge! The "knowing" that is intrinsic to matter and energy since the beginning had to develop for all that time until it was able to "know" a planet like Earth into being. The Temporal Cosmological Psyche, then, is that potential on the part of the cosmos to bring forth Earth. Because life emerged from the dynamics of the planet, this "knowing" or Mind is the basis for all of life, is the immediate Source of life as well as its support.

We are left, then, with the next question. What of the ten billion years of "knowing" that engendered the cosmos, supported its expansion and evolution from energy to elementary particles, to atoms, to molecules, to stars and planets, to life, and to mind? The Pre-Temporal Cosmological Psyche is explainable only as the Mind or Knowing of the Source, of God. We can go on trying to create ideas and words to avoid the notion of a creative Source out of which the cosmos came to be. But, because our minds rebel at an "oops universe," we are by force led to the conclusion that our own minds have the same Source as the cosmos that brought us forth! Our minds search restlessly until they rest in the knowledge of their Source—God. Our intuitions, our feelings, and our thoughts all lead to the Source of everything! And because we are this Mind, we can come to know this Mind in the deep architecture of our souls. This Mind *is* the architect of our souls! Our empirical minds can only come to empirical truths. But the most profound levels of our minds are pre-empirical, pre-temporal, pre-spatial—and we can only say we know ourselves when we know ourselves there. The Tao that is namable *is not* the eternal Tao. We can know the unnamable Tao in the profundity of our own being. Contemplation is the only research program open to us in these areas. But the evidence of this research is plentiful enough if we just search the literature of the world's great religious traditions—and *if we repeat the experiments ourselves!*

Through contemplation we can "see" over the horizon of time and space. We can come to know God, to know Paradise, and to know that we live in God and that to live in God is to live in Paradise. When we awaken to this, we awaken to the full architecture of our souls, because God is the Source and architect of our souls. God is! When we destroy the handiwork of God, which is the entire cosmos, we destroy the architecture of our own body and psyche. We condemn ourselves to sickness and to madness. When we co-create, co-sustain with God, we allow God to regenerate the architecture, the fabric of our psyche. Before us are life and death, sanity and madness. The choice of direction is ours and ours alone.

CHAPTER ONE

The Cognitive Subpsyche

We are only capable of understanding a universe in which beings capable of understanding it could evolve. The only kind of universe that is understandable is one that is able to evolve beings capable of understanding it. (Roszak, 1992, p. 120)

Others say it their own way:

C. H. Waddington points to a "congruity between our apparatus for acquiring knowledge and the nature of the things known" and suggests that the human mind "has been shaped precisely to fit the character of those things with which it has to make contact." Konrad Lorenz goes still further. He notes that the way we experience the outside world, and indeed the "a priori" forms of intuition, are "organic functions based on physical and even mechanical structures of our senses and of the nervous system" and these "have been adapted by millions of years of evolution." Jean Piaget goes so far as to say that our cognitive functions are an extension of organic regulations and must be seen as differentiated organs for regulating our relationship with the external world, which must therefore clearly serve the ends of human life. (Goldsmith, 1993, p. 72)

THIS CHAPTER IS ABOUT THE MYSTERY OF THOUGHT. Even as we think about thought, the thoughts we utilize to do so are themselves a mystery to us. We don't know what a thought is, and yet we know that we think. Humans exhibit what I call Primary Awareness, which is the ability to experience signals from ourselves and from our environment and to then contemplate these signals as objects of awareness. In other words, we can contemplate thoughts, feelings, instincts and physical sensory impressions. In common parlance, this contemplative ability is known as cognition. However, I am calling this contemplative ability Primary Awareness, not because it came first, but because it is most obvious to us in our own experiences of the world. Most animals experience what I am calling Secondary Awareness—they experience thoughts and feelings but cannot experience them as an object of contemplation. The lower animals, plants, and even the minerals of the planet and cosmos experience what I call Tertiary Awareness, which is simple reaction to environmental change and external stimuli. However, humans are unique in that they can experience all three forms of awareness in themselves.

My thesis for this chapter is that the mystery of thought itself is a function of the whole life community. To substantially disrupt the community of life may well mean that in doing so we disorder thought. It should then come as no surprise that we experience various kinds of thought disorders. As Wilber said:

> And precisely because [cognition] exists in this new and wider world, the conceptual mind can repress and dissociate its lower impulses. That is, precisely because the noosphere transcends the biosphere, it can not only transcend and include, it can repress and distort and deny. Not just differentiate, but dissociate. Both individually and at large. Individually, neurosis; at large, ecological crisis. (Wilber, 1996, p. 169)

The first time I came across the term "noosphere" was in the work of Teilhard de Chardin. It was said to mean the envelope of human thought as a planetary structure, used like the terms "hydrosphere," "atmosphere," and "biosphere."

We must all learn to intentionally integrate the three levels of awareness if we are to survive. In doing so, we shall individually and collectively awaken to a radically profound truth that the noosphere and biosphere are inextricably part of one continuum of consciousness. In fact, I believe that Jung was pointing to this:

> Psyche and matter are "two different aspects of one and the same thing" (Jung, 1947, p. 215). "It seems highly probable that the psychic and the physical are not two independent parallel processes, but are essentially connected through reciprocal action ..." (Jung 1912/1928, p. 18). What we call psychic includes both physical and spiritual dimensions (Jung 1929, p. 51). Jung envisions an analogy to the color spectrum between two poles, ranging from the "psychic infra-red, the biological instinctual psyche," to the "psychic ultra violet, the archetype ..."(Jung 1947, p. 215). ... He proposes the existence of a "psychoid level" which is located in the depths of the unconscious where the two poles in some way meet. The psychoid level functions as a kind of transformative interface between psyche and matter. (Chodorow, 1991, p. 44)

The whole of evolution not only creates; it is the architecture of our souls. When I say evolution, I mean human evolution springing from primate evolution, springing from mammalian evolution, springing from reptilian-amphibian evolution, springing from early life, springing from the pre-living Earth, springing from the cosmos, springing from God. Wherever in that sequence there appears a break, or an extinction, that break would appear and be felt at all subsequent levels in some way. To then deal with human cognitive functions we must assume proper functioning of all levels in both the one studying the human in question, as well as in the human being studied. To study human cognition as though it were separate from, say, mammalian evolution as a whole is to study an abstraction, a fantasy. It has no objective reality separated from the larger community. It's like thinking about a solar system that has no sun. We can think the thought but no such solar system exists.

The question I am asking is this. If, as Sagan says, that "after each evolutionary step, the older portions of the brain [I'd add mind] still exist and must still be accommodated. But a new layer with new functions has been added" (Sagan, 1977, p. 53), then functions and dysfunctions we note in the cognitive realm might well come from much deeper zones than we can think about. What if, for instance, we don't yet know that the living communities of mammals are implicated in the existence and functioning of our own limbic systems and we are engaged in making their communities extinct? What if in doing so we are disrupting functions in our own limbic systems which then show up in our cognitive functions as mental illness? A truckload of Zoloft will not even begin to remedy our problem!

In their truly astounding book *Dawn After Dark,* Rene Huyghe and Daisaku Ikeda outline the evolution of life and mind. The following excerpt does, I think, bring the problem into focus:

> Each of us is made up of a superimposition of elements where all the stages of evolution leading to Homo sapiens are inscribed and preserved. This structure retains the series of functions that have appeared during the course of evolution and that indicate the successive complements that have enabled mental life to attain the richness and variety of human psychic activities. It has taken no less than two hundred million years for this slow gestation to advance from reptiles to Homo sapiens. But it must be clearly stated that new faculties have not replaced and invalidated their predecessors. Instead, they have extended their functioning and made possible better adaptation to circumstances. They form an ensemble of increasing richness in which each contributes to the total balance. The older faculties ensure

fundamental functions; the more recent ones, extensions of capacities in the face of the tasks of life. To examine them in chronological order, it is necessary only to observe their stacking in the anatomy of our central nervous system.

The human nervous system preserves elements that first appeared and were successively perfected in the chain of non-human animal life. In addition, the fetus recapitulates those stages in the course of its own development. (Huyghe and Ikeda, 1991, p. 212)

The point in all of this is obvious. The human brain is a product of evolution as a whole. While larger and more complex, it is not dissimilar to the brains of earlier mammals. What makes humans so very different from other mammals is the exceeding complexity of our vast and convoluted neocortical area, not found in many other species.

Early life began on this planet about 3 billion years ago. The animals have been around for about 600 million years. Reptiles appeared about 350 million years ago, and the mammals about half that long ago. Placental mammals appeared about 65 million years ago, following the major extinction event that killed off the larger reptiles. The primate record extends as far back as the early placentals. They acquired several sensing and locomotor adaptations. Somewhere between 10 and 5 million years ago in eastern Africa, certain apes began to walk on two legs. This was the beginning of the hominids. The earliest hominid is Australopithecus aforensis, dating from about 4 million years ago. The eventual rise of species Homo is still not completely understood. Homo habilis dates in Africa from 2.5 million to 1.5 million years ago. Later came Homo erectus and, about 300,000 years ago, Homo sapiens. The modern human appeared around 50,000 years ago. All of this evolution in both structure and functioning is caught up and included in the functioning of human cognition.

Every stage of evolution leaves its imprint and formatting in the architecture of the soul. Indeed, the imprint or formatting is itself that very architecture. Our fascination with the night sky, which in this last century has caused us to explore it, is that imprint or formatting within us. We are from the night sky and to know it is to know ourselves. Our fascination with the dangers and beauties of Earth is also that formatting. We are of the Earth, and Earth is within us and all around us. Our fascination with life forms is our fascination with our own origins. Among the reptiles, mammals, and primates, we exhibit a very special shared origin and destiny. We are a reptile wrapped inside a mammal wrapped inside a primate wrapped inside a human.

Each of us is a community of beings, and we must begin to understand ourselves in that way. Place a reptile, a mammal, and a primate in a cage and watch. There will certainly be an admixture of peace, play, and conflict. When we begin to understand that we are that cage containing all three, we cease to be surprised at the conflict within and among us. At the very time the mammal is reaching out for touch, the reptile is demanding territoriality and boundaries, and the primate is masturbating! I'll share a story to illustrate this point.

Twice yearly I used to take weeks of silence with the Carmelite monks of Nova Nada monastery in Nova Scotia. They have a dog-wolf named Polo. He is a reasonably friendly animal but often insists on his distance. I was petting him once when I first met him. The dog in him pressed up closer and was deeply enjoying the pleasure of a back scratch. In a few moments, however, the wolf remembered who he was. His teeth bared and I remembered, in the hair follicles at the back of my neck, that humans and wolves have a history, a very long history! I was fascinated watching him struggle with his two natures. The wolf wanted to bite me and the dog wanted to be "man's best friend." We have three at odds in us all of the time.

For us to be whole, all three must be allowed their due. When the reptile is silenced, we lose the ability to assert needed territorial boundaries. When the mammal is silenced, we lose the ability to feel deeply and to be fleshy beings. When the primate is silenced, we lose play and so much more that we shall discuss later. My question again is this: Could our loss of instinct and the accompanying instinctual disorders be due to a lack of support for the reptilian formatting in us? Could the extinction spasm we are causing among the mammals, terrestrial and aquatic, be the root cause of our affective dysfunctions? Could the loss of the primate families be the underlying cause of our disintegrating families? Jungian Anthony Stevens speaks to the point: "Our difficulties, neurotic, psychotic, psychopathic, or otherwise, Jung argued, 'come from losing contact with our instincts, with the age-old unforgotten wisdom stored up in us'" (Stevens, 1993, pp. 41–42).

Should we give a rape victim benzodiazepines or should we help her to become aware of and to reassert the reptilian functions of boundary and territoriality? How would we do that? First, we'd listen to her cognitive descriptions of the event. Next, we'd help her to experience catharsis of her mammalian pain at having had her physical being taken by force. Next, we'd address the reptile at the center and help the reptile to speak boldly. We'd bring her whole being into functional unity. If we came to believe that the functioning of the reptile within depended on reptilian function globally, we'd need to defend the global reptile so that our client's reptile within would be supported by the whole reptilian level of functioning. We'd also need to speak for mammals globally if we came to believe that the global mammalian family is involved in the support of our client mammal. The same would be true of the primates. By so doing, we'd be focusing the three lenses of our being. To repeat, our clients are living reptiles with mammals wrapped around them with a primate wrapped around them with a human neocortex in control. The ecology of the whole person demands that the needs of the whole person be met and synchronized. When we do so, the whole architecture of the soul becomes present and the human soul emerges in its rootedness, authenticity, earthiness, and divinity.

The Holomind

A thought or idea is a very mysterious thing. It appears in our awareness seemingly out of nowhere and can either dissipate, like smoke, or take hold of one's cognitive, affective, and instinctual functions. It can dominate one's choices and actions for a lifetime. For example, when we hear "Jesus Christ" or "Gautama Buddha," we might have an idea of an individual man ascend into our awareness. But then Christianity and Buddhism as a whole might come to mind. In those ideas are contained whole architectures of ideas, books, beliefs, histories, and civilizations, not to mention billions upon billions of people who have been caught up in those ideational systems. Undoubtedly, we will have our own ideas about those ideas. This capacity to have ideas about ideas is a unique trait of the human mind that I refer to as the *holomind*.

The idea of holomind was inspired by the thinking of Hungarian author and philosopher Arthur Koestler, who proposed the word *holon* to describe a basic unit of organization in biological and social systems. Holon is a combination of the Greek word *holos*, meaning whole, and the suffix *on*, meaning particle or part. Koestler observed that in living organisms and in social organizations entirely self-supporting, non-interacting entities did not exist. Every identifiable unit of organization, such as a single cell in an animal or a family unit in a society, comprises more basic units (plasma and nucleus, parents and siblings) while at the same time forming a part of a larger unit of organization (a muscle tissue or a community). A holon, as Koestler devised the term, is an identifiable part of a system that has a unique identity, yet is made up of subordinate parts and in turn is part of a larger whole.

The strength of holonic organization, or holarchy, is that it enables the construction of very complex systems that are nonetheless efficient in the use of resources, highly resilient to disturbances (both internal and external), and adaptable to changes in the environment in which they exist. All these characteristics can be observed in biological, psychological, and social systems. The stability of holons and holarchies stems from holons being self-reliant units, which have a degree of independence and handle circumstances and problems on their particular level of existence without asking higher-level holons for assistance. Holons can also receive instruction from and, to a certain extent, be controlled by higher-level holons. The self-reliance characteristic ensures that holons are stable and able to survive disturbances. The subordination to higher-level holons ensures the effective operation of the larger whole.

The holomind is like the wooden Russian doll that is really a doll within a doll within a doll. The structure of our minds is one whole level, say, the human, predicated upon an earlier whole level, say, the primate, predicated upon an even earlier whole level, say, the reptilian, and so on back to the beginning—a beginning that is ever present. Furthermore, the strata of our holomind share not only in the past; they share in the contemporary individuals of the life community who are our distant relatives.

Some psychiatrists and psychologists would have us believe that a thought is the product of a discrete brain, experienced by a discrete person, in a discrete time and place. Therefore, a thought disorder would also have its being within that same person and only within that person. The idea that thought arises from levels of life that are deeper and broader than the individual, such as the human world, the mammalian world, or even the living planet, would seem "unscientific" and, therefore, not real.

However, there is increasing evidence that the individuality of our thoughts is as much an illusion as is the notion that each of us is "a separate self." The biologist Lynn Margulis, and her son Dorian Sagan, tiptoed up to the same realization in their book *Microcosmos:* "Is human thought itself superorganismic, a collective phenomenon?" (Margulis and Sagan, 1986, p. 151).

What if thought arises from the whole cosmos-Earth process? What if the architecture of our souls is constructed of the actual fabric of the cosmos-Earth-life process and that any loose strands in that fabric might be the cause of garbling or distortion or disordering of the thoughts as they occur in our awareness? What if cognitive disordering originates in the pathways through which thought comes to us? What if those pathways are the structure of the natural world, which our industrial enterprise is busily destructuring? What if we are dismantling the architecture of our souls? How then would our thought *not* be disordered? If our conscious function arises out of our unconscious mind and if the structures of the unconscious are the structures of the life community, and if we are destructuring that community, then how can consciousness be anything but disordered? If that function is disordered, then perception, sensation, and reaction will all be disordered as well because consciousness is interrelated with perception, sensation, and reaction. The net result is cognitive disorder on an increasingly global scale with hugely deleterious ramifications for human society and the nonhuman communities of life that are affected by us. Indeed, human society is in the midst of a breakdown.

If, indeed, our minds are ordered along the lines of a holarchy, and if this holarchy participates in the biosphere as well as the noosphere, then there is little doubt that the rampant degradation of our environmental and social contexts will manifest in our primary awareness. Case in point: The incidence of Attention Deficit Disorder (ADD) and Attention Deficit Hyperactivity Disorder (ADHD) is increasing every year. This trend is indicative of an increasing societal dysfunction that is dangerous. If the danger signal is arising from the fact that the child's human family is disintegrating, then the child is having intuitive signaling that what is instinctually needed for human growth and development is disappearing. This instinctual signaling is adaptive and the blocking of that signal by an overreliance upon chemical treatment is maladaptive. Do we avoid the issues of a shameful rate of divorce, of family disintegration, of unparented children by prescribing Ritalin? Do we deny our own moral underdevelopment and denial by drugging our children? Is it fair, then, a few years later, to tritely tell our children, "Just say no!"? To do so is patently absurd because such an approach completely ignores the underlying fractures in the holarchic structure of human development.

Recently, this thought occurred to me: What if all diagnoses could be looked at from both directions, one being a "projected diagnosis" from the clinician toward the client and the other being a "reflected diagnosis" from the client to the context in which the client lives. For example, from the clinician's point of view, the child is indeed suffering from an attention deficit and from hyperactivity. However, from the child's point of view, the family may well be the source of the attention deficit (lack of attention toward the child), as well as the hyperactivity disorder (the family being too busy to give attention to the child in the first place). Who then has ADHD? The child or the dysfunctional parents of the child? Collectively, we could ask the following questions. Is the disintegration of the planet and the life community a symptom of our lack of attention to life itself? Further, is our lack of attention the result of our own hyperactivity in the mad scramble for material gain?

Furthermore, ADD/ADHD could be seen as a milder form of schizophrenia, wherein all social appropriateness and mental function degenerate into bizarre behavior. In extreme cases we observe "word salad" where all linguistic syntax is lost in a fragmentation so devastating that many suffering from this psychosis need to be given heavy sedatives for their own safety and that of their caregivers. The cognitive disorder in ADD/ADHD that exhibits as an inability to stay focused on a given topic of cognition in schizophrenia becomes a complete disintegration of cognition itself. Is medication the solution for schizophrenia? Or do medications enable us to avoid looking deeper? Is our epidemic mental illness problem the human level of the ecological disintegration?

If the human person is the most recent product of the evolution of the life community, then what if the life community out of which we emerge is partially or grossly impaired in both its existence and functioning? It would make sense that if the producer is impaired, then so too will the product be impaired. If the product is the human person, then along with physical defects and disorders (which are rampant), we should expect disorders of our personhood—or personality disorders. If the preconditions for proper and complete personhood are missing, partially or wholly, then personality defects should not come as a surprise to us.

Personality disorders can be thought of as distortions, as expressions of the self that are judged abnormal according to the generally accepted definition of what a self should be. If there is distortion in the way in which we came to be, there will be distortion in our mode of being. If that distortion comes from the breakdown of the life community due to pollution, extinction, and habitat destruction (not to mention macrostructural changes such as rerouting of rivers or subsurface nuclear testing), then we need to look at our definition of normalcy. That is, we must look at our lifestyles if we are ever to understand the true etiology of personality disorders. Treating human cognition will continue to be fruitless if our problem is in the pre-human stages of our ontogenesis. If we act in monstrous ways toward the life community, then we can continue to expect human monsters to be the product of that community.

The pathologies under discussion are associated with the Cognitive Subpsyche; however, the conditions that gave rise to these pathologies may very well be precognitive or transcognitive. What I am saying is that we may not be dealing with the true "why" of their emergence. Naming, numbering, describing, and treating them does little long-term good if we continue to create the conditions that bring them about. Without addressing the deleterious effects upon our mental health that the underlying conditions of social and environmental degradation are having upon people around the world, mental clinicians are masters of triage at best. At worst, they are unwitting collaborators in the devolution of society into a literal hell on Earth. If the underlying causes of these pathologies are the disordering of the life community, then we need to heal the life community. How? By simply allowing it to live. If what I am saying is true, then it follows that all clinicians of the future will need to be at the same time both mental health and planetary health professionals.

CHAPTER TWO

The Affective Subpsyche

WE MOVE NOW TO THE AFFECTIVE SUBPSYCHE, the second layer in Primary Awareness. This chapter is about feelings or affect, another word for emotion. Our most basic feeling is the expression of our own sentience, our own sensitivity, our own awareness. Feelings are a form of awareness that we share with all living things. Even the simplest unicellular organism has an awareness of its environment, and responds to touch and chemicals as well as temperature changes. As we probe deeper into the nature of matter and enter smaller and smaller substates of matter, it becomes clear that matter itself has reactions and is, therefore, for our purposes, aware.

Jung notes that affect is the "glue" that bonds the various ideational or memory components of a complex. Drained of affect, the complex is drained of its dynamism. Jung goes further in discussing affective dynamics in depicting the "emotional core" of complexes as a sort of center of gravity around which psychic contents gather and self-organize. Pieces of personal, human, pre-human, pre-mammalian, pre-geological, and presumably pre-cosmic psychic fragments gather into the "galaxy" of a complex. The following quote from *Dance Therapy and Depth Psychology* by Joan Chodorow treats this theme:

> For Jung, the emotionally toned complex is the key to understanding the unconscious processes that produce psychogenic symptoms. A complex is "a collection of various ideas held together by an emotional tone common to all" (Jung, 1911, p. 599). (Chodorow, 1991, pp. 46–47)

The Affective Subpsyche is the link between the individual and the whole of biological, geological, and cosmic history. We have evolved with cognitive, affective, and instinctual functions. All three ways of knowing are valid. They teach us about ourselves and our relationship to our environment—interior, exterior, and ecological. This is who we are. Without proper integration of emotions (bodily history) and cognitive functions (thought), we become dry and pathological:

> Reason flows from the blending of rational thought and feeling. If the two functions are torn apart, thinking deteriorates into schizoid intellectual activity and feeling deteriorates into neurotic life-damaging passions. (Goldsmith, 1993, p. 73)

So many of my own clients have exhibited complaints about what I have called ecological and cultural grief. Most generations following the baby boomers have this deep sense that they have inherited the ruins not only of Western culture but also of the natural world itself. This grief presents as a certain despair-depression and does not respond to medication or to talk therapy confined to their personal histories. Mention the cultural morass, the planetary degradation, or the affluent baby boomers, and an anger, indeed a hatred, emerges that clears the fog of depression. These generations feel betrayed.

I counsel these clients to go deeper than cognition, to get a "Ph.D." in affective and instinctual knowing rather than yet another in cognitive knowing. They must go deeper in order to establish a footing in their mammalian, their primate, and their biologically grounded knowing functions. From there, they can contact the wisdom of the biosphere, repressed and denied by the noosphere for two centuries or more, but especially since the beginning of the information revolution. From there they can reintegrate the noosphere in a new way that will allow for their survival.

We must consult the elder within, whom Anthony Stevens has named "The Two Million Year Old Self." This deep self contains the wisdom gleaned from the whole evolutionary enterprise. It is from this core of the human animal, and only from this core, that these young people will find the resources to rebuild this world both culturally and biologically. Steven L. Albon puts it this way:

> In recent years, consideration of feeling as the archetypal core of human "being," as the heart of human suffering and transformation, has encouraged men to integrate their feminine sensibility into their sense of self. This is reflected in the content herein and especially in the realization that this project is not just a cognitive exercise in the empirical analysis of affect. Rather, it is an integration of two approaches to knowledge. We have attempted to be affective in the expression of affect rather than purely cognitive about affect. In that sense, the work has been guided as much by our being willing and able to "feel our way along" with these issues as by the rigorous thinking that grows out of our professional backgrounds and interests. (Albon et al., 1993, p. 47)

Integration of our various "minds" or layers of our awareness will provide the necessary energy that will enable young people to recreate their world. We must deepen into our affective and instinctual brains-minds if we are to do so. Our mammalian mind and nature must be connected at each and every stage.

The sixties in American history reflected an experiment in reconnecting to our mammalian nature by embracing more earthy and life-affirming lifestyles. Unfortunately, due to social immaturity and ignorance of psycho-spiritual processes that led to an overreliance upon psychotropic drugs and narcissistic practices, the cultural movement failed to provide the necessary integration of our cognitive minds with our mammalian natures. Although it did succeed in opening Western cultural norms to Eastern philosophies that have had a highly beneficial influence on contemporary cultural, social, and religious philosophies and practices, nevertheless, the period included a fragmentation of the family structures that are basic to sound mammalian personal and social development. Since then, families have become increasingly regulated by the legal interests of a dysfunctionally cognitive culture. The present, with its seeming disappearance of altruistic love, and strewn as it is with the corpses of dead marriages, broken families, and aborted children, is the result of this failed experiment.

Fortunately, human beings are highly adaptive creatures. We can use the best of the failed experiment and mend the rest. We can go forward by returning to our mammalian families with the insight wrested from failure. In fact, our healthy emotional development as individuals and a culture absolutely depends upon a return to family and the kind of love that family fosters. In writing about the mammalian-affective layer of the mind, Carl Sagan said:

> Indeed, with rare exceptions (chiefly the social insects), mammals and birds are the only organisms to devote substantial attention to the care of their young—an evolutionary development that, through the long period of plasticity which it permits, takes advantage of the large information-processing capability of the mammalian and primate brains. Love seems to be an invention of the mammals. (Sagan, 1977, pp. 66–67)

Being that we are mammals, we possess the ability to love. However, that ability can be repressed or dissociated by the dominance of our cognitive capabilities. Therapeutic skills and insights will provide crucial tools in the exploration of these deeper layers of our interior landscape. But Western therapeutic insight is not enough to do the job. The East provides us with a treasure trove of possibilities and paths and we need them all. The following lengthy excerpt explains why:

> Whereas Western psychotherapy's main contribution is in fostering recognition of affective experiences, it is somewhat limited in enabling individuals to discern the various levels of affective processing, many of which operate outside of conscious awareness. Most individuals who complete psychotherapy or psychoanalysis, no matter how extensive their

understanding of subjective meaning, unconscious motivation, and the like may be, still have little conscious awareness of the rapid processing levels in the affective response system, especially the more immediate preattentive expressive-motor and schematic or appetitive/aversive levels of processing that Arnold (1960) and Leventhal (1980) describe. The reason that Western psychotherapy rarely leads to awareness of these high-speed levels of affective processing is that Western psychotherapy does not emphasize disciplined, rigorous attention or awareness training to the same degree that it is emphasized in the great contemplative traditions. ... Attention/awareness training is the cornerstone of any meditation tradition. Precisely because so much emphasis and care are devoted to attention/awareness training in meditation, meditation becomes a vehicle to open up awareness to the rapid-processing levels of the human information processing system normally operating outside of conscious awareness. In this sense, meditation contributes something to our understanding of adult affective development that is rarely found in Western psychotherapy.

Moreover, the endpoint of development in meditation is profoundly different from that of psychotherapy (Brown, 1986). By gaining insight into the workings of the mind on every level through disciplined meditation, the meditator experiences a profound and enduring transformation of the structures of the mind. This relatively permanent new development is called enlightenment. What does enlightenment inform us about optimal development and specifically about affective development? In a sense, this ... is about exceptional human abilities. The classical descriptions of the path of meditation and enlightenment raise the possibility of relatively enduring psychological well-being for the remainder of the life span. (Albon et al., 1993, pp. 374–375)

A deep mindfulness regarding this creation of the mammals' love or caring is emphasized especially in Buddhism. Regardless of what religion a person might belong to or practice, the study of Buddhism and the application of its principles can only serve to deepen one's understanding of our complex nature and thereby enrich our appreciation of the power of our emotions, especially the emotion of love. Of course, becoming a Buddhist is not the only way to practice the spirit of universal love. I do believe, however, that anyone who basically understands the law of life as taught by Buddhism will awaken to the spirit of love. In their book *Dawn After Dark,* Daisaku Ikeda and Rene Huyghe work to understand the huge problems facing us in the modern age and the importance of love as a guiding principle in human interactions:

> Furthermore people who, while regarding human associates with love and care, experience no conscience pangs at killing nonhuman life forms are dangerous. This is true because sometimes one race regards other races as subhuman, as Hitler did non-Aryans in general and Jews in particular.
>
> Giving precedence to love over aggression in relations with all forms of life removes the danger of such a mistake. Human nutritional needs require sacrificing other beings for the maintenance of life. Nonetheless, if love is given precedence at all times, meaningless killing can be avoided; and we will feel profoundly grateful for lives that must be sacrificed for our food. Moreover, realizing the precious price that must be made for our sustenance, we will strive to live so as to be worthy of the sacrifice. (Huyghe and Ikeda, 1991, p. 178)

How we feel on any given day and experience reality during that day depends more on affect than on cognition, more on feeling than on belief. For instance, we don't get up in the morning feeling bad because we are a Democrat or Republican; rather, it is because we are having fearful or depressed or anxious experiences in our affective reality. Life is experienced as feeling and if we are not experiencing our feelings, then we are not aware—we are not experiencing our lives. People without clear affect find it difficult to make and remain in meaningful relationships because they are experienced as boring by others in their environment. A film or musical work that doesn't inspire us to feel is experienced as boring regardless of how deep the thought systems in the piece might be. Sadly, in our times, films become increasingly more violent and/or sexual in order to arouse at least some affect in their audiences, who are often to one extent or another dissociated from their affective functions. Without feeling, life is flat.

To say that our feelings form the core of our experience of reality is to say that experience precedes reflexive thought about experience. Affect, then, precedes cognition. This is true generally in the history of evolution as well as being true in the individual. Ontology recapitulates phylogeny. Mammals precede humans. The limbic system precedes the neocortex. The neocortex supersedes and includes the limbic system. In the same way the limbic system superseded and subsumed the functions of the brain stem or reptilian brain. If affect forms the core of reality, instinct, the reptilian mind, forms the core of the core. While instincts are felt, they are not feelings, in the way I am describing them here. Instincts govern reflexive action. Feelings do not. If my child runs in front of a car, I will act without feeling or reflection upon the feeling, in order to save her. Later, I will become aware of an affective response of fear.

The importance of the emotional life cannot be overestimated. The affective patterns that set us into motion in this life and that provide our lives with meaning were formed long before you were conscious of your own individuality. Spezzano explores some of the thinking behind this important insight:

> Affect theory provocatively suggests a synthesis, elaboration, and clinical adaptation of a radical philosophical theory of mind first presented in modern form by Hans-Georg Gadamer (in German in 1960 and in English translation in 1975) and more recently by Lear (1991). Gadamer

had partially derived his perspective from the earlier work of Edmund Husserl and Martin Heidegger. Husserl's key insight was that "meanings are structures which a person lives before he thinks about them" (cited in Howard, 1982, p. xii). A central premise of affect theory is that these essential human meaning categories are best understood as feeling states.

Heidegger (1927) elaborated Husserl's theory into the fundamental ontological idea that the psychological essence of each individual human life at any moment in time is the outcome of neglecting or realizing specific domains of possibilities. These domains of possibilities are "fore-meanings," meaning categories that exist prior to the individual. (Spezzano, 1993, p. 213)

Although Heidegger and Spezzano point to earlier human structures passed along to individuals as "fore-meanings," it doesn't require a huge leap to understand that there are fore-meanings that were passed to us from mammalian evolution itself. The mammals presumably received even earlier fore-meanings from reptilian evolution and on backward to the planet itself. We can only wonder what happens when the carriers of these fore-meanings are made extinct by human choices. If, for instance, several families of the higher mammals are made extinct, are humans then denied these fore-meanings a priori? Are we then born with less and less bio-wisdom inherent in our beings? In our families? If the supports for fore-meanings are destroyed, are we destroying the very architectures of our own Affective Subpsyches? It is my opinion that these fore-meanings comprise our archetypal affects, of which there are seven.

The seven innate archetypal affects are listed below; their ranges of intensity are shown in parentheses, and the life stimulus of each is shown in italic.

JOY

(Enjoyment-Ecstasy)   *Relationship to the familiar*

INTEREST

(Interest-Excitement)   *Novelty*

SADNESS

(Distress-Anguish)   *Loss*

FEAR

(Apprehension-Terror)   *The unknown*

ANGER

(Irritation-Rage)   *Restriction of autonomy*

CONTEMPT/SHAME

(Dislike-Disgust/
Embarrassment-Humiliation)   *Rejection*

STARTLE

(Surprise-Startle)   *The unexpected*

(Chodorow, 1991, p. 77)

Affect replaces "programmed instinct." This is true because the limbic system includes and transcends the reptilian brain or brain stem. Thus, a new layer of evolution comes on board in the life community with the mammals and then the primates. In my opinion, the affective function does not replace the instinctual function. Instead, it includes instinct and adds something new. This something new is genuine affect, which we can think of as psychic energy, the flow of libido. This flow of libido is one of the main sources of our creativity. It is the glue that holds us in the bond of love. As it disappears, as it seems to be doing, we fall apart. Our marriages fall apart, our cultures fall apart, our psyches fall apart. The architecture of our souls crumbles.

The Primal Self

The core of our emotional sensibilities and our personalities comes to us from the primates and our mammalian lineage. This core is our *primal self*. We, for instance, certainly have transcended the chimpanzee, but the chimpanzee is included in us (we share as much as 99 percent of the genetic code with chimps). When we eliminate them, do we eliminate the living architecture of our souls?

Injuries sustained at this level of the psyche constitute deep wounds that fester into psychopathologies. Affect arises from this primal self and we become conscious of the affect; we experience the affect before we can think about it. In damaging the mammalian families of life, we might be eliminating the embodied centers of this core self that comes to us from "below" us in the chain of being. Jung speaks to the point:

> In its innate form the primal Self remains the same in the mature adult as it is in the new-born infant. Similar perhaps to the structure of the DNA molecule, or Jung's analogy of the preformed lattice in a crystalline solution, the primal Self contains the invisible "groundplan" or innate potential toward the development of the human personality. As we know, the development occurs through the interweaving of innate potential with environmental influence (Jung, 1951, p. 31). (Chodorow, 1991, pp. 80–81)

What Jung is pointing to in the above are the very structures of the primal self. They are passed on to us individually and collectively from the past, a past that includes the primates, the mammals, and all earlier life forms. They give us the ability to "hear" our instincts and to respond to them.

If we are deaf to the pain of the planet, which is "heard" through our instincts, we might continue to destroy the very basis of our own being, the architecture of our own souls.

The Cosmos As Self

Deeper still, the self that I most truly am you most truly are as well. When I journey "down" through all the identities that make me me, I come to the fundamental awareness of them. That awareness is the field upon which all the other identities are experienced. That awareness is present within the whole created order. It is the way God can be simultaneously aware of everything and everyone in the whole creation. Self is shared by all. In the words of Daisaku Ikeda:

> Our selves and all other selves partake of the fundamental cosmic energy that creates all phenomena. When this fundamental energy appears in the ordinary world as lifeforce, the various selves assume their individual identities as stars, planets, humans, or other living beings. The energy possessed by the self pours forth as life-flow, which creates life-space and life-time. The self and the manifestation of its fundamental energy give birth to space and time. There is no space or time apart from life activity. This principle must be understood before one can fully understand the identity of the self and the cosmos or the concept of eternity in every life-moment. (Ikeda, 1982, p. 86)

The life of the cosmos is the life of all that lives at this present moment—yes, but also the past or memory of the cosmos is the past and memory of all beings in the cosmos. If this is so, then Earth remembers her own past. She remembers the dinosaurs in the lizards. She remembers the primates of the past in the primates of the present, the mammals of the past in the mammals of the present. The way the past felt in the way the present feels. As Ken Wilber has pointed out in his stunning work *Sex, Ecology, Spirituality,* the universe is an expanding *and* deepening holarchy whose primary dynamics could be called transcendence and inclusion. The universe grows by transcendence of the past by the present but also by inclusion of the past in the present.

I am asserting that our present epidemic of affective pathologies might be better understood by looking at the species "below" us in the holarchy that we are eliminating. When we make species extinct, we eliminate embodied memories and perhaps our ability to have healthy feeling lives in the present as well as in the future. Could depression be nothing more or less than felt psychic sinkholes as the architecture of life is collapsing beneath us? Could fear be the warning signal of and from an unraveling biosphere? Do we want to block these signals with drugs?

Looking at the affective pathologies (called mood disorders, anxiety disorders, and adjustment disorders), we shall want to ask some new and deeper questions. Given that the affective disorders can be reduced to two basic categories, (1) depression and (2) fear-anxiety, then what is the source of these two chronic feeling states? I suspect that a sense of desertion and abandonment is the affective context in which an increasing number of us live our lives, and that this sense arises as a symptom of our loss of paradise (i.e., the natural world and healthy affective relations with the community of life). What steps need to be taken in order to address that loss? No amount of cataloging and treating individual affective disorders will ever resolve our woes, if we are sent back into an alienated concrete jungle that does little to feed our souls. We might look at the pain of our upbringing or the pain of our present situation for years. Still, if the real source of the pain is the loss of the bondedness with nature, each other, and with our source in God, then all our counseling will only leave us the whining victims that so many of us have become.

CHAPTER THREE

The Instinctual Subpsyche

Together the patient and I address ourselves to the two mil-
lion-year-old man that is in all of us. In the last analysis,
most of our difficulties come from losing contact with our
instincts, with the age-old unforgotten wisdom stored up in
us. (Carl Jung)

STEVENS CONTINUED JUNG'S THOUGHT: "Secular urban
life breeds disalliance with the unconscious, and disalliance with the
unconscious is synonymous with loss of instinct and rootlessness"
(Stevens, 1993, p. 70).

We intuit. This chapter is about instincts and the voice of instincts,
which is intuition. Returning again to our model of the triune brain, or
triune psyche, we can review the archeology of our souls. In the outer
cortex of the brain we see the history of human evolution. This most
recent development of biological and cultural evolution is the center of thought as we experience it, i.e., self-reflexive thought. Beneath
the cortex lies the limbic system or paleo-mammalian cortex. Here is
where our experience of affect—our feelings—arises. In that cortex we
experience the lived history of the whole mammalian event on Earth.
In our own bondedness with our young, we can catch a glimpse of
primate-mammalian bondedness generally. I have suggested that the
larger mammalian family generally shares the embodiment (literally)

of the whole history and evolution of the mammals. Deeper still, we find the brain stem. We can think of the brain stem as a light bulb screwed into the top of the spinal cord that brings the light of wisdom from the collective history of the reptiles, birds, and fish to bear on the deepest interior of our souls. The reptiles embodied the earliest wisdom of life, down through the earlier marine life forms and still further down to the worms and unicellular and even prokaryotic life forms. These, in turn, contain the creativity of the pre-biological Earth, which itself embodies the whole creative memory of fifteen billion years of cosmic evolution, which embodies the creativity of God.

We are the embodiment of the history of life, and the instincts are the embodiment of that history at the instinctual level. Carl Sagan described the R-complex found in the human brain in his book *The Dragons of Eden*. This R-complex is part of what he called the "old brain," but it is still very much "performing" in humans today:

> … we should expect the R-complex in the human brain to be in some sense performing dinosaur functions still; and the limbic cortex to be thinking the thoughts of pumas and ground sloths. … it would be astonishing if the brain components beneath the neocortex were not to a significant extent still performing as they did in our remote ancestors. (Sagan, 1977, p. 63)

Sagan continued his argument by describing the kinds of behavior we observe today that are still governed by the R-complex, which:

> … plays an important role in aggressive behavior, territoriality, ritual and the establishment of social hierarchies. … this seems to me to characterize a great deal of modern human bureaucratic and political behavior. … it is striking how much of our actual behavior—as distinguished from what we say and think about it—can be described in reptilian terms. We speak commonly of a "cold-blooded" killer. (Sagan, 1977, p. 63)

These R-complex behaviors are determined by instinct, which is a fixed pattern of action triggered by a deep and unlearned signal inherent in the organism, presumably from conception. How many times have we heard the statement "I need space?" The need for a place seems fundamental to all living things. Recent *in utero* filming technologies have shown human fetuses withdrawing from saline solutions injected into the territory of the womb in order to abort them. They scramble and scream in an attempt to withdraw from the assault on their habitat. They are searching frantically for safe space. So, even before the fetus has conscious self-awareness, they are already instinctually (unconsciously) self-aware of what is needed. This is so because instinct arises out of the formative experiences over the vast reach of evolutionary time, even from matter itself. Instinct is "mind" present in pre-living as well as living matter; thus, instinct includes the wisdom of the cosmic process, the earth process, the life process, and the cultural process of man.

We are composed of the energy, matter, mind, and purpose of the cosmos. The cosmos had some ten billion years of energy, matter, mind, and purpose even before Earth came to be. Earth contains the memory of all that time and expansion. When life awakened on Earth, life also contained that whole eleven billion years. Part of that deep well of experience, life began its evolution and branching. All of that is recalled in the living community. All of that is recalled in the depth of the human mind. The physical organ responsible for keeping all of that knowledge present in us is the brain stem. The structures of this knowledge present in our deep psyches are instincts. The signals emanating from these instincts are called archetypes. Our felt experience of these archetypes is called intuition. From Jung:

> That this is so is immediately understandable when we consider that the unconscious, as the totality of all archetypes, is the deposit of all human experience right back to its remotest beginnings. Not, indeed, a dead deposit, a sort of abandoned rubbish-heap, but a living system of reactions

and aptitudes that determine the individual's life in invisible ways—all the more effective because invisible. It is not just a gigantic historical prejudice, so to speak, an a priori historical condition; it is also the source of the instincts, for the archetypes are simply the forms that the instincts assume. From the living fountain of instinct flows everything that is creative; hence the unconscious is not merely conditioned by history, but is the very source of the creative impulse. It is like Nature herself—prodigiously conservative, and yet transcending her own historical conditions in her acts of creation. No wonder, then, that it has always been a burning question for humanity how best to adapt to these invisible determinants. If consciousness had never split off from the unconscious—an eternally repeated event symbolized as the fall of the angels and the disobedience of the first parents—this problem would never have arisen, any more than would the question of environmental adaptation. (Jung, 1960, p. 157)

In his groundbreaking work *The Voice of the Earth,* Theodore Roszak brought this kind of thinking into the Freudian sphere. In a radical revision of the way in which we look at Freud's id, Roszak suggests that the id is a sort of ecological compass pointing humans back to proper relationship with their source, Earth, and cosmos:

The id is that very protohuman psychic core that our evolution has spent millions of years molding to fit the planetary environment. Its seeming unruliness deserves a deeper understanding if only because it grows from a long evolutionary history. In the course of that history its dominant characteristics must have been selected for some good reason. ...

The id, as Freud recognized, is a deeply conservative component of the psyche. But lacking ecological insight, he misconceived the locus of that conservatism. At one stage in his theoretical development, he connected it with the father-son rivalry of the primordial horde; at another, he reached back to connect it with the death instinct, a longing to return to the inanimate state. But between these two waystations in the history of the cosmos there lies a broad historical-evolutionary zone during which life and mind emerged from the innate system-building tendencies of the universe. In that vast interval, all the patterns if environmental adaptation were meticulously laid down as basic properties of living things and of the planet as a whole. *Seen from this perspective, what the id conserves from its long maturing process is our treasury of ecological intelligence.* Its intractability stems from its deeply ingrained resistance to all social forms that endanger the harmony of the human and the natural; its untamed "selfishness" represents a bond between psyche and cosmos whose distant origins reach back to the initial conditions of the Big Bang. Just as there is a "wisdom of the body," which often has a better sense of health than medical science, so too there may be a "wisdom of the id" that knows what sanity is better than any school of psychiatry whose standard of normality is essentially a defense of misconceived social necessity. (Roszak, 1992, pp. 289–290)

Drive and instinct, then, are to be understood as the most basic modes of volition. They re-present to us the basic will of creation generally: to become and be sustained in existence. The brain stem is the rudder that stabilizes and guides the trajectory through existence. If we engage too much in the thinking with the neocortex, we silence the voice of the rudder and begin losing our course and heading for disaster. We no longer are able to live "receptively and acceptively" in our habitat "alert to its every signal, obedient to its every demand," as Roszak says, and we unknowingly begin to destroy our habitat as a result. This is the true root of the ecological crisis we are experiencing. We can no longer feel most of the wisdom gained over fifteen billion years of evolution. We can't identify with our own context. We can't feel the murderous pain we inflict on the whole community of life. Horribly, the community itself is the support for our own bodies and psyches. Destroy the context and you destroy the architecture of our souls.

Instinct and Morality

Nonhuman animals do not live beyond the range of their instincts, and thus, they remain in appropriate relationship to the other species and to the nonliving components of their environment. A lioness might appear ruthless when she takes down a wildebeest, but she will never leave an entire landscape strewn with skinned and tongued bison. She kills to eat. Only the human can take this instinctual drive and, precisely by thinking about it and lusting for the affective thrill of killing, enter into non-instinctual behaviors such as superkill. When we use our minds and feelings to overindulge our instincts, we are not acting like animals. We are acting like perverted humans.

It is precisely to the animals that we owe the proper limits of our instinctual psyche. The self-reflexive version of these limits is contained in our global religious traditions as moral laws. The loss of functional practice of those traditions is a major source of our loss of contact with our instinctual base. Instinct is the inward governance of the living community, a voice from the Source of life, itself, the tried and true wisdom of the evolutionary enterprise. Since the life community has risen into self-reflexive thought, i.e., since the emergence of the human, instinct becomes subject to human understanding and choice. At that point, when instinct becomes conscious, we can begin to talk about morals. In the introduction to his good-natured book *Origins of the Sacred*, Dudley Young points to this same phenomenon:

> The word I use for these measures is "lawlines," and in the beginning this is literally what they are, lines drawn in the mind and on the dancing ground to regulate the flow of energies no longer governed by the codes of primate instinct.

What is being sought in these chapters is effectively the grammar of primitive experience, the ways in which magic, myth, and ritual were used to allow us to talk to the gods without being swallowed by them. (Young, 1991, p. xx)

When we ignore the signals of this instinctual psyche, we do so at our own peril. From Jung:

Archetypes were, and still are, living psychic forces that demand to be taken seriously, and they have a strange way of making sure of their effect. Always they were the bringers of protection and salvation, and their violation has as its consequence the "perils of the soul" known to us from the psychology of primitives. Moreover, they are the infallible causes of neurotic and even psychotic disorders, behaving exactly like neglected or maltreated physical organs or organic functional systems. (Jung, 1960, p. 266)

In our age, we ignore the lawlines at the peril of the whole biosphere, and all of human culture as well. When we become unaware of the Instinctual Subpsyche, we dim or mute the voice of intuition. To do so is similar to a spinal tap in that after the central nervous system is neutralized we can operate on the body with no experience of pain. When we block out these deep signals from the psyche, we can disassemble the life community and, in doing so, disassemble our own psyches and remain blissfully unaware that we are doing so.

Instinctual Pathologies

We are plagued by what I call instinctual disorders—pathologies associated with the instinctual psyche. An instinctual disorder is a disordering of basic life impulses, a garbling of basic life messages about danger, eating, drinking, sexual behavior, familying, and ecological peril. While not naming them as instinctual disorders, the DSM IV, an excellent psychotherapeutic diagnostic guide, does list some of these disorders. It is, however, a partial list. I will provide a more complete list below. First, those listed in DSM IV:

- Substance related disorders
- Eating disorders
- Sleep disorders
- Sexual/gender disorders

I would add:

- Abortion as contraceptive practice/in utero technologies
- Nuclearism/ecological disorder
- Loss of religion/niche/territory

Although instincts can be thought about cognitively, and can therefore become expressed as morals, instinctual disorders cannot be treated cognitively. This is because instinct is a different voice from thought. Consider the first category of instinctual disorder, substance related disorders, especially alcoholism. What alcoholics think about their problem is of no help whatever in recovering from it. In fact, the recognition of bankruptcy in this area of thought is a prerequisite for recovery. You'll hear alcoholics say at AA meetings: "My best thinking earned me a seat in AA." The same is true regarding affect. What an alcoholic feels about the drinking problem is of little help and can even be an impediment to recovery. To dwell on feelings of shame can, and often does, lead the alcoholic back to the bottle in a failed attempt to numb the pain. It is only when both thought and feeling are surrendered that the deeper instinctual function can be activated and reassert the instinct to live. That instinct brings the person to recovery.

The effectiveness of Alcoholics Anonymous rests on this point. It is the brain stem and its equivalent Instinctual Subpsyche that responds to AA's therapy. In other words, the alcoholics recover through a moral psychology. They say as much in the section called "The Doctor's Opinion" in the AA "Big Book": "We doctors have realized for a long time that some form of moral psychology was of urgent importance to alcoholics" (Alcoholics Anonymous, 1976, p. xxv).

Instinctual disorders are caused by exceeding the boundaries of instinctual or moral law. These laws are formatted in the Instinctual Subpsyche and remain formatted there as a permanent structural inheritance from the life community over the whole of the evolutionary enterprise—biological, geological, cosmological, theological. They are structures in the architecture of the soul and they signal consciousness regarding human limits. The correspondence between the Instinctual Subpsyche and the Affective Subpsyche is a felt experience of truth. The Cognitive Subpsyche then thinks about that signal and codifies it conceptually. This whole psychic correspondence is called *conscience*.

Morals are self-reflexive instincts. They are intrinsic to the human. While the counseling establishment has tried to become "value free," we have overlooked this need for a moral psychology. Moral psychology cannot be confused with moralizing. Moralizing has no place in a counseling environment but—and this is a big *but*—morals as a function of the psyche certainly do. They are the rudder and compass of the psyche. They contain the deeper wisdom of the life community itself from which we emerge. There are cognitive therapies to treat thought disorders. There are affective therapies to treat mood disorders. Moral therapies treat instinctual disorders. From the point of view of depth, both psychologically and biologically, morals are of fundamental importance. As Thomas Moore rightfully points out in his popular book *Care of the Soul:* "It is not possible to care for the soul while violating or disregarding one's own moral sensibility" (Moore, 1992, p. 187).

Because morality is instinct, then morality is niche. It is the voice of the lawlines provided by that psyche which is our Source. What then of the ecopsychology of instinct? What are the instincts trying to tell us? How do we articulate and give therapy to that which is deeper than thought or language? We must become aware of our intuition, the voice of our instincts. However, we want to avoid making the instincts themselves conscious—that would cripple us with sexual neurosis, performance anxiety, and so on. But what happens when we have created a world so dominated by our cognitive faculties that our instincts no longer even comprehend it? What happens when our instincts no longer tell us what we need to know regarding our safety or adaptability? What happens when cognitive knowledge is so very complex that instinctual wisdom cannot adapt to the environment created by it? Goldsmith addresses this concern in his book *The Way:*

> The problems that confront us become increasingly "counterintuitive," to use Jay Forrester's expression. ... Whereas our ancestors had no difficulty in understanding their relationship with the living world, we have no means of understanding our relationship with the surrogate world we have created. What are the implications, for instance, of subjecting our children to X-rays; or permitting a nuclear power station to be built in the vicinity of our homes; of using CFC-emitting cosmetic sprays that erode the ozone layer which shields our planet from ultra-violet radiation; of cutting down the world's tropical forests; or indeed of countenancing the industrialization process itself? ...
>
> It is not only our sense and our intuitive faculties that fail us before the brave new world to which economic development is giving rise; our very instincts cease to serve as a guide to adaptive behavior. (Goldsmith, 1993, pp. 248–249)

It is only when there is a functional match between the inner and outer environment, the inner soul and outer culture, the inner and outer awareness and sensitivity that our whole being—cognitive, affective, and instinctual—can function within the context of the biosphere. Once again the words of Theodore Roszak make the point simple and clear:

> The human must establish a *transactional bond* with the natural; there must be give and take, courtesy and respect. One bargains with nature, apologizes for intruding upon it, begs pardon on the animals one hunts and kills, tries to make good the losses one has brought about, offers sacrifice and compensation. Sanity is just such a matter of balance and

reciprocity between the human and not-human. (Roszak, 1992, p. 79)

Do unto others as you would have them do unto you. The idea that sanity is a "balance and reciprocity between human and not-human" is an ancient moral code that many people—indigenous, agricultural people—would find quite familiar. However, my fellow contemporaries would want to split hairs on the matter. This is the problem. As Sagan points out, "human beings are quite capable of resisting the urge to surrender to every impulse of the reptilian brain," which is very socially oriented, but he cautions that "it does no good whatever to ignore the reptilian component of human nature, particularly our ritualistic and hierarchical behavior" (Sagan, 1977, p. 64). He believed that this understanding can help us therapeutically to understand "the ritual aspects of many psychotic illnesses" as a possible failure of the neocortex to override the R-complex.

In many ways, Sagan was asking the same questions that I am. If there are discrete disorders of the Instinctual Subpsyche, then how are we to treat them? They are not cognitive, though they are interpreted by our Cognitive Subpsyche. They are not affective, though they are felt by our Affective Subpsyche. They are instinctual and need instinctual therapy.

What is an instinctual therapy? The answer is a moral psychology and its corresponding therapy. In order for an instinctual disorder to be understood and treated, it must first be allowed to enter into our felt experience (the Affective Subpsyche) and then to be interpreted cognitively (the Cognitive Subpsyche). Because of the inspiration of AA's founder Bill W., we indeed have these instinctual therapies in our midst. They are known as twelve-step programs. Further on in this chapter I shall explain how they work. Right now, I want to name and briefly describe the disorders I am calling instinctual.

One commonality among all addictive-instinctual disorders is the ritual behaviors common to them. In my opinion, these dysfunctional ritual behaviors spring from the loss of a functional religious system and its attendant rituals. We in the West, who have lost functional contact with the cup of wine (i.e., blood) and the plate of bread (i.e., divine flesh), have fallen into an epidemic need for rituals to replace them. These show up as eating disorders, substance abuse and alcoholism, and other forms of repetitive ritual behavior. Below I shall treat a description of some of the more obvious instinctual disorders and will show how each of them contains in some fashion a ritual underpinning. What twelve-step programs provide is a ritual meeting of groups in a fellowship and a spiritual path, or therapy, that restores the Instinctual Subpsyche to its proper functioning and role in the larger personality.

So, then, let's start with the first and greatest of all instinctual disorders, the loss of religion, and move through the seven types.

1. Loss of Religious Affiliation or Experience

The first things we know about ourselves come from religious beliefs and rituals. Religions provide us with codes of morality, which come from the voice of the brain stem, or Instinctual Subpsyche, and create for us codified systems of instinctually correct behavior. They allow the human to surrender the will, and sink into the deeper levels of the psyche. The major systems East, West, and Native provide humans with ways to live that have, over time, been proved adaptive. To separate ourselves from genuine religious experience is to separate ourselves from the morals and behaviors that are based on instinctual formatting. To do so is to break with functional relationship with that wisdom which is our Source and which predates our individual conception: i.e., instinct. Perhaps this disorder is the "mother" of all the other instinctual disorders. Religions, after all, offer guidelines about substance use, overdrinking, dysfunctional behaviors, sexual behavior, and eating rituals; they also offer guidelines for familying, prohibitions against abortion and guides for the proper protection of our young, prohibitions against greed and the root impulses for ecological destruction. The loss of religious experience *is* the loss of human instinct and the fundamental root cause of all instinctual disorders. The loss of religion is also the loss of ritual, which only guarantees that rituals will present themselves in neurotic ways.

2. Chemical Dependencies and Behavioral Addictions

Regardless of what zone of the body-mind is targeted for "pleasure" by a given drug, these substances have one thing in common: They all end in time with death of the body itself, which is, of course, the death of the mind as well. This is an affront to the most basic instinct of all, the instinct to remain in existence. The will to be seems to precede life itself. Even a rock seems to will to be in the space it occupies. Still, chemical addiction can erode even that most basic of human drives.

Behavioral addictions are themselves chemical dependencies, though few people in my experience treat them that way. The chemicals in question are somatic chemicals released in the body under the stimuli of fear or excitation. A gambler really doesn't care if he wins or loses. He's in it for the rush of "feel-goods" following a win or of the "feel-sads" following a loss. A sex addict isn't addicted to a member of the opposite sex. He is addicted to the somatic chemicals of arousal (the more so if amplified by fear) that are released by the behavior of the chase of or surrender to a sexual partner. Given the knowledge we have of HIV/AIDS and sexually transmitted disease, the chase after unsafe sex is itself against the instinct to live. The ritual component here is the chase itself and the repetitive behaviors of coaxing, seduction, and even brute dominance, in order to arrive at the place of orgasm. The ritual is all about control.

3. Sexual and Gender Identity Disorders

The instinct to join with another in sexual behavior is fundamental to our need for pleasure and closeness as mammals as well as being fundamental to the propagation of our species. To be without any solid identity in this regard can be a torture like no other. To have an identity so disordered as to place oneself in legal danger every time one expresses oneself creates a hellish existence of repression, and/or covert behaviors that leave one perpetually lonely and frightened. Those who suffer from sexual disorders often lead tortured existences, feeling compelled by their own instincts to participate in behaviors that are often illegal, dangerous, or both.

4. Eating Disorders

Eating is basic to anything that lives. Eating is central to human social life. Eating is a fundamental pleasure because it satisfies a fundamental instinct. The eating disorders basically fall into two categories: (1) compulsive overeating disorder, and (2) starvation disorders—anorexia and bulimia.

An overeating disorder is an attempt to satisfy all human needs by eating and eating and eating. The other is its flip side—"I shall eat nothing." The anorexic or bulimic person suffers from a delusional need to create a fat-free body. Beneath that deluded behavioral system are rituals of starvation and vomiting that create the illusion of control. Surrender of that illusion in a twelve-step program is perhaps the best hope for recovery from either. The victims of these disordered instincts destroy their health and eventually die if the instinct in question is not allowed to reassert itself in a healthy way. As Marion Woodman's work has described with such clarity, eating disorders can only be healed by a return to a functional spiritual life, including religious ritual.

5. The Loss of the Familying Instinct

Our ability to procreate is given us by our DNA. Our ability to make families is an art passed on culturally and religiously. In the U.S. more marriages and families fail than succeed. Much of this is due to instinctual disorders such as the ones mentioned above. Certainly chemical dependencies and behavioral addictions are responsible for many marital break-ups. But it goes deeper than that. Our loss of enthusiasm about familying, our stance that familying is just one of many "lifestyle choices," seems to go against the biological, spiritual, and instinctual needs of human young. The will to be in a family and the instinct to protect and parent our children seems to be losing its power to bond us. We seem to be denying instinctual needs by blocking them with cognitive-legal constructs. Here again there is the loss of ritual behavior. The most fundamental ritual in the human psyche is the meeting, courtship, public stating of vows, and private consummation of our marriages. This fundamental ritual, which expresses itself wherever humans couple, is often replaced by the rituals of sexual addiction and "recreational sex." Likewise, traditional family rituals of eating together, celebrating special times together, and working and playing together are being replaced by violent games before which we are entranced at our individual computer modules, alone.

6. Abortion

The loss of the familying instinct has contributed to, and, at the same time, causes a further disorder that we call abortion. Separated from all of its rhetorical props, abortion is the destruction of humans in a pre-born stage of development. I view the whole pro-choice movement as a massive cognitive denial system that tries to shield us from what abortion really is at the instinctual level. The desire to engender and protect our young is basic to us all, male and female. The will to destroy our young represents a profound instinctual disorder in us all, male and female. Whether we're the one paying for, performing, or having an abortion, we are participating in a highly pathological and pathogenic behavior that cannot and will not ever be adequately silenced by the affective or cognitive psyche. It is behavior that's against the individual's instincts and the species' instincts alike. The Cognitive Subpsyche throws up rational reasons why we should abort. The Affective Subpsyche can be made to produce sentimental feelings about "protecting potential abuse victims" from the families into which they would be born. This writer is one of those children born into an abusive system. My recovery from that experience has given me "characterological" gifts that are the source of what I now think of as the best part of me. To deny a person the legitimate struggle that life demands of them is to deny their potential heroism.

As a clinician, I have sat for a decade sharing the pain of horrendous wounds in women. When over time their cognitive defenses wither and the truth of what has happened to them and to their children emerges from the Instinctual Subpsyche, they feel betrayed, not only by the child's father, but by a culture that arrogates the right to a choice that is destructive. I have witnessed women trying to deal with the loss of as many as eight children. In the words of one of them, "I have killed my family." No one will ever convince me that abortion is an adaptive behavior.

I remember in 1983 going to a conference in which there were speakers from many different traditions. As a Native American named Bill Waupaupau was speaking, we the audience fell into a deep and complete silence. He was a speaker who possessed what I think of as true spiritual authority. We found ourselves in the spell of his truth. In commenting on the white culture of North America, he said, among other things, that it is unnatural for a people to kill their young.

7. Ecological Disorder

In the same way that the human womb is the primary habitat of all humans, the life systems of the exterior planet are the primary habitat of all that lives. To pollute, clear-cut, burn, tear up, or in any way to *superkill* our natural inheritance is suicide. No governments, economies, or courts have the right to allow behaviors that militate against our environment. Suicide is an abhorrent act and to will environmental destruction is, in the long term, suicidal. Again, like all instincts, it flies in the face of basic life instincts and is, therefore, an instinctual disorder.

Twelve-Step Programs: Re-Ordering Disorders

Twelve-step programs, coming from and including Alcoholics Anonymous, all represent approaches in which disordered instincts can become re-ordered. Below we shall take a brief look at each of those twelve steps.

STEP ONE

"We admitted we were powerless over alcohol, that our lives had become unmanageable."

From AA's *Twelve Steps and Twelve Traditions* (called "Twelve and Twelve," or even more simply, "12 & 12"):

> No other kind of bankruptcy is like this one. Alcohol, now become the rapacious creditor, bleeds us of all self-sufficiency, and all will to resist its demands. Once this stark fact is accepted, our bankruptcy as a going human concern is complete.
>
> But upon entering AA we soon take quite another view of this absolute humiliation. We perceive that only through utter defeat are we able to take our first steps toward liberation and strength. Our admissions of personal powerlessness finally turn out to be firm bedrock upon which happy and purposeful lives may be built. ... we shall find no enduring strength until we first admit complete defeat. ...
>
> When first challenged to admit defeat, most of us revolted. We had approached AA expecting to be taught self-confidence. Then we had been told that so far as alcohol is concerned, self-confidence is no good whatever; in fact it was a total liability. Our sponsors declared that we were the victims of a mental obsession so subtly powerful that no amount of human willpower could break it. There was, they said, no such thing as the personal conquest of the compulsion by the unaided will. (AA, 12 & 12, 1978, p. 21)

When any one human instinct is expected to deliver too much personal pleasure or satisfaction, or if any instinct is denied and blocked off, an instinctual disorder results. Because the instincts are components or organs of a mind that precedes our own individual conception, that instinct can become completely out of our control. In such a case we become *instinct possessed*, controlled by a single instinct. When we are instinct possessed, all other faculties of the personality—thought, affect, or will—can become subverted and drawn into orbit around, and forced to support, the instinct(s) in question.

We can "know" that we drink, eat, or gamble too much. We can "feel" the tragic loss of our family, job, self-respect, and physical health. We can marshal the will behind decisions to stop the questionable behavior, and still, the possession with the impulse to drink, eat, gamble, or starve ourselves will completely dominate our reality. Our thinking will keep us in denial and assure our path to insanity and death. It is only when the post-conception mind, the cognitive and affective minds release the will from the illusion of control over the instincts, that the instinct(s) will regain proper functioning in support of the whole architecture of the soul.

Step One is that release. We acknowledge our powerlessness over the instinct. It is simply the recognition of reality, the first step out of the madness of unreality. Instincts create us. They are the pre-conception bud from which the post-conception body-mind will blossom. The instinctual mind is the intelligence that governs the action of conception, cell differentiation, and all processes associated with embryonic development. Instincts are the voices of the soul. Instinct is the voice of our Source. The addict in surrender recognizes that he or she needs to be recreated. The instincts, being the Source, are also the recreators of ourselves. In the surrender of Step One, the addict recognizes that he or she needs to be reconstellated by the instinct. The reconstellated psyche will then heal the body, emotions, and the mind. Full cognitive, affective, and sometimes physical bankruptcy can often be the cost or precondition of this release from the illusion of control. Those who cannot admit this powerlessness often go mad and die. The power needed to prevent madness or death is the higher power that is accessed by surrendering.

STEP TWO

"We came to believe that a Power greater than ourselves could restore us to sanity."

From AA's "Big Book":

As soon as we admitted the possible existence of a Creative Intelligence, a Spirit of the Universe underlying the totality of things, we began to be possessed of a new sense of power and direction, provided we took other simple steps. ... We found the Realm of Spirit is broad, roomy, all inclusive; never exclusive or forbidding to those who earnestly seek. (AA, Big Book, 1976, pp. 55, 46)

Another way to put Step Two would be: "Came to believe in that which pre-exists me, my thoughts, feelings, memories, and will." The Instinctual Subpsyche is the locus of all pre-conception memory, i.e., life, Earth, and cosmos. When the will to resist the addiction by means of cognitive and affective functions is surrendered, the illusion of control is broken and we begin to intuit this "power greater than ourselves." This greater power, pre-existent to ourselves, is what people mean by the word God. The voice of God can be heard deep within, from the Instinctual Subpsyche.

Imagine again that light bulb screwed into the top of the spinal cord. Imagine it being switched on so that its glow radiates through the mammalian and cognitive brains and outward as a field of light surrounding the person. That field of light contains all the biological, geological, and cosmological wisdom remembered in each of us since the "grain" of the cosmos emerged from the mind of God. With that glow comes the feeling of belonging and safety, and with safety comes trust or faith. Our instincts released, relaxed and in equilibrium, we are released from addiction and from most affective and cognitive disorders associated with addiction.

STEP THREE

"We made a decision to turn our will and our lives over to the care of God, as we understood Him."

The following prayer is the prayer of surrender, the third-step prayer:

"God, I offer myself to Thee—to build with me and to do with me as Thou wilt. Relieve me of the bondage of self, that I may better do Thy will. Take away my difficulties, that victory over them may bear witness to those I would help of Thy Power, Thy Love, and Thy Way of life. May I do Thy will always!" We thought well before taking this step making sure we were ready; that we could at last abandon ourselves utterly to Him. (AA, Big Book, 1976, p. 63)

With faith and trust we can surrender to that which we trust. We surrender our will. How different is that from what we learn from Skinner or Ellis? But just think of it—the surrender of one's will—the surrender of the much vaunted "right to choose." The alcoholics' choices earned them seats in AA! We use our right to choose, to surrender our right to choose; the will is disengaged from the cognitive and affective functions. We simply give up.

We also surrender our lives. Career, sex, finances, religious beliefs— everything is surrendered to God. We realize that "we are now on a different basis; the basis of trusting and relying upon God. We trust infinite God rather than our finite selves. We are in the world to play the role He assigns" (AA, Big Book, 1976, p. 68).

This isn't some trite and starry-eyed religious hysteria. This is a life-and-death, real deal, giving up on one's own life agenda in favor of whatever agenda is given us by God to fulfill. We even surrender the way in which we are to believe in God and allow God to reveal our way through the fact of abstinence. We allow God to reshape us at the instinctual-moral level. We have no theologies. We leave even our way to understand God up to God. It is Zen in its surrender of all conceptual apparatus regarding this most important of life issues. "We earnestly pray for the right ideal, for guidance in each questionable situation, for sanity, and for the strength to do the right thing" (AA, Big Book, 1976, p. 70).

For many alcoholics and addicts it is as though they've truly exhaled for the very first time in their lives. A new type of person emerges, not the "in-your-face" reborn person, but a truly new person, calm and confident in the buoyant realization that trust in God is warranted and functional. We come to see in our own lives and experience how practical it is to "cast out one's own will and one's own ideas" (AA, 12 & 12, 1978, p. 35). We see all around us that "the facts seem to be these: The more we become willing to depend upon a Higher Power, the more independent we actually are" (AA, 12 & 12, 1978, p. 36).

STEP FOUR

"We made a searching and fearless moral inventory of ourselves."

From the Big Book:

> *There is a solution.* Almost none of us liked the self-searching, the leveling of our pride, the confession of shortcomings, which the process requires for its successful consummation. But we saw that it really worked in others, and we had come to believe in the hopelessness and futility of life as we had been living it. When, therefore, we were approached by those in whom the problem had been solved, there was nothing left for us but to pick up the simple kit of spiritual tools laid at our feet. We have found much of heaven and we have been rocketed into a fourth dimension of existence of which we had not even dreamed. (AA, Big Book, 1976, p. 25)

During the experience of addiction, during any cognitive or affective disorder as well, there are terrible experiences of anguish. We say, do, and feel things that later become additional sources of suffering. The memories of these experiences are all stored in the psyche, stored in the same layers where they were experienced, i.e., in the cognitive and affective layers. The pain of an instinctual disorder is similarly stored. In order that the three zones of the psyche return to a relaxed, fluid, compensatory relationship with each other, these contents must be emptied. This is the purpose of the fourth step, or moral inventory. We list all cognitive, affective, and instinctual memories that engender either shame or guilt. Shame is the affective memory of things done to us. Guilt is the memory of things done and done to harm others. In emptying them all, the will is freed from the activities of repression and denial. The psyche returns to an unimpeded and unified functioning of all three zones.

The great wonder of the twelve-step therapies is that they go deeper than any and all other forms of counseling of which I am aware. They also go deeper than classical analysis to the extent that, in the Jungian approach at least, they go beyond the archetype, the picture of the instinct, to examine the instinct itself. The following quotation from the opening of Step Four explains it clearly:

> Creation gave us instincts for a purpose. Without them we wouldn't be complete human beings. If men and women didn't exert themselves to be secure in their persons, made no effort to harvest food or construct shelter, there would be no survival. If they didn't reproduce, the earth wouldn't be populated. If there were no social instinct, if people cared nothing for the society of one another, there would be no society. ...
>
> Yet these instincts, so necessary for our existence, often far exceed their proper functions. Powerfully, blindly, many times subtly, they drive us, dominate us, and insist upon ruling our lives. Our desires for sex, material and emotional security, and for an important place in society often tyrannize us. When thus out of joint, people's natural desires cause them great trouble, practically all the trouble there is. No human being, however good, is exempt from these troubles. Nearly every serious emotional problem can be seen as a case of misdirected instinct. When that happens, our great natural assets, the instincts, have turned into physical and mental liabilities. (AA, 12 & 12, 1978, p. 42)

It goes beyond the Freudian model in that it focuses on all the instincts rather than emphasizing the sex drive only. It goes beyond the Adlerian model in that it focuses on not only the will to power, but on all other human drives as well. It goes beyond professional psychology in that it is all written in terms nearly anyone can understand. It goes beyond religion in that it effects genuine salvation without theology or a professional religious class that controls the tools of spiritual growth. It returns the care of the soul to the soul itself in relationship to God.

In the same way that many in the medical field still remain prejudiced toward chiropractors, many in the professional psychology field still cast a condescending look toward the twelve-step programs. Like chiropractic treatment of the spine, which realigns the spinal column so that the flow of life moves correctly through the body, twelve-step programs work in the same way. They work by realigning the cognitive, affective, and instinctual psyches. Will they cure schizophrenia? Perhaps not. But they help!

As AA points out throughout its literature, it is the instincts that are the problem in addiction. "Every time a person imposes his instincts unreasonably upon others, unhappiness follows" (AA, 12 & 12, 1978, p. 44). And as the instincts rage out of control, they create a "soul-sickness" in the individual. Once the instinctual disorder is named and accepted, then the inventory-confession process can begin.

The moral inventory required in this fourth step is a sweeping one. "To take inventory in this respect we ought to consider carefully all personal relationships which bring continuous or recurring trouble. It should be remembered that this kind of insecurity may arise in any area where instincts are threatened" (AA, 12 & 12, 1978, p. 52).

The Big Book actually gives a model of an inventory, which I have included here because it is a valuable tool:

I'M RESENTFUL AT:	THE CAUSE:	AFFECTS MY:
Mr. Brown	His attention to my wife	Sex relations
		Self-esteem (fear)

(AA, Big Book, 1976, p. 65)

STEP FIVE

"We admitted to God, to ourselves, and to another human being the exact nature of our wrongs."

AA's 12 & 12 contains this passage about Step Five:

> Few muddled attitudes have caused us more trouble than holding back on Step Five. Some people are unable to stay sober at all, others will relapse periodically until they really clean house. Even AA old-timers, sober for years, often pay dearly for skimping this Step. They will tell how they tried to carry the load alone; how much they suffered of irritability, anxiety, remorse, and depression; and how, unconsciously seeking relief, they would sometimes accuse even their best friends of the very character defects they themselves were trying to conceal. They always discovered that relief never came by confessing the sins of other people. Everybody had to confess his own. (AA, 12 & 12, 1978, p. 56)

Following the inventory phase comes the confessional phase. The fifth step, which requires sharing ourselves fully with another person, takes courage, but AA's experience shows that it is only when all secrets are shared that a person finds relief. This practice of confession is, of course, not a new one; it has been practiced for centuries, especially in the Catholic traditions.

Following the complete disclosure of Step Five, most of those who suffer from instinctual disorders seek out counseling to complete the problem of resolving cognitive and affective suffering. In time, the introjected pain is released and we experience the joy that comes from feeling well. What we have done is to have emptied our post-conception memory-experience in order that our pre-conception psyche can recreate order, balance, and proper functioning in the post-conception mind. We have realigned the layers of the primary zone of our psyches.

Step Six

"We were entirely ready to have God remove all these defects of character."

Again, from AA's 12 & 12:

> Since most of us are born with an abundance of natural desires, it isn't strange that we often let these far exceed their intended purpose. When they drive us blindly, or we willfully demand that they supply us with more satisfactions or pleasures than are possible or due us, that is the point at which we depart from the degree of perfection that God wishes for us here on earth. That is the measure of our character defects, or, if you wish, of our sins. (AA, 12 & 12, 1978, p. 65)

When we are instinct possessed, the will is engaged in forcing the cognitive and affective faculties to serve the instinct. This creates habits or grooves in our thinking and feeling processes that condemn us to focus our thoughts, our feelings, and our will on the behavior that results from the particular instinct gone wild. Basic drives such as eating, drinking, sexuality, or security (life instinct) become mono-values in our lives, dominating and destroying our health, self-esteem, and even our ability to live. We surrender the will, cognitive and affective functions, our whole post-conception psyche, and ask God to remove the habits or grooves in our thinking that perpetuate our obsessions with the instincts in question.

STEP SEVEN

"We humbly asked Him to remove our shortcomings."

Combined, Steps 6 and 7 provide us with a second-stage release from the rampaging instinct. A further "letting go" takes place wherein the Cognitive Subpsyche and Affective Subpsyche relax and "float" fully in compensatory relationship with the pre-conception psyche, the Instinctual Subpsyche. The instincts resume their normal functioning at the base of the psyche, providing the "voices" that support the life of the organism. These voices are also the source of life energy from the larger biological, geological, cosmological, and theological context of the individual. At this point, the architecture of the soul is in place.

Does this bring the former sufferer to a state of perfection? Certainly not. What it does is to allow the victim of instinctual possession to return to a normal, reasonable state of functioning.

STEP EIGHT

"We made a list of all persons we had harmed, and became willing to make amends to them all."

STEP NINE

"We made direct amends to such people wherever possible, except when to do so would injure them or others."

STEP TEN

"We continued to take personal inventory and when we were wrong, promptly admitted it."

Steps Eight, Nine, and Ten are all restitution steps:

Seldom did we look at character-building as something desirable in itself, something we would like to strive for whether our instinctual needs were met or not. We never thought of making honesty, tolerance, and true love of man and God the daily basis of living. (AA, 12 & 12, 1978, p. 72)

In these steps, we shift our focus from our interior selves to the world around us. We begin to list anyone or anything harmed by us while our instincts were on rampage. Step Eight asks us to make a list of those we have harmed. Step Nine asks us to make restitution to those people. And Step Ten asks us to continue to keep a watch on our natural tendency to allow our instinctual drives to overstep their proper boundaries. These steps ask us to make restitution and continue our self-examination. "Since defective relations with other human beings have nearly always been the immediate cause of our woes, including our alcoholism, no field of investigation could yield more satisfying and valuable reward than this one" (AA, 12 & 12, 1978, p. 80).

Having done these steps, individuals have a chance to become the person they were supposed to be before the instinctual disorder took over. Their spiritual growth from that point on depends on the effort they choose to put into their own evolution. In this, they are like everyone else. Instinctual therapy levels the field and allows the person the choice to live and grow. But that alone is a far cry from suicide by addiction. As the intuitive voices begin again to rise to feeling and thought, we begin again to have values to which we could anchor ourselves and begin to build our characters around them.

STEP ELEVEN

"We sought through prayer and meditation to improve our conscious contact with God as we understood Him, praying only for knowledge of His will for us and the power to carry that out."

From AA's 12 & 12:

And when we turn away from meditation and prayer, we likewise deprive our minds, our emotions, and our intuitions of vitally needed support. As the body can fail its purpose for lack of nourishment, so can the soul. We all need the light of God's reality, the nourishment of His strength, and the atmosphere of His grace. (AA, 12 & 12, 1978, p. 97)

Having experienced what life can be like lived in God's will, i.e., lived under the guidance of the pre-conception psyche, we come to see that only through a lifelong discipline of prayer and meditation can we continue to heal, to be nurtured and given continued growth by the grace of God moving through us. Step Eleven represents our attempt to continue and deepen our contact with God and to live by the light flooding forth from our Source deep within.

STEP TWELVE

"Having had a spiritual awakening as the result of these steps, we tried to carry this message to alcoholics, and to practice these principles in all our affairs."

Growth continues:

And as we grow spiritually, we find that our old attitudes toward our instincts need to undergo drastic revisions. Our desires for emotional security and wealth, for personal prestige and power, for romance, and for family satisfactions—all these have to be tempered and redirected. We have learned that the satisfaction of instincts cannot be the sole end and aim of our lives. If we place instincts first, we have got the cart before the horse; we shall be pulled backward into disillusionment. But when we are willing to place spiritual growth first, then and only then do we have a real chance. (AA, 12 & 12, 1978, p. 114)

Step Twelve is a reminder to all people who have been released from an instinctual possession that they must continue to grow. In other words, they are informed regarding the real purpose of life. And the energies of that growth are to be given away to the next person who suffers.

Now what about the rest of the Twelfth Step? The wonderful energy it releases and the eager action by which it carries our message to the next suffering alcoholic and which finally translates the Twelve Steps into action upon all our affairs is the payoff, the magnificent reality, of Alcoholics Anonymous. (AA, 12 & 12, 1978, p. 109)

The twelve steps are considered to be a revelation to humans by God, their source. As I mentioned earlier, they are truly revolutionary in that they democratize both psychology and religion. Leadership in twelve-step programs comes only from true spiritual authority. Ordination or degrees truly mean nothing whatsoever. A plumber can lead the priest, a prostitute may save the life of the principal. The last become first and the first, last. Eternity erupts into time through the healed psyches of the humble. The architecture of the soul begins to be realigned and is restored to strength. It had to be what Christ meant by the Kingdom of God among us.

In summary, given the powerful influence of the Instinctual Subpsyche throughout the architecture of our souls, it is important that certain insights are clearly stated:

1. The Instinctual Subpsyche pre-exists the individual. As the egg and sperm wed, the whole cosmos/earth/life community expresses itself in the creation of a new being. It is that very psyche that provides the formatting that makes embryo genesis itself possible. This is true of each and every living being. In the same way that the whole universe acts gravitationally when I drop my pen, the whole universe acted in my conception. It begins by creating the first cells, organizes them into what will become the spinal cord, which in turn will support basic physical functions such as heartbeat and breathing as well as basic psychological functions such as instincts.

2. As this theological, cosmological, geological, and biological Instinctual Subpsyche organizes the growth and differentiation of the individual, the whole evolutionary event is recapitulated. It is from this psychic core that mammalian history unfolds in the body-psyche reflected in the brain by the emergence of the limbic system or paleocortex. As the process further unfolds, the Cognitive Subpsyche emerges and a human individual is born.

3. As the cognitive apparatus develops *ex utero*, the fullness of the human psyche blossoms into being. Our affective and cognitive functions emerge as we develop and because of them we have feelings and thoughts about our experience of living. These thoughts and feelings comprise the contents of our memories from conception to death.

4. Sound morality is sound instinct because the lawlines of the life community are encoded as instinct.

5. Pathologies of the Instinctual Subpsyche are expressions of transgressions of the lawlines—the universal moral codes deeply embedded in all of us that precede the secondary moral norms that are relatively determined by our respective cultures.

6. Instinctual pathologies cannot be therapeutically addressed by cognitive or affective therapies; rather, they require instinctual therapies that realign the person with the lawlines.

7. The twelve-step programs are very effective instinctual therapies.

In the next three chapters, we will examine the three domains of our Secondary Awareness: (1) personal—my thoughts and feelings about me, (2) familial—my thoughts and feelings about my family, and (3) cultural—my thoughts and feelings about mine and other's cultures. It is important to understand that these domains of awareness are premised upon the memories of our cognitive, affective, and instinctual experiences that arose in the stream of our Primary Awareness. They are quite powerful in their own right because our personal, familial, and cultural awarenesses (identities) color our thoughts, filter our feelings, and harness our instincts. In other words, they have the power to fashion a heaven or a hell of life.

CHAPTER FOUR

The Personal Subpsyche

> But Jesus knew all people and did not trust himself to them; he never needed evidence about anyone; he could tell what someone had in him. (New Jerusalem Bible, John 2:24–25)

WE REMEMBER. We all have a story. Our biographies are our memories of who we have been, what we have thought, and how we have felt. On writing about the personal unconscious, Jung once said that it was only a potential zone of the psyche at birth. It only became actual when contents, remembered or repressed, made the zone actual. He envisioned the personal unconscious as the upper layer of the unconscious mind, the deeper layer being called the collective unconscious.

While my own understanding of the Personal Subpsyche is certainly derived from Jung, it is nonetheless different in very significant ways. Chief among them is the understanding of the Personal Subpsyche as the upper layer of the zone of the psyche, which I am calling Secondary Awareness. Below the Personal Subpsyche are the Familial Subpsyche and Cultural Subpsyche. The three layers together form the personal underpinnings of psychic life. They represent environmental influences as opposed to genetic or inherited influences. They are the formatting present in a person that mediates between the boundaries of the zones of Primary Awareness and Tertiary Awareness. When they are empty we are transparent, and have arrived at the condition of the newborn babe.

When they are full, those around us are often more aware of what we hold inside than we are.

Contents held in Secondary Awareness—repressed thoughts, feelings, and even deeper feelings associated with instinct—often create a surrounding sense of who we really are. Others might feel uneasy around us, or even be convinced that we are hiding something from them, or being fake in the way we present ourselves to them. Thoughts, feelings, and instincts held out of Primary Awareness exert a certain force field all around us. This is especially true in the case of repressed violent contents. Others around us can feel or sense these stored secrets. Animals can as well. All mammals can sense insincerity and other signals in other mammals. When we are emptied of these contents via confession of them, we become transparent again. That very transparency is radiant because awareness present beneath denied contents is radiant. That radiance is the presence of God in us, but more truly as us. Jesus, Buddha, and Krishna, and all avatars and masters, are able to "see" what is within us because they are awareness itself; they are Spirit in the flesh.

We are all transparent to God because God is the very transparency of our body-spirit. But I am also holding that we are transparent to ourselves. Our deepest selves, our emptied selves, are the transparency and radiance of God, of Spirit. The healthy or proper development of the zone of Secondary Awareness would be formed in the following way. From conception through childhood our families provide the formatting contents of the secondary zone. Our relationships in our families day by day create the very structures of our Familial Subpsyche. This layer is made up of the residual effects of countless interactions within our familial environment, and is an imprint of our experience of that family culture or system. That imprint includes, of course, our place in it, our role or function in the larger system. For this reason we know things about other family members that strangers might never know. We share a family psyche.

Families too are imprinted or formatted by even deeper influences inherited from the culture of which they are a functioning part. Families are the vehicles of enculturation or the lack of it. The Christian-ness, the Moslem-ness, or Jewish-ness of our cultural milieu is imprinted in us by the family. Those imprints form the formatting of the architecture of our souls. Attitudes regarding other cultures will be instilled in us at the structural level of the psyche, at the assumption level by the culture we are born into. All of this happens in the family. Attitudes toward animals and plants, toward Earth and cosmos, and toward God as well come to us from the culture through the family. To have no culture because our family chooses not to transmit one to us, or to have no family, is to be left without a systematic or shaped structure that can become this Secondary Awareness in us. We remain "in potential" only, and are shaped haphazardly by whatever influences us, good or ill.

Whatever contents we deny or disown in Primary Awareness—whether cognitive, affective, or instinctual in nature—are forced out of awareness and remain in Secondary Awareness. When this happens Secondary Awareness becomes a barrier to the deeper spirit-self we inherited at conception. That inherited pre-conception self is what I am calling the Tertiary Awareness. As we lose touch with our depth, we tend to forget the deeper self and continue to block out our awareness of it by further repression. Eventually, Primary Awareness is isolated to a greater or lesser degree from this deeper self. We become isolated in our cognitive faculties because the source of our deeper felt and intuited adequacies are separated from awareness and kept separated by the barrier that Secondary Awareness has become. We forget who we are. We slowly become liars, to ourselves and to others.

Whatever we disown in Awareness and then repress, was at least momentarily known to us and thus remembered. As we invest sometimes small, sometimes great, amounts of psychic energy in holding something out of consciousness, it takes on a powerful existence in the personal subconscious. It remains there gathering the energies of repression around itself, until it grows into the size of a psychic storm, a typhoon, a tornado. At that point it exercises such a hold on us that we become victims of symptoms that point to a major pathological psychic event. Either we succumb to the paralyzing numbing of a depression, or we experience anxiety symptoms as the energy system of the repressed content presents itself emotionally. In the case of depression, the content is acting in the way a cancer acts on the body. It absorbs the energies of one's psychic life and robs consciousness of needed energy. Depression results. As these gathered energies become more powerful than the conscious ability to repress them, they present themselves as anxiety. In either case, we know what is repressed because we repressed it! To take it out of the "shadow" zone, we need only allow it back into the zone of Primary Awareness. In Ken Wilber's words:

> Yes, there are now aspects of the self's being that it doesn't own or admit or acknowledge. It starts to hide from itself. In other words, the self begins lying to itself. A *false self system* begins to grow over the *actual self,* the self that is really there at any given moment, but is now denied or distorted or repressed. Repression, basically, is being untruthful about what is actually running around in your psyche. And thus the *personal unconscious* begins its career. And thus unconscious is, in part, the locus of the self's lie. As we earlier put it, aspects of awareness are split off—"little blobs," little selves, little subjects, are forced into the subterranean dark. These little blobs remain at the level of development they had when they were split off and denied. They cease to grow. They remain in fusion with the level where they were repressed. They hid out in the basement, and the door to that basement is guarded by the lie.
>
> So aspects of your potential, sealed off by the dissociation, begin eating up your energy and your awareness. They are a drain. They sabotage further growth and development. They are dead weight, the weight of a past age that should have been outgrown. But instead, protected and sheltered by the lie, they live on to terrorize. (Wilber, 1996, p. 161)

What Wilber means by the lie of a false self is that this shadow zone of repression is not really a part of the organism until it is created by repression. It is not part of the self created by God, but is a self created by one's will to repress. And because the contents repressed are usually associated with shame (what someone had done to us, e.g., molestation, violence, neglect) or with guilt (what we have done to others, to animals, to Earth or to God, e.g., the seven cardinal sins), the false self is a very painful lie to live with.

The false self is built from "above"—from Primary Awareness. As these contents create the zone of Secondary Awareness (below or subconscious), the deeper zone of the self that I have called Tertiary Awareness becomes separated from our Primary Awareness. In order to become aware of our deeper selves, Secondary Awareness must be emptied.

The false self is inflated from "below" in that it forms a sort of psychic membrane that inflates as it prevents the movement of the life force from Tertiary Awareness to Primary Awareness. When we comment that someone has an inflated ego, an inflated view of herself or himself, we are observing this inflation of the psychic membrane that blocks the life force. Such blockage predictably leads to psychic, behavioral, social, and/or physical disorders that are often expressed in a violent manner—be it violence on the street or when these contained energies erupt into the body tissue as cancer. Violence, then, is not the problem; rather, it is the symptom of a fundamental disorder. Thomas Moore addresses the point:

> The word *violence* comes from the Latin word, *vis*, meaning "life force." Its very roots suggest that in violence the thrust of life is making itself visible. If that fundamental vitality is not present in the heart, it nevertheless seems to appear distorted by our repressions and compromises, our fears and our narcissistic manipulations.
>
> It would be a mistake to approach violence with any simple idea of getting rid of it. Chances are, if we try to eradicate our violence, we will also cut ourselves off from the deep power that sustains creative life. Besides, psychoanalysis

teaches, repression never accomplishes what we want. The repressed always returns in monstrous form. The life current of the soul, *vis*, is like the natural force of plant life, like the grass that grows up through cement and in a relatively short time obliterates grand monuments of culture. If we try taming and boxing in this innate power, it will inevitably find its way into the light.

"Repression of the life force" is a diagnosis I believe would fit most of the emotional problems people present in therapy. (Moore, 1992, p. 127)

The real self is born of God in the same way that the cosmos is born of God. Conception is the temporal signal that creates a window in eternity from which someone is conceived. As people move from eternity into time, they remember the whole of reality, i.e., the pre-conception psyche that consists of the birth and evolution of the cosmos, Earth, life, everything that has thus evolved from the basis or foundation of their psyche. In the words of Anthony Stevens, writing about Carl Jung:

When at eighty-two, he began his autobiography with the words "My life is a story of the self-realization of the unconscious," it is significant that he wrote *the* unconscious, not *my* unconscious, for what fascinated him was the universal human unknown that, generation after generation seeks incarnation. ...

Jung's discovery that schizophrenic delusions had mythic parallels was for him an intellectual watershed. It convinced him that Freud's view was so narrowly personalistic that it blinded him to the existence of the suprapersonal psyche shared by us all by virtue of our humanity. Jung called it the natural mind, a dynamic and universal substratum on which our private world is built. (Stevens, 1993, pp. 8, 10)

The individual created in the pre-temporal, pre-spatial Source gathers to himself or herself the whole of cosmic evolution and then adds to it by his or her own life experiences. Recently we have begun to realize that there is a profound deeper order to "chaos." A pre-temporal and pre-spatial chaos is the order of God, which existed prior to the creation event and expresses itself in the order of the whole creation. We are that pre-temporal and pre-spatial chaos expressed as order. In the "flash" of conception each of us emerges from this pre-temporal and pre-spatial chaos. The science of chaos sees order beneath apparent disorder. I hold that the ultimate chaos, or God, pre-exists the ultimate order, the cosmos, and that each of us emerges from Source-God through the whole cosmos memory in a split second of experience that provides us with a pre-conception memory of the entire cosmos and its evolution.

The personal, familial, and cultural layers block off our pre-conception memory of all that memory-formatting when they are filled with repressed contents. Therefore, emptying of the Personal Subpsyche of its contents allows us to become aware of the introjected contents of our experience of family and of culture. As these contents are emptied we begin to feel deep instinctual signals from the deeper zone of Tertiary Awareness. Those signals will ascend toward Primary Awareness through the formatting structures of Secondary Awareness. In other words, we become more aware! As more contents are emptied, awareness continues to expand. We become aware of our deeper pre-conception psyche, our primateness, our mammalness, our membership in the whole biospheric community, our earthiness, our cosmic and divine lives. When Primary, Secondary, and Tertiary Awareness are one, we come to see that Awareness is one, that Awareness is the glow of beauty, the feeling of truth, and the presence of God. The three zones of awareness are, after all, one Awareness. This unified Awareness is the goal of unitive psychology.

Citing Jung in *The Lemur's Legacy*, Russell refers to this emptying of our psyches of repressed contents as our central task in living: "Man's task is to become conscious of the contents that press upward from (the unconscious). ... As far as we can discern, the sole purpose of human existence is to kindle a light in the darkness of mere being" (Russell, 1993, p. 11).

Jung correctly understood the need for emptying the Personal Sub-psyche. He also understood that the deeper unconscious contained the history of the animals, planet, and even the cosmos. What is less clear is whether he understood the possibility of what I am dealing with in this book. Yes, the removal of the blockage between the upper and lower levels of the psyche will lead to a reunified psyche. But what if the very structures of the deeper psyche are being disassembled? We might have the psychic symbols, the archetypes, present in our psyches, but what if their living counterparts are being extinguished? If, for instance, the structuring of our psyches depends upon the correlates of a living community of primates, basal mammals, reptile-amphibians, and ultimately of the whole life community, would the elimination of these correlates ultimately eliminate, through forgetting, the very organs of our own psyches? If so, no amount of emptying ourselves of our personal contents can bring back or replace these correlate beings. If our own affective cortices depend upon the mammals, then the mammals themselves are organs of our psyches. If the Instinctual Subpsyche depends upon the reptiles and earlier life forms, then these reptiles and earlier life forms are organs of our psyches. In that case, how would we possibly escape thought and mood disorders? We'd have to think of ourselves as disordered no matter how empty we became. In that case, we would be structurally disordered. Emptiness, then, would only make us more aware of our disorders.

Still, in order to at least become aware of our deeper selves, ordered or disordered, we must empty ourselves. Presumably, the Christian sacrament of confession-reconciliation was meant to serve the same purpose—emptying. Guilt-ridden sinners would come before the understanding and merciful representative of Christ. Then they could let down their guard and allow the painful contents to come forth and be given the healing touch of another's forgiveness and acceptance. The priest, in turn, could invoke his power to forgive in the name of the whole Catholic Church—in the name of God! For the believer, this represents a whole lot more than the relief of unburdening oneself of painful repressed contents. It amounted to communal restoration and the full forgiveness of God. In other words, it represented the dissolution of karma. Karma, the law of cause and effect, holds that a person's action and responsibility for that action is recorded on the very fibre of the cosmos. But God, Source of the cosmos, is Lord of Karma. In the Catholic confessional the chains of karma are broken and individuals are freed to be their real, original self again. Naturally, sorrow must be real. The depth of true sorrow is the measurement of sincerity of the confessee. Sorrow is the felt emotional charge that surrounds the sin event. It is the charge of sorrow or guilt that brings the repressed content to the fore.

The Buddhists have *Shunyata*, often translated as emptiness or void. I have always felt that either definition was incorrect and misleading. My skepticism was confirmed in 1993 at the Parliament of World's Religions in Chicago. There, Buddhist Maseo Abe gave a talk that focused on this very word and explained that Shunyata is best translated as *emptying*. He explained the word by quoting the Pauline corpus in which Paul spoke of Christ emptying himself of his divinity and taking on the human condition.

Emptying is what we do in therapy, in twelve-step programs, and in confession. Having emptied ourselves of the toxins of repressed personal contents, we gain access to the next two layers—the Familial Subpsyche and Cultural Subpsyche. Both are layers in what I am calling the post-conception psyche. But they are deeper and less conscious than the Personal Subpsyche. In fact, they provide the assumptions that often govern the choices we make, which result in the need for repression of personal contents. So, if we were brought up black or white in the pre-Civil Rights South, we'd be likely to have, as familial and/or cultural assumptions, inferiority in the case of blacks, superiority in the case of whites, as a feeling-level assumption. In either case, our deluded assumptions would cause pain in our personal lives and begin the need for repression early on. To empty the Personal Subpsyche in either case would open the possibility of having a clearer view of the deeper deluded assumptions on the part of those who preceded us. This ability to "see" the deeper causes of our woes would grant us the opportunity to begin the painful process of structural change.

If there has been no real cultural structuring at all—no religion in our families of origin—the first task of the therapist following cathartic emptying of the Personal Subpsyche would be to help the client in building a cultural self. If there was no proper family structure, as in the case of an adopted person or someone who experienced parental divorce, the family structures need to be built. Some form of group therapy would be indicated.

But in all cases, those of us who are alive presently must go further. We must:

- Empty the Personal Subpsyche
- Heal the Familial Subpsyche, creating structures where necessary
- Heal the Cultural Subpsyche, creating religious structures where necessary

These three must be done so we can begin the work of reconstructing Tertiary Awareness. In other words, we must help to heal our shared environment in order that our individual souls can heal and become whole. We must accomplish this not only for ourselves but also for our families, for our children, and for our grandchildren. This represents what Thomas Berry has called the "Great Work."

CHAPTER FIVE

The Familial Subpsyche

Whatever has happened in your family shapes you. Events that occurred long before your birth, never mentioned in your family during your lifetime, may influence you in powerful, though hidden, ways. Take, for example, a child who dies before another's birth, for whom the next child becomes a replacement. If the "replacement" child tries to leave home as a young adult, the entire family may go into crisis. Yet no one links the upheaval to the loss that occurred years earlier. Every fact of your family's biography is part of the many-layered pattern that becomes your identity. (McGoldrick, 1995, p. 30)

WHO AMONG US HAS NOT CAUSE TO WEEP over their parents? Their families? Most of us have more than a little to say regarding our families. Our differences with family members can range from irritation, to years and even decades of bitter estrangement. Still, even in the most bitter cases, let someone else criticize a family member and we find our feelings becoming defensive. We seldom feel neutral when someone attacks a family member. In fact, we feel personally attacked when someone does so. This is because our experience of our families becomes part of who we are as the Familial Subpsyche.

Even in utero, we are affected by whatever happens to the family that surrounds us, and in which we are embedded. We hear their voices before we hear our own. We experience their affections or discord with each other before we experience our own affections or discord toward any of them. We are affected by their moods, laughter, grief, hatreds, shame, and bliss before we have the ability to reflect upon our experience of them. We know them before we know that we know them. They shape us before we have any choice in the matter.

In a profound and immediate way we experience our mother's point of view toward any and all members of the family—and indeed, we live in her world. In the same way that our bodies experience the ebb and flow of her body processes, reacting to whatever enters or does not enter into the habitat of her body, our soul is embedded in her—whatever she feels we feel. Whatever contents are stored in her memory are, at the feeling level at least, stored in our own. If she is ashamed, we feel shame. If she is afraid, we feel fear. If she feels safe, we feel safe. Her experience is in a real way our own experience. In a sense, we remember our experience of her experience in a deeper place within us than we experience our experience of ourselves.

The impact and subsequent internalizing of our mother's or family's experience becomes the immediate foundation of our personality. We store these primitive feelings in a layer of ourselves that goes deeper than the Personal Subpsyche. There, stored feelings become the assumptions that underlie our own self-concept.

Those contents stored in the Familial Subpsyche are recorded in us post-conception; however, they are structures that pre-exist our conception in that they exist in the people who conceive us and in the culture that conceived and shaped them. They form deep formatting structures imprinted in our psyches that often determine our predispositions to certain behaviors, thoughts, and feelings. Our psyches interpret those structures at subconscious, mythic, or assumption levels, and then we act out of those subconscious or assumption level dynamics.

Our families and cultures provide the stories that will guide us through our conscious lives. These stories clarify our place in the family and, eventually, in the world. The family members, even the pets, play roles in the unfolding drama. These familial and cultural stories or myths are learned at such deep levels of our psyches that we are not aware of even knowing them. The following excerpt further elucidates the point:

> The family is the crucible in which the imperatives of genet-
> ics and the mythology of a civilization are amalgamated
> into the unique mythic framework that shapes each person's
> development. Personal myths are the individual's legacy
> from the past and a source of guidance and inspiration for
> the future. They are pregnant with the hopes and the disap-
> pointments of prior generations. Operating largely outside
> of conscious awareness, personal myths are internal struc-
> tures that organize perceptions, govern emotions, coalesce
> thoughts, and mediate behavior. Personal myths continually
> evolve and are responsive to purposeful intervention. (Fein-
> stein and Krippner, 1988, pp. 130–131)

This lack of awareness of the roles that have been cast upon us by the needs of the family myth in which we mature is necessary for our families and us to function. If the roles were up for debate upon reaching childhood, adolescence, and adulthood, then the family system would fragment into a squabbling mess of immaturity and confusion. We grow by accepting, embracing, and exploring our roles with their concomitant obligations and relations. To be brought up in a family circle that is sup-portive, stable, fluid, and adaptive lends to becoming a stable, supportive, fluid, and adaptable person. As we mature, becoming more aware of how each role we played in the family myth prepared us for life in the world, we can better appreciate the wisdom inherent in the process.

Unfortunately, there is no guarantee that a child will be born into a healthy family myth. If one is caught in an unhappy myth and a miser-able role, then life can be a prison of infinite proportions. To be brought up in a broken or violent home is to be subjected to shattering experi-ences that will always tend to leave us broken or shattered in the depths of our own personhood.

In the present age, we have become so accustomed to divorce that we forget that the child experiencing divorce loses his biological right to both parents, his right to his siblings, his right to the safety of the familial nest within the nest of the neighborhood within the nest of the town or city, and so on. The psychic foundations of children of divorce are seriously fractured—without any choice in the matter! There is little wonder why the souls of our young people are full of confusion and rage.

The Human Courtship Ritual

At the root of the disintegration of the family, with its corresponding disintegration of the culture, we find the erosion of ritual. In this case, the ritual we are losing is more than just the culturally embedded ritual of marriage. What we are losing is the more fundamental biological ritual of familying that enables us to bond and mate in permanent ways. Consequently, our ability to live day by day with our children, transmitting to them the familial and cultural histories, erodes. In losing the two-parent family, we lose the richness of its dual mythologies, as Huyghe named them, "the all-forgiving maternal" and the "paternal which cultivates intellect, emotions and will." Our children are growing up in family myths that seem like the "Clash of the Titans," wherein the mother and father are estranged from each other and vilified by each other. All the while, the children are losing familial stories that would guide them in their growth toward becoming mature, loving, and nurturing adults. The erosion of the familial stories reinforces the erosion of the cultural rituals attendant to love, courtship, sexuality, and the raising of families. With the weakening of both the familial and cultural formatting, our children become increasingly narcissistic, barbaric, and materialistic.

We need to understand the human courtship ritual. All life forms seem to have some form of specific behavior that takes place around mating. These behaviors are ritual communications between the males and females that allow each of them to understand what the other is asking for, and to respond either positively or negatively to the request. Should the response be positive, subsequent behaviors continue this process of arousal that eventually leads to union, fertilization, and biological evolution. Humans, having developed morality and culture as governance for these instinctual drives, likewise have a mating ritual, though we don't often think about it in this way.

Our mating ritual has six basic stages. As they evolve, one to the next, they perform a bonding function that joins us at the deepest levels possible. To abort the ritual at any of the preliminary stages is to abort the bonding and—in my opinion—to largely guarantee a divorce. (Divorce, the breaking into two, happens when the bonding process ends, not when the legal procedure commences years or decades later.)

A real marriage is, at the spiritual level, comparable to conception. In conception, two distinct genetic bundles come together and fuse into a completely new being. DNA is shared. Cytoplasm is shared. A complete union, indestructible and eternal, is formed—a person emerges. When we bond properly, similar things takes place at the instinctual-spiritual level. Recognition, courtship, announcement to the community, community-religious ritual, and private ritual of consummation then take place. In consummation the bond is materialized, and the two become one.

Since the sixties in the U.S. there has been a progressive weakening of this ritual unfolding and, therefore, necessarily of the bond of marriage. The family is a shattered biocultural institution. Because we can think the idea of physical sex only doesn't mean that that thought is grounded in affect, instinct, or biology. It's an idea. I can think, for instance, of an Earth with no sun or moon. It's an idea! But my ability to even think it is dependent on a real Earth in union with the real sun and the real moon. This Earth, this planet, is the truth. My ideational Earth is an abstraction, a lie, the absence of truth. Our ideas about "free love," "recreational sex," and the inevitable "right to choose" that is their consequence, seem in the mind of this author to be cognitive constructs. We seem to create them in an attempt to elevate abstractions and semantic deceptions into truths. These do not seem to be working for us—they are certainly not working for our young, born or pre-born.

So, let's take a look at the six stages of our mating ritual:

1. Meeting
2. Recognition
3. Courtship
4. Public announcement (engagement)
5. Public ritual of marriage
6. Private ritual of consummation

Meeting

Meeting, it goes without saying, is the a priori condition for relationship. We meet people daily—in traffic, in stores, at restaurants, in work contexts, in virtually every context we find ourselves in every day of our lives. Still, with all these meetings, few of them become significant relationships in our lifetime. I, myself, have not loved deeply more than half a dozen times, perhaps less. In each case, however, I was aware of a deep bonding attraction in the first meeting. In every instance where I pushed for early sex, the relationship became complex and died. The many clients I have seen over the years report similar experiences. Meeting in this way is more than meeting. It is a significant encounter, a revelatory experience of a biospiritual nature. Our bodies and our souls respond with heightened levels of awareness. We know something about ourselves and about this person that we didn't know prior to meeting. Nonetheless, we cannot really articulate what it is that we know. We recognize something about this person. This recognition is the driving energy of the next stage.

Recognition

Usually this period of time following meeting is a very stressful experience. Every weakness and embarrassing content from our Cultural, Familial, and Personal Subpsyches is thrown into high relief. This happens because the deeper zone of the self, that of Tertiary Awareness, literally lights up "beneath" the zone of Secondary Awareness. The contents (good and bad) of the Secondary Awareness are projected into Primary Awareness and we begin to juggle our personal assets and liabilities in order to bolster or negate our claim to being worthy of relationship with this person. Many people are so crippled by contents of Secondary Awareness that they will back off from even attempting courtship. Others will move ahead in a decent and calm manner, convinced of their own basic worth and value. Still others might be stimulated into acts of violence such as rape, if the contents within them are sufficiently volatile. In any case, this period is a time of recognition, of re-*cognizing* who we are in our depths, below cognition.

The instinctual cortex, the brain stem, lights up with re-cognized mating signals that have supported the overall evolution of life for millions of years. The affective brain is overloaded with contents thrown up from Secondary Awareness and the Cognitive Subpsyche tries to manage all these signals, usually causing us to make fools of ourselves during the re-cognizing overload. If everything works out, we find ourselves on a date. Then begins courtship.

COURTSHIP

Movies these days keep telling us that courtship begins with a sexual experience. Well, it does to the extent that all of the above is deliciously sexual. But they are lying to us when they tell us that the courtship stage begins with a genital exchange. If that is the case, we run the risk of aborting the whole bonding process. Most people I've counseled—male and female—report knowing that they've lost the relationship the moment they've moved into genital experience. There is a pain signal that we seldom can name as pain that arises from the depth of the psyche signaling a breaking of the bond. At this point, the relationship is in all likelihood over. The only times I've observed this not being the case is when one and then both partners admit that they don't feel good about crossing the genital boundary at that time. When it happens that they truly step away from further genital behaviors (and this is terribly difficult to do in that it feels like an attempt to make evolution run backward), the relationship has a reasonable hope of survival.

For reasons coded into us by nature itself, and reflected in our cultural-moral coding, the process of interior bonding is impaired by exterior bonding early on in the relationship. It creates a sort of barrier (divorce) between the two people and the spiritual "cytoplasm" is prevented from flowing back and forth. We can think that this should not be the case in the same way that I can think the idea that I should be able to walk on the underside of clouds. My ability to think it does not mean that it exists other than in my thought. The time of courtship is the time of bonding our interiors, our depths. It is the period of the real work of relationship building. If, after a reasonable period of courtship, we discover that we are still compatible and attracted, we make a public announcement of our intent to become one, to marry.

PUBLIC ANNOUNCEMENT TO THE COMMUNITY

> Marriage is proclaimed publicly so all members of the social group are aware that an inviolate consort bond has been established. Marriage bonds are negotiated. As for our ancestors, the formation of this sexual bond requires an exchange of goods: a man gives money, food, property, or the promise of protection and security in exchange for sexual access. (Russell, 1993, p. 171)

This public announcement in our culture is called engagement. A diamond ring announces this period to the world. It is a ritual passage to a deeper level of commitment. The diamond signifies the many facets of our personalities and the durability we are claiming exists in our relationship. It is a time for family, friends, and the larger community to grow used to the idea of these two people forming a permanent union, and the community is given the opportunity to support or not support the union. It is also during this period that the couple might begin to experience their exterior bonding by engaging in the early phases of sexual behavior. The need to know if they are bodily compatible can be satisfied during the engagement process. Having bonded on the inside, they test the bond on their outsides before coming to full communion with one another. Courtship bonds their interiors. Engagement bonds their exteriors. The following two stages complete their communion.

PUBLIC RITUAL OF MARRIAGE

All cultures without exception have some form of marriage ritual. Even completely secular versions of marriage, such as those done by Justices of the Peace, include witnesses and vows, and are usually done in a formal atmosphere of at least some solemnity. In the marriage ritual, the community (sometimes represented by only two witnesses but represented nonetheless) comes together around the two individuals in order to proclaim that they are a couple. This is usually conducted in a religious context signifying not only the bonding of the two people, but their bonding to the community and the community bonding to Spirit. Marriages then take on a planetary and indeed a cosmic dimension in these ritual experiences. It's not about stained glass and organs. It's about the recognition that our love for each other is a function of the whole cosmic-spiritual process. But when all this bonding is done, the marriage is still not complete. There is yet another, final seal to the process.

PRIVATE RITUAL OF CONSUMMATION

Consummation is the experience of full sexual union and the exchange of DNA. The couple, having bonded in mutual recognition, in courtship, and in the community, now comes together to share the force of life itself in the carnal enjoyment of each other. What the couple has done in bonding spiritually and emotionally, they now do in bonding physically. Again, they become one. Man, woman, all humans, all primates, all mammals, all forms of life, the planet, the cosmos, and their source are joined in conception. Evolution moves forward. The significance is incalculable. It represents the core meaning of our lives individually, as a community, as a species, as a life form. The pleasure is significant of the depth of union that occurs in consummation.

When children are born to a couple so joined in the soul-field of a genuine couple bond, a new holon or soul-field emerges, and includes the child in the bond. This is a family, a new holon, a human nested hierarchy of love. The family is a holon within the larger holon of the community. The community is a holon within the larger holon of a culture. Cultures are holons within the context of the other cultures. The biosphere of Earth is a holon containing countless billions of sub-holons that make up the life communities of Earth. The human family is a biocultural reality. Cultures formed of these holons are viable cultures.

The Family As a Cultural Unit

Family myths and subconscious beliefs not only bring conscious and subconscious contents together, they bring culture and biosphere together as well—biosphere is brought "up" into culture or noosphere. Where this does not happen, there opens a lesion between the biological inheritance of the human (i.e., the primate-mammalian-reptilian, organic, pre-organic, geological, Kosmological, and ultimately the Source of the pre-conception psyche) with neocortical realities located in the human. This "unplugging" of the deepest psyche from the most recent psyche might be the root cause of our present crises with mental health. We simply cannot functionally disconnect ourselves from the overall history of our evolution without suffering deeply. We cannot deny our depth needs, the biological history that is our source, without seeing the results of that deprivation at the surface. As Anthony Stevens put it:

> If we are to understand the psychiatric disorders from which our contemporaries suffer, therefore, we have to consider in what ways Western society frustrates the needs of the two-million-year-old—that is to say, the primordial man or woman—within. Many possibilities immediately come to mind: the disruption of community-based kinship bonds

as a result of migration, job mobility, experiments in town planning, and so on; the disruption of families through divorce and separation, together with the rapidly increasing incidence of single-parent families; the lack of adequate provision for the secure and intimate care of children whose mothers go out to work; the loss of myth, ritual, and religion; the lack of contact with nature, the seasons, and the primordial environment. (Stevens, 1993, p. 68)

We are social animals. We evolved that way and selection created us as familial and cultural beings. The great stories of our past civilization enterprises are the link between our geobiological selves and our neocortical-cultural selves. We cannot rid ourselves of them without creating a rift between the modern culture-bound human and the equally necessary animal dimension of our being. We cannot deny the fact that we have evolved since the period of the great religious cultures. As Joseph Campbell has stated, meaning in primitive times was located in the group, whereas in our times, meaning is located in the individual. This requires individuals "to consciously participate in charting their own guiding mythologies" (Feinstein and Krippner, 1988, p. 132). But, if we do this without taking into account the deeper levels of our psyches, we do it to our peril. Hinduism, Buddhism, Taoism, Confucianism, Judaism, Christianity, Islam, indigenous belief systems, and all religions from the past provide the socket into which the pre-conception psyche plugs. They are the architectural bridge between the collective present and the collective past. The collapse of that bridge threatens to functionally disconnect the new brain from the old brain, the new psyche from the old, the psyche from the body, the human from the Earth.

When the cultural story is abandoned, the family story collapses—it lacks context and support. As the family, the psychic nest of the human, collapses, we are all thrust upon our individual strengths alone. The present culture is the result of this collapse. Humans cannot make it alone. We become sick, addicted, and suicidal as a result of our "anxious solitude."

With all the self-focused demands about so-called "rights" to having one's needs met, "rights" to choose, "rights" to career and personal fulfillment, we seem to be losing a sense of responsibility for our young. Regardless of where one stands on the abortion issue, it seems to me that honesty predicates the admission that family life in the United States has become less and less stable since the 1973 decision to "decriminalize" abortion. The reason for this might be that the primary species-level imperative of all life forms is the creation of the future in the form of young. When we foreclose on our young, we foreclose on the future. It is a legitimate goal to control the growth of population globally. How we do so is a profound moral (instinctual) and, I'd add, biological issue.

The building of truly bonded relationships with one another through an appropriate unfolding of our courtship ritual enables men and women to remain together long enough to become friends—lifelong friends. Following the initial high-energy events of falling in love and procreating, this lower-energy bonding of friendship provides the lifelong support for the psychic nest of the family. These friendships are built upon a mutual caring and concern for each other's needs, whether spiritual, cognitive, emotional, instinctual, or physical. The young are given a model of goodwill and decency and have the security of a well-bonded nest. I recall my wife, Carol, sharing with me a piece of advice from one of the first parenting books we read while awaiting the birth of our first child. The authors stated that the best thing parents can do for their children is to love each other. I have found this to be true in my twenty-five years of marriage. It is the advice I give my clients.

When we are honest, most of us are able to admit to a fairly rich and far-ranging sexual fantasy life. While this is true, and while it sometimes creates not a small amount of tension in our lives, most humans have settled on monogamy as the optimum constellation for familying, and for permanent happiness. The following excerpt further elaborates this point:

> A small degree of polygamy could exist, but it would be
> severely limited. It is interesting that although it still occurs
> in a number of minor cultures today, all the major societies

(which account for the vast majority of the world population of the species) are monogamous. Even in those that permit polygamy, it is not usually practiced by more than a small minority of the males concerned. It is intriguing to speculate as to whether its omission from almost all the larger cultures has, in fact, been a major factor in the attainment of their present successful status. (Morris, 1967, p. 83)

With the evolution of a lifelong friendship, the greatest satisfaction seems to be made available to the greatest number of us. We've all heard "there are no perfect marriages." It's true. But because it's true is no cause to abandon the institution altogether.

This wide-ranging and complex fantasy life might be nothing more than our memory of our primate origins. Thus, the reality of biological or physical monogamy seems to be belied by an internal or psychic promiscuity. Monogamous marriage seems to work best when we can admit to this dual nature of ours. We are happiest when embraced by the context of a family culture. Still, we are haunted by fantasies that try to lead us elsewhere; however, when we follow the promptings of these fantasies, we more often than not create individual, familial, and cultural disruption, experienced as pain and pathology. We cannot escape our primate or mammalian inheritance. The "primammal" (primate-mammalian) truth within us, transcended and included in our evolutionary leap to culture and self-reflective consciousness, must be included in our overall understanding of who we really are. Too often, religious leaders spin the illusion that there is some sort of "transcendence" of our sexual condition—transcendence in their usage meaning a leap over or away from sexuality. It is not true! No one escapes his or her sexuality without extreme psychopathology. Evolution occurs in a transcendence of the present and inclusion of it in the future. We are mammals. We are primates. We are culture-creating humans. Included in our being is a longing for many mates; and yet our souls long for monogamy. Both are true and must be treated gently, and with mutual forgiveness. Friendship, honesty, and goodwill—also human attributes—make this possible.

Pathology of the Familial Subpsyche

The Secondary Awareness psyche is a post-conception structure of consciousness. It can be imagined as three concentric layers forming a single band that constellate between the structure of Primary Awareness and the structure of Tertiary Awareness. One's personal memories—whether cognitive, affective, or instinctual—form the center of the band and are the most available to Primary Awareness. The second band is composed of familial memories—cognitive, affective, or instinctual. The third and furthest band, which we shall deal with in the next chapter, is the cultural band that provides the context for the familial and personal layers. So, sickness in the family becomes structural sickness in the individual. Sickness in the culture becomes the context for sickness in the family and, therefore, in the individual.

Most readers are familiar with the family structure of the addicted home. In such a system, each member takes on a specific and rigid role in order to play out a specific function of the family culture. The alcoholic-addict and the spouse-enabler are at the nucleus of the system. One child becomes the family hero, usually a people pleaser who presents the family's "best face" to the world. Next comes the rebel, who plays the part of trying to act out the sickness in the family system by bad behavior and rebellion. Then there is the "lost child," a sort of imploded person who lives a lonely and alienated existence within the family and without. There's also a mascot or clown who acts out the family's sense of humor and lightens reality for the other members. The point is that each member becomes frozen in place, restricted to a role in the family, with a set script and rigid expectations. The only person in the system who exhibits any freedom is the alcoholic-addict, and she or he is enslaved to the substance of addiction.

The pathology in such a family is systemic, but it is experienced in the individual as his or her illness:

> The members of the pathogenic family are differentiated
> in their roles and form an interacting and self-maintaining

system within which it's scarcely possible to point to one member as causative for the characteristics of the system as a whole. Indeed, the assigning of cause or blame to one or other member of such a plexus presents problems rather similar to those presented by the question "Who is the most sick?" The identified patient is most overtly sick, but the family system itself is undoubtedly strange and the strangeness may be specifically located not in the individuals but in the premises governing the differentiation of their roles. (Bateson, 1991, pp. 114–115)

Even the threat or attempt at suicide is a function of the whole system or group. Chaos theorist Linda Chamberlain says this:

Bergman (1985) defined suicide threats as just another symptom that serves to maintain equilibrium in the family. Suicidal behavior may serve as a means of preventing change (chaos) and maintaining stability (order). For example, a child's suicide attempt may unite parents who are conflicted. ...

The appearance of suicide may be a way to increase the chaos in the system to a crisis point that will necessitate the family taking some new action to re-establish order, such as making contact with a psychotherapist. (Chamberlain, 1995, pp. 117–118)

Too frequently, people serving the restorative function in a sick family succeed in the attempted suicide. Their lives are given for the family in a misguided attempt to pull the family toward help. Tragically, the suicidal death of a family member often does little or nothing to thaw the system that is frozen.

It all comes down to this. We cannot produce healthy children in unhealthy families. We cannot produce healthy families in cultures devoid of their moral-instinctual moorings. Healthy humans need to be nested in healthy families. Healthy families are created by a proper adherence to the human courtship ritual, which is included in religious ritual. Healthy courtship rituals are a function of culture. So, we now turn to the Cultural Subpsyche, the deepest layer of Secondary Awareness.

Chapter Six

The Cultural Subpsyche

But it is nonetheless clear that if an ethical unconscious did not exist, no amount of police force or bureaucracy could hold any society together. We form ourselves spontaneously into family, clan, band, tribe, guild, village, town. This is social ecology in action. (Roszak, 1992, p. 229)

HUMANS CREATE CULTURE. What the pack, the flock, or the herd is to different animal species, culture is to humans. We form tribes based on a unified code of behavior, unified ritual, and unified relationship to the surrounding environment. When we evolve beyond the tribal experience of culture, we form larger organizational structures called religions. Our cultures are the product of our religions. Religions are the self-organizing dynamics between us, the transpersonal dimension of our psyche. All cultures are sacred cultures in that they are organized around a vision of God. So-called "secular cultures" are cultures in decline, cultures in pathology.

Our biological evolution proceeds from instinct to affect to cognition. While I am aware of oversimplifying the issue, I shall nonetheless assert that tribal religions mediate our instinctual relationship to the environment, that our religious cultures (Buddhism and Christianity come to mind) mediate a compassionate or altruistic relationship to each other and our environment, and that with the abandonment of both of these we have found ourselves in an information glut. The information age separated from affect and instinct might be one cause of our dissatisfaction and epidemic meaninglessness. It is not as though cognition is negative or without value in and of itself. Still, separated from our deeper forms of knowing and their deeper forms of religious experience and ritual, cognition alone isolates us from each other and our environment.

In unitive psychology, it must be remembered that every developmental level we achieve is dependent on those we have transcended and included. So it is with evolution in the natural order. Physical cosmic law was transcended by, and included in, the earliest life forms, known as bacteria or prokaryotes. Prokaryotes were transcended by, and included in, complex cells known as eukaryotes, such as amoebas and paramecium. Eukaryotes were transcended by, and included in, multicellular life forms known as invertebrates, such as worms. Invertebrates were transcended by, and included in, vertebrates, such as fish and reptiles. Vertebrates were transcended by, and included in, mammals. Mammals were transcended by, and included in, primates. Hence, all of life and all physical law was transcended by, and included in, humans. Herding, packing, flocking, and trooping life was transcended by, and included in, human culture. If we destructure primate troops, mammalian herds, bird flocks, and fish schools, will our cultures disintegrate and sink? So it is when we lose the tribal and religious inheritance we've received from the past. Our souls, missing these deeper influences and their formatting, collapse into chronic depression and anxiety disorders. A sinking of the deeper structures must result in a sinking in the upper structures. Collapse and disintegration, whether in the material or the non-material worlds, are inevitable when we attempt to disrupt the flow of soulful and cultural formatting.

The imperative to make culture, much like the urge to flock or herd, is genetically passed. But cultural structures, moral codes, and rituals are not passed genetically. All humans will always develop culture. The specifics of the cultures we inherit from the past, however, are not included in our genetic gifting. A child orphaned at infancy in Buddhist

Vietnam can be brought up in Mormon Utah. The child, though Asian genetically, will be a Mormon culturally.

The idea prevalent since the sixties that children should be brought up unprejudiced by a tradition so that they can later, "in freedom," choose their own path, is flawed. The opposite of cultural transmission isn't freedom, it's forced neo-barbarism. The lack of culture is barbarism. What I mean by neo-barbarism is the missing formatting structures of the Cultural, and therefore Familial and Personal, Subpsyche.

These structures are learned in the context of the family's religious tradition and ritual. Without these teachings and their resultant cultural transmission, children are without the inner ethical and moral vocabulary that enables them to understand their place in the world and the transpersonal dynamics of relationship with others around them.

Deeper still, they are lacking the structures that enable them to connect to and relate to the other life forms in their area. Missing this deep formatting, they are without the ability to interpret signals coming from Tertiary Awareness. In street gangs, we observe this inability to interpret signals coming from the primate level of our being. Dominance hierarchies once again exert themselves without mediation of compassion or altruism. In short, cultures mediate nature, families mediate culture, and without this mediation a person is lost and dehumanized both naturally and culturally. We see this alienation from life and from other humans all around us. A psychology that does not address these deep pathologies cannot heal.

Does God Remember?

I'd like to return to the beginning of the book for a moment. I've said that there are three levels of awareness: Primary, Secondary, and Tertiary Awareness. These, of course, are ways in which Awareness manifests itself in the created order, and therefore in us. But the awareness itself is one, and it suffuses or permeates the whole cosmos, Earth, and all levels of life and culture. The level of awareness present in an amoeba is certainly different from the level of awareness present in a horse. But the awareness itself is one. It is the evolved complexity of the horse that allows awareness to exhibit itself in greater depth than in the amoeba. I hold, following Ken Wilber and others, that the awareness precedes space/time. This is in fact what is held by most religions around the world. This truth is eloquently declared in the opening lines of the Gospel of John: "In the beginning was the Word, the Word was with God, and the Word was God. ... Through him all things came into being, not one thing came into being except through him. What has come into being in him was life, life that was the light of men" (New Jerusalem Bible, p. 1744).

Awareness is the presence of Spirit. Past is the memory of Spirit. The memory of Spirit is nonlocal and, therefore, available to all. Jung's groundbreaking work on the collective unconscious and archetypes shed a great light on understanding how Spirit remembers:

> The collective unconscious contains the whole spiritual her-
> itage of mankind's evolution, born anew in the brain struc-
> ture of every individual. ... The unconscious ... is the source
> of the instinctual forces of the psyche and of the forms or
> categories that regulate them, namely the archetypes. All the
> most powerful ideas in history go back to archetypes. This is
> particularly true of religious ideas, but the central concepts
> of science, philosophy, and ethics are no exception to this
> rule. In their present form they are variants of archetypal
> ideas, created by consciously applying and adapting these
> ideas to reality. For it is the function of consciousness not
> only to recognize and assimilate the external world through
> the gateway of the senses, but to translate into visible reality
> the world within us. (Jung, 1960, p. 158)

So, is Jung correct in saying that there is a collective unconscious? Yes, I'd say so. Does it manifest in archetypal structure throughout the created order? Yes. Can we remember these structures? Yes, to the extent that we can feel or intuit earlier memories of awareness, and bring them "up" into thought. As we do so, we make culture and store what we remember in the Cultural Subpsyche. Families help us to remember these deep stories of life. The culture formed of these remembered stories supports the ability to remember. Each of us has the propensity to remember culture and store it in the Cultural Subpsyche, but we must be reminded of that information in order to remember and store it. It is the function of religion to remind us of these deep stories that are our Source. Otherwise, we forget. In any case, we will create culture, whether the culture of the street gang or the religions of the ages.

While I feel uncomfortable with computer-versus-human comparisons, they nonetheless sometimes provide a working metaphor. We are born without the cultural, familial, or individual stories of Secondary Awareness. The "hard drive" of Secondary Awareness is formatted and ready; however, it is empty. The cultural, familial, and personal content must be "written" onto the hard drive. Without the cultural story inherited in the family, the individual is without the ability to "read" his or her deeper identity and, consequently, he or she is unable to completely engage the cultural milieu of the world at large.

As I said in Chapter Four, the zone of Secondary Awareness is also the locus of storage for repressed cognitive, affective, and instinctual contents. When enough repression and denial have taken place that this zone is "filled" with "static," the person so affected finds his or her ability to integrate Tertiary and Primary Awarenesses blocked. In staying with the computer metaphor, it is as if the memory files have been corrupted. All that is needed in this case is a profound experience of confession—whether in counseling, a twelve-step program, or a religious context. When this happens, the hard drive of Secondary Awareness is "rebooted" so that the person can experience the reintegration of all three zones of identity.

The biological aspect that allows us to store cultural, familial, and personal contents is the human body with its triune brain. Because we have a brain stem, we can incorporate the contents of the pre-human created order. Because we have an affective cortex, we can incorporate the contents of the mammalian order. Because we have a cognitive cortex, we can incorporate the primate and cultural order. Because we have the potential zones of Cultural, Familial, and Personal Subpsyches, we can store and utilize the past. Cultural contents stored become the context for familial contents. We store in the Cultural Subpsyche the stories about God, who God is, what God does. Even in utero we begin this process because of what we take in from the family context that surrounds the mother's body. Imagine the different experience it must be for a person in utero to hear-feel the murmuring of family prayers, the chanting of the *om,* the listening to Verdi's requiem? Now imagine the sounds of family discord mixed with acts of domestic violence, the swearing and beating, the blasting television or AM radio? The experienced difference between these two realities becomes the fundamental reality of the being within. Imagine what abortion or war is like from within. My wife fell off some rocks into shallow water when she was eight-and-a-half months pregnant. She landed belly first on a slightly submerged rock. My daughter has a deep fear of waves. Can I prove the two events are connected? No. Do I believe they are? Yes, certainly.

Ex utero, the child begins to experience stories of God—or the lack of them. Ritual and prayer, or the lack of them. These contents, or the lack of them, are stored and give shape to the Cultural Subpsyche. That shaping will form the window through which the contents of Tertiary Awareness will find expression. An empty disk equals an empty screen. Without the stored contents of the Cultural Subpsyche, we cannot interpret the signals coming from the animals, the life community, the Earth, the cosmos, or from God. We are lost in a confusion of feelings, or worse yet, a feeling vacuum, a meaningless cosmos. If we are not lost, it is because someone taught us the stories of God (or the gods, depending upon one's religion) and gave shape to the Cultural Subpsyche. Training and participation in the sacraments, such as baptism and communion, provide for Christians the basis upon which a religious story can be built and formatted in the psyche.

The experience of a family story is built upon these foundations of a cultural story. An individual story is built upon a familial story. We cannot build an adequate self without a family self and a cultural self.

Counseling or psychotherapy must certainly include the emptying of the painful feelings about oneself repressed and stored in the Secondary Awareness zone. However, if we do not include the rebuilding of the structures of the family and culture, we do little indeed to help anyone. As we empty the pain of the cognitive, affective, and instinctual levels of the self, we need to be able to offer personal relationship, a familial context, and a religious or cultural story in order to reformat the subpsyche. Chodorow elaborates upon this point quite clearly:

> The functions of the cultural Self include Henderson's four basic cultural attitudes: the aesthetic, the religious, the philosophic and the social—as well as a central, emerging, self-reflective psychological attitude. Each of the attitudes may be understood as a particular form of the imagination. And each offers a way to experience the life of the spirit. ...
>
> Henderson (1984) characterizes the four main cultural attitudes: "The ethical consistency of a social attitude, the logic of a philosophical attitude, the transcendent nature of a religious attitude. ... the sensuous irrationality of the aesthetic attitude" (p. 49).
>
> The aesthetic attitude seeks the world of beauty. The religious attitude seeks the realm of the sacred. The philosophic attitude seeks principles of universal validity. The social attitude seeks a state of communal well being, utopian communitas. As we see, the cultural attitudes lead us to the age-old ideals of ultimate human value: the Beautiful, the Holy, the True and the Good. The functions of the cultural Self are mirrored in the external cultural forms of Art, Religion, Philosophy and Society. (Chodorow, 1991, pp. 86–87)

The "cultural self" is the transpersonal self, the self that is more than just "me," the connective tissue that bonds me to a people, a place, and a time. This self is passed from generation to generation or it is not passed at all. Much of what is diagnosed as depression or anxiety is nothing more or less than the grief and terror at the loss of this self. I once heard a man say on a morning radio talk show, "When men (people) have no religion they believe in anything." The depth and truth of this statement riveted me in place. Religions are the vehicle for transmission of the transpersonal self. As Thomas Moore put it:

> I have also taken the Renaissance approach of not separating psychology from religion. Jung, one of our most recent doctors of the soul, said that every psychological problem is ultimately a matter of religion. Thus, this book contains both psychological advice and spiritual guidance. A spiritual life of some kind is absolutely necessary for psychological "health."... Another aspect of modern life is a loss of formal religious practice in many people's lives, which is not only a threat to spirituality as such, but also deprives the soul of valuable symbolic and reflective experience. Care of the soul might include both a recovery of formal religion in a way that is both intellectually and emotionally satisfying. One obvious potential source of spiritual renewal is the religious tradition in which we were brought up. (Moore, 1992, pp. xii, 211–12)

Of course, the last sentence of the excerpt begs the question "What if I was not brought up in a religion?" Having been raised without religion suggests that the soul has been deprived of stories that enrich one's life with insight into one's self and the human drama in which one participates. This deprivation is not insurmountable; however, it will require effort, learning, and a spirit receptive to grace. One must become a pilgrim and begin the journey by confessing ignorance and asking for help. This first step opens the heart and mind to the wisdom that is deep within, as well as outside, as the architecture of the soul. As it is said, knock and it shall be opened to you; ask and it shall be given. Every one of us is much more than we think we are because we share in a transpersonal reality that contains all that has ever been, is, and will be.

This transpersonal self is the web of bondedness that makes a culture what it is. It provides a distinct cultural identity. However, there are commonalities between human cultures and those commonalities create another dimension of the person, i.e., a transcultural self. There are also relationships between cultures and the animals and plants that support and interact with humans in culture. These relationships form a trans-species dimension of our selves. We are many selves "all the way up, all the way down." Our psyches include and transcend a great many Subpsyches. Ken Wilber elucidates the matter very well:

> ... this cultural space exists for all holons, even though it might be simpler and less complex. So there is *intersubjectivity woven into the very fabric of the cosmos at all levels.* This is not just the Spirit in "me," not just the Spirit in "it," not just the Spirit in "them," but the Spirit in "us," in all of us.
>
> And, as we will see when we return to environmental ethics, we want to arrive at a *justness* for all sentient beings: the deeper *good* for all of *us.* (Wilber, 1996, p. 114)

In order to understand the architecture of our own souls, we must come to see the cosmos as a series of webs within webs within webs. The macro structures of the cosmos are bonded in a gravitational web that holds the cosmos together in its expansion. Life on Earth is a single phenomenon held together by the water, soil, and light of this solar system. Human cultures are webs composed of human families, themselves webs. Human culture as a global phenomenon is a single web of human meaning, bonding the planet in a noospheric web of meanings. Ecosystems are webs. Bioregions are webs. Continents are webs. Webs within webs within webs. The individual certainly has meaning, but only within the context of ever more meaning-filled and inclusive webs.

So, if cultures are webs within webs all the way up (to the present) and all the way down (to the beginning of the cosmos and before, into the mind of God), then I'd like to look at human culture as a single phenomenon, an evolution of ever more meaningful and inclusive webs. For my purposes (and I recognize that the following is simplistic), I shall talk about culture as exhibiting three stages:

- The Tribal Instinctual
- The Religious Affective
- The Cognitive Informational (Breakdown or Integration?)

THE TRIBAL INSTINCTUAL

Tribal religious practice represents the bridge from Eden to Culture. In Genesis, chapter 3, in the New Jerusalem Bible, we find the first humans ascending to self-reflection. They are aware of their nakedness. This awareness differentiates humans from their proto-human forebears, probably chimpanzees. As nature takes up residency in the human cognitive cortex, reflection becomes possible and life is able to view and reflect upon itself. In the next chapter of this book, we shall see that the chimpanzees actually use language, have the rudiments of culture, and, according to recent research, are capable of self-reflection! These discoveries make permeable the line we've traditionally drawn between ourselves and other primates. Either we are higher-order chimpanzees or chimpanzees are lower-order humans. Whichever way you view it, the appropriate attitude is reverence in that our Maker or Source, at least in the Hebrew Bible, is said to have found it "good." If evolution is the nature of reality, then evolution was begun and is sustained by God. The fundamentalist-creationist stance is more about not wanting to be born of chimps than it is about a defense of God's manner of creating humans. If there is no boundary between the human primate and the other primates, then we are not separate from the rest of the life community. If we come from chimps—and it appears we do—then our appropriate attitude is to "honor thy father and mother," whether or not they swing from trees! Our bumper stickers should read: Evolution: God Made It. I love It. That settles It!

In any case, this shift from non-reflective to self-reflective life forms did not separate us from the earlier life forms. It differentiated us—it did not separate us. All of early life was still being transmitted through the brain stem. Reptilian instincts, all the way back to cellular sentience, which included the pre-biological planet, were brought forth from ten billion years of cosmic creativity, which began with the fire-ball and came from God. All of these levels of creativity are still present to the human through the brain stem. Through the limbic system, which transcends and includes the brain stem, the whole mammalian-primate substratum of feelings, instincts, and wisdom are present. The whole process was called up into the cognitive cortex and was able to be reflected upon, and this reflection was itself the beginning of culture.

Culture is Awareness aware of itself. Once Awareness becomes self-aware, it remembers. This remembering finds a window in Secondary Awareness through which God (Awareness) remembers. In tribal instinctual cultures this remembering is done through ritual, dance, and custom. The drumming, dancing, body painting, and ritual are ways of keeping the past present. These traditions comprise the symbol system through which the pre-human and cultural worlds are kept present in Awareness. The tribal traditions are passed from generation to generation (or not passed), and successive generations can thus remember (or forget!) their relationships to animals, plants, the planet, the stars, and the gods. They are the unitive, the ecopsychological links to Earth and cosmos.

The ability for us to remember the past is a gift of genetics. But the contents of the culture are not genetically stored. If a single generation forgets to pass them on, they begin to be forgotten. They are not lost, for they exist nonlocally in the Awareness memory, but we lose direct cognitive access to them in our ability to remember. The result is that we forget our connection to the animals, the plants, the planet, and the stars. They are before our eyes but are no longer connected to us behind our eyes and skin, within our souls. We experience our existence as separate from them, as alienated.

Presently we are called to integrate tribal, religious, and cognitive layers of the psyche in a full-blooded experience of Awareness—Primary, Secondary, and Tertiary. We are called to grow up as a species, to become whole.

THE RELIGIOUS AFFECTIVE

Religion is basic to humans. Like schooling in fish, flocking in birds, herding in cattle, creating troops in primates, forming clans in human tribes, the forming of religions is a basic instinct in developing man as a whole. Even atheists celebrate anniversaries and birthdays, which are ritual reenactments or remembrances of great passage points. Even when we attempt to desacralize our ritual behavior, we go on behaving ritually. This deep imperative in us arises, it seems, from the root of life itself. This tendency is passed along to us not only genetically, but through the brain stem as well. The instinctual urge to gather with others in religious assembly and/or ritual celebration is very strong. In fact, denial of this urge to the sacred in life will give rise to an inflation of self, which is to say an egotistical self-absorption, and all the evils that attend the inflated self. (For further reading on this topic, I suggest M. Scott Peck's *People of the Lie.*) The fact is that we are so deeply embedded in sacred structure that to deny it is like denying that the body is mostly composed of water, when indeed water comprises approximately 65 percent of the body. Ken Wilber addresses this issue with passion from his Buddhist perspective:

> When you are ultimately *truthful* with yourself, you will eventually realize and *confess* that "I am Buddha," I am Spirit. Anything short of that is a lie, the lie of the ego, the lie of the separate-self sense, the contraction in the face of infinity. The deepest recesses of your consciousness directly intersect Spirit itself, in the supreme identity. "Not I, but Christ liveth in me"—which is to say, the ultimate I is Christ. This is not a state you are bringing into existence for the first time, but simply a timeless state that you are recognizing and confessing—you are being ultimately *truthful* when you state, "I am Buddha," the ultimate Beauty.
>
> And the ultimate cultural fit or justness is, "we are all members of the Community of Spirit." *All sentient beings*— all holons in fact—contain Buddha-nature—contain depth,

consciousness, intrinsic value, Spirit—and thus we are all members of the council of all beings, the mystical church, the ultimate We. Which is ultimate ethics, the ultimate Good.

And the ultimate objective truth is that all beings are perfect manifestations of Spirit or Emptiness—we are all manifestations of the ultimate It, or Dharma. Which is the ultimate Truth.

The ultimate I, the ultimate We, and the ultimate It—Buddha, Sangha, Dharma. (Wilber, 1996, p. 132)

For the Christian, the ultimate self is Christ, as when the apostle Paul said, "Not I but Christ living in me." For the Christian, Dharma is the revealed truth in scripture. *Sangha* refers to the great gathering, the Church including the communion of saints and the created order. Christians believe "in God the Father Almighty, maker of Heaven and Earth." Earth and heaven, as well as all life forms, are the Father's church. As Christ reminded us, not a sparrow falls but His Father knows it. By whatever name—Buddha, Dharma, Sangha, God, scripture, and the church/temple—the basic truths of humans are plain to see for those willing to open their eyes. We exhibit divinity as our supreme identity. We arrive there by revealed truth in scripture and we are a religious tribe. Jesus Christ actually uses the word "flock."

Now, given the fact that all humans feel this basic religious urge or instinct, it must also be said that the "way" in which this urge is experienced is different in different contexts or cultures. In fact, this difference of expression *is* the difference in cultures. One voice, many songs. Pope John Paul II put it this way:

With regard to religion, what is dealt with is in the first place religion as a universal phenomenon linked with man's history from the beginning, then the various non-Christian religions, and finally Christianity itself. The Council document on non-Christian religions, in particular, is filled with deep esteem for the great spiritual values, indeed for the primacy of the spiritual, which in the life of mankind finds expression in religion and then in morality, with direct effects on the whole of culture. The Fathers of the Church rightly saw in the various religions as it were so many reflections of the one truth, "seeds of the Word," attesting that, though the routes taken may be different, there is but a single goal to which is directed the deepest aspiration of the human spirit as expressed in its quest for God and also in its quest, through its tending towards God, for the full dimension of its humanity, or in other words for the full meaning of human life. The Council gave particular attention to the Jewish religion, recalling the great spiritual heritage common to Christians and Jews. It also expressed its esteem for the believers of Islam, whose faith also looks to Abraham. (Pope John Paul II, 1979, p. 20)

So, unitive psychology holds that any form of "mental health," including, of course, emotional and instinctual health, must be integral with the religious instinct. Opening ourselves to organized religion is critical to finding our way down to Tertiary Awareness of our psyches. If we do not find our way to our depth we shall continue to disintegrate as cultures, as individuals, and as a planet. Unitive psychology stands with and in the wisdom of Alcoholics Anonymous as the latter implores its members to drop their deep prejudice against organized religion. Following is a quotation from the "Big Book" of Alcoholics Anonymous. It is only one among many that could be cited from the AA literature:

We, who have traveled this dubious path, beg you to lay aside your prejudice, even against organized religion. We have learned that whatever the human frailties of various faiths may be, those faiths have given purpose and direction to millions. People of faith have a logical idea of what life is all about. Actually, we used to have no reasonable conception whatever. We used to amuse ourselves by cynically dissecting spiritual beliefs and practices when we might have observed that many spiritually-minded persons of all races, colors, and creeds were demonstrating a degree of stability, happiness and usefulness which we should have sought for ourselves. Instead, we looked at the human defects of these people, and sometimes used their shortcomings as a basis of wholesale condemnation. We talked of intolerance, while we were intolerant ourselves. We missed the reality and the beauty of the forest because we were diverted by the ugliness of some of its trees. We never gave the spiritual side of life a fair hearing. (AA, Big Book, 1976, pp. 49–50)

What then does all of this mean? It means that religion must become experiential, which is to say mystical. To wake up is to come to experience the whole created order as the body of God's Spirit. Spirit descends as cosmos; we ascend as Spirit. Without the instinctual Spirit integrated we get trite, soppy, affect-only religion—or worse—dry cognitive "enlightenment" religion. We see them both around us. They are both pathological. They are not only pathological; they are pathogenic. They not only fail as the cultural autoimmune system, fighting off cultural pathologies; they themselves engender new illnesses such as fundamentalisms. Inane religious practices or rabid fundamentalism are two poles of a collective spiritual pathology.

THE COGNITIVE INFORMATIONAL

Little need be said about this present cultural period because we find ourselves in its midst. The so-called information revolution has set us adrift in a wash of cognitive contents. These cognitive contents separated from the deeper evolved realities of feeling and instinct leave us stranded in a shallow experience of life. Facts without feelings and instincts are meaningless in and of themselves. Meaning is a by-product of connectedness, of relationship—to others, to other cultures, to the animals and plants, to the planet, to the cosmos, and to God. No amount of information can satisfy the human yearning for this connectedness. No amount of *gnosis* can replace the experience of love and of God. T. S. Eliot once said that all our information brings us nearer to death, and still no nearer to God. Knowledge in and of itself can only satisfy when it becomes wisdom. Wisdom is felt knowledge in action.

The goal of unitive psychology is to integrate all the various layers of our existence or self. In the Cultural Subpsyche layer, all three periods of cultural evolution must be integrated. Thus, our present Cognitive Informational culture must be integrated with the cultural period of the Religious Affective, which must be integrated with the Tribal Instinctual cultures. Tribal Instinctual must include an integration of our primate nature, our mammalian nature, our reptilian nature, and our bondedness with early life, the planet, and the cosmos. Wholeness can only come from this sort of psychic chiropractic, this aligning and integration of our layered selves. Primary Awareness must integrate Tertiary Awareness through our emptying and integrating Secondary Awareness. As we do so, we begin the early integration phase of Western culture.

With the post-modern period behind us, we begin a whole new phase of Western experience, the second Renaissance. With the rise of Western science and its stunning record of achievements came the devaluation of Western religious experience. With this devaluation of our own native expression of the sacred, we alienated ourselves from the gateway to our own depth. Experiencing this as a collective identity crisis, we've spent decades now running frantically to Taoism or Confucianism, Hinduism or Buddhism, fundamentalism within the spheres of Judaism or Christianity or Islam. Seeking a connection with Earth, we've run to Native American religions and other tribalisms, attempting to revive "matrifocal" cultural systems and to integrate them with Gaia in an attempt to integrate science and religion. All of this was in an attempt to find or create ways to meet our needs. What I think we really need, however, is to relax and integrate our own systems of religious consciousness by seeing them within the larger context of the other systems. By understanding the other systems, we can integrate our own into that larger model and allow our own to evolve again with the others in mind. We can come to a complete re-viewing of Western religion. That, however, is the subject matter of another book!

To sum up, each of the periods discussed in this Cultural Subpsyche layer gives the human a specific inheritance. To describe what I am trying to say in this chapter, let me use a simple visual image. If the human psyche is seen as a telescope, our Cultural Subpsyche is a series of lenses through which the deeper energies of our Source pour. If these lenses are out of focus, i.e., are not transmitting the Light of our Source correctly, the psyche will not be whole. Each cultural period represents a different lens and for this layer of the psyche to operate correctly, the person must integrate the inheritance, or light, for each cultural period. So, the present culture of the Cognitive Informational period has a lens that gives the light of knowledge. The cultures of the great religions, the Religious Affective period, gives the light of feeling. The cultures of the Tribal Instinctual period give the light of instinct. When this light, our Source, flows freely through each of these three lenses, we can begin to talk about an integrated Cultural Subpsyche, which then opens backwards to the primate, mammalian, reptilian, and pre-life energies of Earth, cosmos, and God. It also opens forward to facilitate the energizing of all the layers above it.

CHAPTER SEVEN

The Trans-Primate Psyche

WE ARE PRIMATES. Unless one believes that it pleases God to ignore all intelligent inquiry into our biological history, unless one finds stubborn ignorance a reasonable basis for faith, unless one wishes to deny one's own selfhood and make a mockery of how God indeed did bring things about, we are left with the simple fact that we are primates. God is said to have found the entire creation good. Why then should we find it bad to arise from the diverse community of Earth's biosphere? To deny our real origin is to deny the wisdom of God's plan. To claim such a denial as an act of faith is futile.

The primates include all prosimians—lemurs, lorises, galagons, and tarsiers—as well as all anthropoids, New World monkeys, apes and humans, macaques, and Old World monkeys. In all, the primates include 222 species, with humans most numerous by far. The primates emerged from pre-existent ancestral mammals, most likely from tree shrews. The tree shrew is a squirrel-like insectivore that lives in trees and spends most of its life looking for insects. From the tree shrew the primate evolved and radiated throughout the Cenozoic.

It comes as no surprise then that we should share many common characteristics with the primates. The more I go on studying the primates, the more human feelings, attitudes, and behaviors come to look more "primitive." I'm sure that this is true for those who, like Shirley Strum and Jane Goodall, have lived with and come to deeply love baboons and chimpanzees. I shall look at several types of primate behavior that shed light on our own behavior throughout this chapter.

But my question in this and in all other chapters remains the same: What if the actual troops of primates collectively support and embody a level of mind from which we have evolved? What if there is a common psychic structure supported by the other living primates?

Recently, I came across the philosophical idea termed *adequatio*. The term relates to the idea that each species and each individual within each species has certain "adequacies" through which they will perceive and experience the world. As one author put it, " I don't see the world as it is, but as I am." The spectrum of adequacies allows us to experience the various spectra of reality. Einstein had adequacies that allowed him to understand the fundamental structures of the cosmos. I'd argue that Beethoven had similar adequacies in a musical vein. Males and females have differing and similar adequacies at the species level. Also at the species level, humans have adequacies so spectacularly different from the other primates that it is no wonder that we'd think of ourselves as extraterrestrial in our origin. Our differences from the other primates, and from other animals generally, are of an order of magnitude as to make us appear discontinuous with them. But we are not. We are primates!

A brave soul, Mae Noell, had the courage to step out of the narrow base of "Christian" fundamentalism to declare that chimps are at least very close cousins to humans. Her views stand against most religious and social views on the matter of chimp and human evolutionary relatedness. However, with more than fifty years of direct exposure to one of the world's largest privately owned groups of captive apes, it would not be an understatement to say that Mae knows apes—at least those held in long-term captivity. Her thoughts on the matter bear some reflection, so let us consider what she shared with Jane Goodall:

> Over breakfast one morning at a Florida coffee shop, Mae Noell gave me her forthright opinion about the Temerlins' disposition of Lucy. She began by explaining that even though she is a Christian fundamentalist, a Baptist, her lifelong intimacy with chimps has taught her something other Baptists might not understand: that "this critter is a very

close cousin, *very* close cousin. He is a human being except
for his ability to talk and understand morals. He can't understand morals and the Bible ... but he is a very close cousin.
The truth is, he's got the same number and type of teeth
that we've got, same muscles, the same bones, and they've
recently found that they've got the same blood types. How
much closer can you get?" Chimpanzees, she continued are
"always distressed about the fact that you don't have a big
thumb on your foot. They just cannot stand it that you don't
have a thumb on your foot. But I really feel that they are
people—of a lower grade. And I've been criticized for that."
(Peterson and Goodall, 1993, pp. 209–210)

In mistaking ourselves as other than animals because of the spectacular adequacies we exhibit (e.g., our ability to send ourselves and other
primates to the moon) and in misunderstanding that all life forms and
even pre-living matter are all expressions of divine life, we have sought
to escape our earthly connection to the life community. We've built our
homes in the noosphere and forgotten our foundations in the biosphere
and physiosphere. When we lose functional contact with our primate
nature, we lose functional contact with the whole life community. When
functional, instinctual contact is lost, we lose affective contact as well
and begin to experience reality in a shallow cognitive manner.

Conversely, when we embrace our animal nature, reconciling the
ancient schism of human versus animal within us and discarding the
age-old prejudices toward our more primitive behaviors, then we open
to levels of mental clarity, emotional depth, and physical vitality that
are richly and soulfully fulfilling and healthy. In doing so, we see our
distant relatives in the primate populations and our hearts open to
their life paths and our minds delight in understanding social behaviors that are fundamental to both humans and primates.

The primate community continues to operate from its sixty-five-
million-year history in and around us, and its psychic, behavioral, and
social substructures present in our architecture are formidable. With

study of the chimps, monkeys, gorillas, baboons, and other primates, we begin to dimly perceive our own reality as being determined in its larger profiles by these deep primate substructures.

> The ancestral ape pattern of social organization appears like a parody of some forms of human social organization. Actually, human social organization has been inherited with only slight modifications from that of our ape ancestors. Humans are risen apes, not descended angels. Our societies echo strongly the troops of ancient apes. Social dominance of males has been characteristic of human evolution and is characteristic of virtually every human culture. (Russell, 1993, p. 156)

When we look around at reality with these substructures in mind—in other words, when we look at our world from the standpoint of our primate selves—things look very different. An example or two will illustrate this point. At the time of the writing of this chapter, President Clinton was going through his ethical difficulties and impeachment proceedings. Looking at President Clinton's sexual behavior, it is easy to judge it from the point of view of our higher adequacies such as religion, justice, and constitutional law. However, when we temporarily suspend our higher adequacies and observe President Clinton's behavior through the primate lens, we see an amiable, dominant male, possessing a brilliant intelligence and enviable interpersonal skills, gaining access to the females of the troop, as any silver-back gorilla would do, with impunity. Less dominant males used the higher adequacies, such as law, as a way to dethrone this "silver-back" president. They framed their attack in high-flying rhetoric drawn from religious sources, which one wonders if even they adhered to. Seen from a transprimate perspective, the real motivation of their attack was a hierarchical struggle for dominance.

We could look at World War II in a similar way. A group of sick males became possessed with an insane idea based on race hatred and fueled by the pseudo-spirituality of Nazi mysticism. They formed huge troops, aggressed upon their nearest neighbors, and continued their aggression until another group of males confronted and defeated them.

The females stayed home, conserving the core of the coalition while the Allied males toppled the aggression of the Axis males. The scale of the enterprise was different, but not unlike the tensions worked out in many primate troops, with the possible exception of Bonobos.

I'm not saying that we should abandon our higher adequacies or surrender to our lower adequacies. That is regression. What I'm asserting is that to focus only upon our higher adequacies without integration of our lower ones is pathological. It creates, and sustains, a tear in our individual psyches and in our species—and thus in our cultures.

Because of our amazing adequacies, humans, as I said above, have thought of themselves as somehow separated from the animals. We have supported this idea of ourselves by pointing to four major differences between primates, especially chimps, and ourselves. These four major differences are held to be: (1) use of tools, (2) culture, (3) a sense of self (self-reflection), and (4) language.

These differences may not be so seminal after all. In the BBC program *Monkey in the Mirror,* each of the four differences was examined in detail and tested. It was discovered that chimps do indeed use tools, both to fish for insects and to crack nuts. Moreover, different troops use these tools differently and pass on these different "styles" of insect fishing and nut cracking to succeeding generations via transgenetic cultural coding. In other words, they exhibit rudimentary cultures. Further, chimps are shown to recognize themselves in a mirror. Unlike monkeys who always see another monkey, a stranger, in the mirror, chimps see and recognize themselves. Last, we have for a long time comforted ourselves in the feeling of being separated from the animals because of our use of language. Not only can chimps use linguistic symbols, but they also comprehend sentences and combinations of these symbols.

We are primates, and until we integrate the primate zone of ourselves with all higher zones, we will continue to watch helplessly as these dimensions of ourselves go about their "monkey business." Mr. Clinton's "monkey business" cost him international humiliation. Our rates of divorce, marital infidelity, single parenting, and fatherless children can in large part be traced to our unfinished "monkey business."

Until we complete the integration of our whole being (the goal of all real spirituality), we shall continue to suffer the individual and collective ignominy of our neglected primal nature.

The business of integrating our whole being is the business of the human primate. We are the primates who have sufficient adequacies to seek and discover God. We form religions from those discoveries; hence, it only follows to see ourselves as religious primates. The calling of every religious primate is to recognize the sacred within the profane, and using this knowledge to further the sacred story of evolution with illuminated intent.

It is critical, then, that we bless the whole story through remembering the fullness of who we are. In the following chart, borrowed from Robert Jay Russell, we can gain understanding of the ancient and rich lifeline from which we are descended. Figure 1 shows the classification of species that gave rise to the human primate, Homo sapiens.

Superkingdom Eukaryota (large, nucleated cells; not bacteria)

Kingdom Animalia (animals; not plants)

Phylum Chordata (animals with a hollow nerve tube like a "spinal cord")

Subphylum Vertebrata (animals with backbones)

Class Mammalia (mammals, not birds or reptiles, etc.)

Subclass Eutheria (mammals whose embryos develop with a placenta)

Order Primates (not dogs, or cats, or shrews, or rodents, etc.)

Suborder Anthropoidea ("higher," haplorine primates, not prosimians)

Superfamily Cercopithecoidea (Old World monkeys, apes, humans)

Family Hominidae (humans, not apes)

Genus Homo (three species, with only one alive today)

Species Homo sapiens (modern humans)

Figure 1. The line of descent to Homo sapiens

This evolutionary line of descent is a sacred lineage worthy of our respectful remembrance. We are composed of eukaryotic cells, not prokaryotic cells, although we do share our bodies with bacteria (pro-karyotes) and are dependent upon them for our health. We are animal cells, not plant cells. We are chordates, as are all vertebrates. We are mammals whose young grow in utero prior to birth. We are of the order Primates, and the suborder Anthropoidea, which means "higher primates" exclusive of prosimians. We share in the superfamily Cerco-pithecoidea, which includes Old World monkeys and apes. Our family is Hominidae—the humans. And our genus is homo, which means man. We share our genus with three other genetically similar groups, Homo habilus, Homo erectus, and Neanderthal, but they did not survive. Today, we are the only human species, Homo sapiens.

As I noted earlier, the family lineage has been around for about sixty-five million years. In that time we've developed and inherited several fundamental traits. These fundamental traits are the roots of the larger contours of our present behaviors as individuals and as a species. They are not going away! Figure 2 shows the geological span of our tenure on this planet.

A misunderstanding of Christianity is at least partially responsible for our misunderstanding of ourselves in relationship to the other animals. A different reading of the third chapter of Genesis in the Bible can yield an entirely different set of meanings. Instead of our understanding of "the fall" as a loss of paradise, we could interpret this chapter as ascension into self-reflection. The angel with the burning sword would then be sealing us with the higher adequacies of Primary Awareness, not separating us from the earlier adequacies of Tertiary Awareness. In other words, we were sealed into an irreversible evolutionary leap that would provide us with a higher adequacy called self-reflection. We invisibly became a species with a large cortex and the new adequacies made possible by that cortex. We were given the ability to choose—like it or not. Chapter 3 of Genesis is about ascension into self-reflection rather than a fall. It's about a new adequacy given to the human animals and not about an expulsion from the animals.

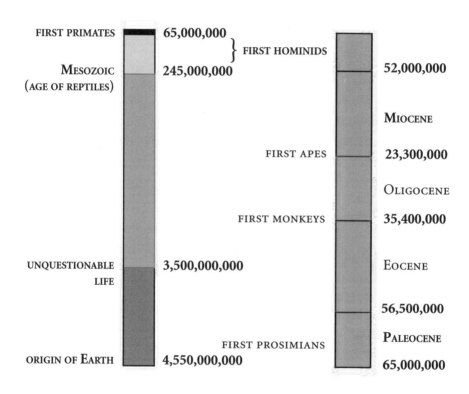

FIRST PRIMATES   65,000,000
} FIRST HOMINIDS

MESOZOIC   245,000,000
(AGE OF REPTILES)

52,000,000

MIOCENE

FIRST APES   23,300,000

OLIGOCENE

FIRST MONKEYS   35,400,000

UNQUESTIONABLE   3,500,000,000
LIFE

EOCENE

56,500,000

PALEOCENE

FIRST PROSIMIANS

ORIGIN OF EARTH   4,550,000,000

65,000,000

Figure 2. Geologic time span for primates

We are animals who have evolved from animals. That beautiful and powerful fact has yet to sink in fully to the public consciousness. As we enter the twenty-first century, we know that, like the shape of our skull or the pattern of teeth in our jaw, our behavior too has evolved. We can often trace and understand patterns of behavior between species with almost as much certainty as we can trace the evolution of their physical form. Yet knowledge of the behavioral evolution of our species has yet to be widely exploited in our service. (Russell, 1993, p. 6)

It is not too much to say that the chimp-like ancestors of humans experienced a giant evolutionary leap. We didn't become other than the chimp; we transcended and included them in ourselves. In Shirley Strum's words:

Jane Goodall's study of wild chimpanzees at the Gombe Stream in Tanzania, begun in 1960, revealed many new behaviors closely resembling those of humans. Although primarily fruit eaters, chimpanzees did occasionally hunt and eat prey. They used tools and even shared food, two characteristics previously thought to be uniquely human. In addition, genetic studies, especially sequencing DNA, demonstrated an even closer biological affinity between chimpanzees and humans. Some scientists estimated that chimps and people share 96% of their genetic material, while other scientists raised the percentage to a startling 99%. (Strum, 1987, p. 73)

The whole sixty-five million years of primate evolution ascended into self-reflective consciousness in the human. We are not the sum of our cognitive adequacies alone. We are sixty-five million years of primate experience built upon even earlier mammalian experience that included and built upon earlier reptilian experiences, and so on all the way down. If we are to know ourselves we must know our whole selves. Anything less is superficial and trite. Again in the words of Shirley Strum (1987):

> Prosimians, monkeys, lesser apes, the great apes, earlier hominids, true humans and modern humans, every step along the evolutionary sequence showed that there were important lessons to be learned about human behavior. (Strum, 1987, p. 71)

And, however we try to distance ourselves from our chimpanzee cousins, they continue to express themselves in all our human institutions.

> If paleontologists are correct, human behavioral history has been separate from that of the apes for at least 16 million years. If molecular anthropologists are correct, human behavior and chimpanzee behavior were one and the same less than four million years ago. (Wilber, 1997, p. 52)

So it all comes down to two questions:

- Are we vastly different from other primates due to our different adequacies? Yes.
- Are we primates nevertheless with a sixty-five-million-year behavioral history inherited from the primates? Yes!

Yes on both counts! Wholeness, then, requires that we integrate our adequacies with our basal primate nature. We are not like the rest of the animals in our adequacies. We truly are different; however, the acceptance of our vast differences with respect to the remainder of the life community does not have to incur separation from them. We are primates, we are mammals, and we incorporate within us the reptilian, multicellular, unicellular, pre-biological, pre-geological, and pre-cosmological levels of evolution. Anthony Stevens puts it this way:

> For in the course of human evolution at no time have we ceased to be mammals or primates. Indeed, as neuroscientist

Paul MacLean has demonstrated, the human brain incorporated still-functioning and much earlier mammalian and even reptilian brains. It is said, very truly, that a patient entering the consulting room brings a crowd of people along. What MacLean has shown is that the patient also brings in a horse and a crocodile. (Stevens, 1993, p. 21)

It is our peculiar and powerful intelligence that created the differentiation between humans and other primates. It's as though the degree of encephalization opened a window from God, a window not present in the biological structures of other primates or mammals. The light from that window is the blinding light of our intelligence that is able to become aware of its Source and origin. In humans, God became self-aware in flesh. In the various incarnations, East and West, Jesus Christ and Krishna being the most obvious, God becomes self-aware to a degree that realization of ontological oneness dawns where a primate becomes aware of its supreme and divine nature. No wonder we feel separate, given the millennia spent in ignorance. But we are not. In realizing our biological oneness with the whole created order and our oneness with its source and vivifying spirit, we come to realize that the whole cosmos is a single divine organism and we are the self-awareness of the whole. It is this peculiar light that Buddhist Daisaku Ikeda is pointing to in the following:

If the hominoids had remained in the forests, they would either have starved to death or been vastly reduced in number. Their departure made it somewhat easier for those that remained to evolve into the apes and orangutans and chimpanzees today, but it remains a fact that man's ancestors are the only creatures who attempted to solve the environmental problem by an exercise of will. From the biological viewpoint, their "moment of decision" was mutation leading toward the development of man. This successful mutation continued to develop more and more human characteristics and eventually to display what we think of as the light of human intelligence. Though we may think of the first step as resulting from frequent consecutive mutations, we cannot avoid the conclusion that the life-activity leading toward human evolution was different from the life-activity in countless other species that have appeared and disappeared in the course of evolution as a whole. Physical impulse of instinct led other creatures to produce one new species after another, but the transition from beast to man was not an unconscious development. It involved the working of some sort of inner intelligence—a light that did not shine in other species. (Ikeda, 1982, p. 206)

It comes down to this: Whichever way we choose to frame it, humans remain primates. If the other primates were necessary for our emergence, they may be involved in our support. If they are part of our support and we make them extinct, we continue to disassemble our own emotional and mental structures. We continue to go mad individually, culturally, and as a species. If what they've given us is taken away, what we've gained may be lost.

What truly has changed between the chimpanzees and us is that chimpanzees cannot choose to emulate nature in one moment, and then destroy the animals and plants that comprise their ecological and psychic niches in the next moment. We can. One human culture will deify nature, and the next will commodify it. This uniquely human trait for worshiping nature in one age, then obliterating it through commercially sanctioned genocide and environmental destruction in another age arises from the same cognitive capacity that makes us human—the ability to objectify reality and think about it, otherwise known as self-reflection.

Faced with the unprecedented levels of maladaptivity we see all around us, we must be willing to ask new questions, even if some of those questions seem or even turn out to be ridiculous. If we don't risk the new questions, we'll be left with only old answers that clearly are not helping us to solve our individual or cultural or ecological dilemmas.

The Primal Roots of Familying

Emotional bonding or attachment begins, in an evolutionary as well as ontogenetic sense, with the crucial mother-infant bond. There is abundant evidence in the literature on both nonhuman primates (Kaufman and Rosenblum, 1969; Hinde and Spencer-Booth, 1971) and humans (Spitz, 1946; Bowlby, 1973) that disruption of this relationship, even when the infant is physically well cared for in the absence of the mother or other primary caretaker, results in serious emotional distress that is likely to leave scars.

In the chimpanzee, as in man, the period of emotional dependence on the mother has been extended considerably beyond childhood. Not only the infant, but also the juvenile and the young adolescent, will show distressed searching behavior accompanied by whimpering and sometimes crying if he or she becomes separated from the mother. (Goodall, 1986, p. 203)

The mother-child bond begins at the moment a mother becomes aware of her pregnancy. Instincts surface in her to begin the embrace of the new life growing inside her body. There are always fears attendant to the process, but the instinctual bonding begins pre-consciously. Should the cognitive "choice" be made on the mother's part to "terminate the pregnancy," that instinctual bond must be withdrawn— the mother must deny her relatedness to the life growing inside her. We cannot prove that the human young within are self-aware of the abandonment, but they must feel it, whether or not they can reflect on the feeling. Animals know when they are going to be killed. Given the nonlocal nature of feelings, we can begin to wonder if all fetuses know that one or several have been abandoned to death. In my clinical work I have noticed a collective rage, usually repressed and felt as grief or depression, in all generations that have followed the 1973 decision of *Roe v. Wade*. I've even heard of children who are convinced that their parents aim to kill them. Are they experiencing a collective fear felt by all conceived souls that their lives or deaths reside in the choice of their parents? How can we give therapy to a rage that deep?

Shirley Strum points out that this family bonding is fundamental to baboons. In concentric circles, which remind one of Confucius, she observed how the family bonds are the core of baboon social life. She puts it this way:

> Attachments between baboons derive from interaction, from spending time together. The more time, the stronger the bond: family ties are more intense than the bonds of friendship and these in turn are stronger than the ties of the group as a whole. Even at its weakest, the bond remains tough and enduring. (Strum, 1987, p. 52)

The first circle for us all is the circle of the womb, then comes the family circle, then the circle of friends, and then the circle of community followed by the circle of the other life forms, and finally that of the planet and that of the planet's circle around the sun. Strum goes further. She claims that her own relationship with the baboons is a form of friendship. It certainly brings to mind the biophilia idea:

> Yet slowly and almost imperceptibly I had become deeply involved with the animals. Just being with them created a strong emotional bond. It was nothing like the feelings I would have for a pet; they were not pets. They were friends, in a very unusual sense. (Strum, 1987, p. 54)

During the years I was studying with Thomas Berry, we used to go to a diner on Broadway to eat our breakfast together on Sunday mornings. One such morning he told me this story. When Confucius was dying his disciples came to gather around him. One among them said something like: "Master, you have taught us for many years and have used many words. We'd like you to reduce your entire teaching down to one word for us." Confucius thought a moment and then said "reciprocity." If Shirley Strum is correct, even wise Confucius is indebted to baboons.

"With baboons, as with humans, friendship is based on reciprocity" (Strum, 1987, p 55).

The Primal Roots of Emotions

Certainly the most emotionally complex primate on earth is the human. Still, Goodall and Strum, as well as many other researchers, report that the other primates have complex emotional lives. They seem to exhibit, at one level of complexity or another, all the emotions we feel—joyous and painful and all the shades in behavior. Strum, for instance, points out the behavior of a baboon, whom she had named David, who had experienced rejection from a female:

> It is difficult to tell whether baboons are neurotic in the same way humans are. David, however, came closest to what one might imagine a neurotic baboon would be like. He took failure badly; when females rebuffed him, we would lurk behind bushes and rocks. (Strum, 1987, p. 112)

Goodall reports genuine laughter among the chimpanzees and other primates:

> I'm referring to real laughter, fully recognizable laughter the kind where you lie down on the ground and shake in a paroxysm of clear amusement and simple pleasure. I have seen wild chimpanzees in an African forest laugh; I have seen a wild-born, orphaned bonobo laugh. I am told by an expert from the San Diego Zoo that orangutans laugh, too, in quite the same way. And I have come to believe that humans share with only four other animals species the astonishing ability to be overtly amused and to express that amusement with semivocalized convulsions. (Peterson and Goodall, 1993, p. 181)

Both Goodall and Strum also report powerful communication through the eyes. As in the case of humans, other primates can express curiosity, love, and threat or hatred through the eyes. Consider the following from Goodall and Strum, respectively.

> I sat on the couch, and a young female chimpanzee was brought into the room. Her human surrogate parents, Jane and Maurice Temerlin, stood by to see what would happen. Lucy came and sat close beside me on the sofa, and simply stared into my eyes for a long, long time. It gave me a strange feeling. I had to wonder, "What is she thinking? Is she looking for something to do with my character? Is she wondering who I am? Why I'm here? What is she getting from this deep, searching gaze?" Staring directly into the eyes is not common behavior for animals. Most animals won't. But chimpanzees permit you to gaze into their eyes, and they will return the scrutiny. (Peterson and Goodall, 1993, p 203)
>
> I encountered plenty of challenges. What did the look Rad was giving Sumner mean? When Sumner pushed Rad away from a Grewia tree laden with fruit, Rad's eyes seemed to shoot lightning; he'd raised his brows and opened his eyes very wide so that the sun caused his white eyelids to flash. It was a devastating look, utterly clear in its meaning. (Strum, 1987, p. 26)

The Primal Roots of Abstraction, Imagination, and Self-Awareness

Perhaps most incredible of all, Goodall suggests that chimps have an imagination—they can contemplate the future. They can plan.

> At Gombe, on three separate occasions, adolescent males have been encountered as they performed charging displays in the forest, far from their companions. And Figan, it will be remembered, practiced Mike's display techniques with an abandoned kerosene can, by himself, in the bushes. Who are

we to say that these actions were not performed expressly to terrorize a host of imaginary chimpanzees? (Peterson and Goodall, 1993, p. 590)

Due to the research done recently by Goodall and many others, the old prejudices regarding the differences between humans and other primates has been debunked. While pre-human adequacies are significantly different from human adequacies, the same basic rudiments apply in human and pre-human primates. Chimps learn by observation, by mimicking, by positive and negative reinforcement, or reward and punishment. They learn by trial and error. Chimpanzees are able to perceive the relationships between things—in other words, they have insight. Raised in human environments, chimps learn to sew, to mix drinks, even to smoke! They learn to communicate through sign language and are then able to teach each other. They are capable of cross-modal transfer, the ability to recognize by touch what we see with our eyes. They are capable of concept formation, or abstraction and generalization. They recall the past and plan for the future. They possess spatial memory—the ability to form mental maps of environments. They retain the memory of these maps over long periods. They are fully capable of symbolic representation.

Perhaps most incredible and threatening to our separate species sense is the primate sense of self, certainly present in chimps. To have a sense of self, an animal must be able to adopt the perception of another toward himself. In the BBC nature series *Monkey in the Mirror,* we observe startling evidence of their self-sense. A female chimp became aware of her own teeth and of paint on her head as she stares into a mirror. Not only can chimps become self-aware, but they can also infer on others—that is, they can understand what needs to be done by another in order to accomplish a task. Chimps are capable of intentional communication including visual communication requiring complex formation and interpretation of facial expression. They have a whole vocabulary of auditory calls as well, and they know when to suppress their calls. While they have no vocal box and therefore cannot speak, they certainly can understand language and follow instruction. In the words of Gerald Edelman:

> *Homo sapiens* is the only animal with a true language, although higher primates appear to use individual symbols with some degree of semantic reference (not just simple significance). These primates, such as chimpanzees, lack rich syntactic resources, but they do display some evidence of self-awareness. The emergence of this trait suggests that chimpanzees have at least the beginnings of higher-order consciousness with some capacity for forming a self-model in relation to a world model. True language is thus probably not absolutely necessary for the emergence of higher-order consciousness, although it is required for its later elaborations. (Edelman, 1989, p. 187)

I want to conclude this section with an incredible example of chimpanzee adequacies with language. In this case Lucy, a famous chimpanzee, exemplifies a considerable grasp of self-reflective language skill:

> She eventually acquired a vocabulary of more than a hundred signs, including nouns, pronouns, verbs, modifiers, and emphasizers. With that basic vocabulary she asked questions, made direct statements, invented entirely new signs and spontaneously combined some of her old signs to create new ones. One time she defecated on the floor. Her teacher, Roger Fouts, turned to the evidence and asked her, in sign language, "What's that?"
>
> Lucy feigned innocence, "Lucy not know."
>
> Roger insisted, "You do, you know. What's that?"
>
> Lucy yielded, "Dirty, dirty."
>
> Roger continued, "Whose dirty dirty?"
>
> Lucy, referring to another teacher, lied, "Sue's."

Roger persisted: "It's not Sue's. Whose is it?"

Lucy retreated into a deeper lie: "Roger's."

Roger persevered: "No! It's not Roger's! Whose is it?"

Lucy, at last, submitted: "Lucy dirty, dirty. Sorry Lucy."

(Peterson and Goodall, 1993, p. 207)

The Primal Roots of Socio-Political Society

Year-round production of testosterone in males produces a danger-ously high level of male aggression and competition for females. This aggression has to be displaced outside of the troop (community) in order to maintain sane measures of place and stability within the troop. The mechanism for displacement would present itself in the twofold preoccupation of males even to this day, human and nonhuman alike. Hunting provides joint effort among males with its corresponding bonding, and war enables groups of males to displace aggression on other groups of males.

When one considers male power coalitions, the first institutions that come to mind are the armed forces. Until recently, these institutions were all male. Political parties, again until recently all male, and still all male at the top, are another example of this overall male dominance. Equally interesting is the phenomenon of the monastery, where, vow-ing lifelong celibacy, males gather together, to consider the great ideas and the great reality of God. Too often these males are particularly weak individuals who exhibit inadequacy in forming lasting relation-ships with women and in competing for a living in the marketplace. There are those who truly do forsake women, children, and career by choice, but these are rare individuals.

As one continues to consider primate social and political behavior generally, parallels and precedents to human behaviors among the other primate groups become apparent. Consider, for instance, the following:

Nothing divides the male coalition more than sexual access to females. Each member of this power coalition is a competitor whenever a female in the troop becomes sexually receptive. Accordingly, tensions within the male power coalition run very high. About once a month, the tensions build and threaten to physically pit each male against the other—potential pandemonium that would disrupt the entire troop with ruinous consequences. So, when the male tensions are palpable, the coalition joins in together what can only be described as a ritual of male bonding. Holding one another, they hoot and scream in near-sexual excitement. Then the males march off, away from the core of the troop's home range, in search of nearby prey. Their prey of choice—a lone infant deer or unguarded baby monkey—is never a match for a band of these 40–50-kilogram (88–110-pound) males. They violently and cooperatively dispatch the victim, pummeling the hapless creature with their fists, tearing it apart with their powerful hands.

When finished, they return together, prey in hand, to the core of the troop. What follows is as socially important as the hunt. The male with the prey in hand will pass portions of the victim to the other males, high-ranking females, juveniles, and infants who beg a portion. The power coalition shares the meager spoils of the hunt. Importantly, chimpanzees normally forage independently; they do not share food. Sharing the spoils of the hunt is a social bonding function, primarily bonding the potentially divisive males together until tensions again make another bonding hunt necessary. (Russell, 1993, pp. 148–149)

We find ourselves looking through the primate lens, when we suspect that presidential decisions regarding the timing of a conflict are based upon the momentary expediency of distracting the population from other presidential problems. At such times, we mistrust the plausible cognitive reasons given by our Presidents when they make these choices. We have this deeper "gut" suspicion that war is being used to displace in-group male aggression.

We will never be able to integrate these primate dynamics and come to understand them unless we first understand that we too are primates and that we possess them. Then, perhaps, having accepted their presence within us, we just might be able to transform them into symbolic forms of war such as the Olympics, or evolve beyond them altogether. In the same way that we must acknowledge and deal with our sexuality, the sexuality of primates, we must also deal with our warring nature. Primate sexuality and primate warfare are part of the architecture of our souls. We will never understand-integrate-transcend them until we first admit that we possess them. To deny them is to repress them. To repress them is to dissociate them from our higher faculties of consciousness. To do so is to force them into a "loose cannon" type of sub-personality, semi-autonomous and self-willed. We must cut a deal with our earthly nature. Jane Goodall realized this as she came to understand the real nature of the chimpanzees:

> In 1976, a surprised and saddened Jane Goodall reported that chimpanzees make war. She watched in horror as the male coalition of one troop huddled in excitement, "grinning hugely," then marched toward the edge of their territory in search of members of a neighboring chimpanzee troop. Upon locating a sufficiently small subgroup of their neighboring troop, the male coalition attacked them in merciless force, beating, biting and slamming bodies against trees. (Peterson and Goodall, 1993, p. 151)

The following quote from Dudley Young's book *Origins of the Sacred* brings home the point made above that perhaps both war and murder arrive in us via the chimps and other earlier primates. They might "flow over" the threshold of Eden and be responsible for Cain and Abel. If they do, we had better protect the threshold and those on the other side of it from extinction. We need to understand our inheritance from the primates if we are to integrate and transform it.

Of course evolutionary thinking has always countenanced competition, both for the ecological niche and among conspecific rivals for the best grazing. What is quite new is the idea that by the time of the chimpanzee, such competition was already looking much like war as we know it. And the fact that at Gombe and Mahle it was undertaken for fun and for profit refutes the idea that war arises with scarcity: the best grazing is always scarce if you actually enjoy fighting for it. To say that the chimp will occasionally go to "war" is to say that he is sometimes a social predator, like the lion and the hyena, capable of classifying his conspecifics as prey. What makes the Gombe story truly horrifying is that the war was in effect a civil war: the two troops had originally been united, and so the murderers were in fact stomping their former friends. And just as I suggested earlier that the chimp's brain is responsible for his adopting predatorial ways, the expanding brain will remain crucial as early man moves onto the savannah; not only for the refinement of weaponry and gladiatorial prowess, but for the acquisition of those cooperative skills that make any hunting pack so formidable. However disagreeable, the evidence is fairly clear that the human brain began its prodigious expansion at the same time as we became serious hunters, about 2.5 million years ago. (Young, 1991, p. 58)

Again, we have only two choices: (1) to repress and deny that we are primates, or (2) to accept and integrate the simple fact that we are primates.

Too often religion has been used to deny and repress our animal nature in order to focus on the divine nature that we also possess. But if God simply designed us this way, if evolution is understood to be the progressive evolution of Spirit in matter, then our animal nature *is* our divinely ordained nature. To accept that we are primates is then to accept God's will for us as our flesh. The dualisms of St. Paul would then be transcended in a unitive vision of who we really are as creatures of God. First, like Jesus Christ, we are incarnate—we have a body. Second, like Jesus Christ, we have an immortal soul that outlives that incarnation. St. Paul describes this as warring sides of our nature; Jesus creates far fewer such dualisms.

Integration rather than control of our nature seems closer to the unitive understanding of "I and the Father are One." If we are primates, divine primates, then so too were Jesus Christ and Krishna! Our job is not to deny but to unify. The body is holy and the dwelling place of Spirit. It is also a primate with periods and erections! When the mystery we create with clothing is dispelled with nudity (not to say pornography, which is not instinct based but cognitively based), there we are! Primates! We need our religions—humans are very sophisticated primates, religious primates. Our religions provide the guidance, the behavioral channels that we need to keep us on the pathways of our instincts. But we must say "no" when our religion attempts to make us think of ourselves as though we have no bodies. Sixty-five million years of evolution will not be controlled or overturned by two thousand years of religious doctrine, Christian or otherwise. However, male primate aggression lacking the bridle of a functioning religion or moral system is not desirable either. A constant and systematically applied religion or moral system harnesses the energy of the primate, and in the integration of the two sides of our nature, we discover who we really are.

Aggression, however, is not the only reality among the pre-human primates. Primatologist Shirley Strum observed levels of cooperation among baboons that even she hadn't expected to find. In her wonderful book *Almost Human,* she returns again and again to this theme of cooperation and political and social finesse among baboons. Many of her observations flew in the face of traditional wisdom regarding primates:

> My shocking discovery was that males had no dominance hierarchy; that baboons possessed social strategies; that finesse triumphed over force; that social skill and social reciprocity took precedence over aggression. (Strum, 1987, pp. 157–158)

And, as she points out, the implications are that pre-human primates already had the ability to form groups with social cohesion that are "governed" more by political skill than by tyranny. Thus, we can think of government as intrinsic to our nature. I think we can view religion in the same way. Strum again:

> The implications were breathtaking. I was arguing that aggression was not as pervasive or important an influence in evolution as had been thought, and that social strategies and social reciprocity were extremely important. If baboons possessed these, certainly the precursors of our early human ancestors must have had them as well. (Strum, 1987, p. 158)

As is becoming more and more clear, in primate and even mammalian research generally, there is a great deal more going on among non-human animals than we have ever appreciated before. Certainly, more than nature as red in tooth and claw! Perhaps the animals continue to evolve in consciousness (and therefore adequacies) as we ourselves do. So our ability to perceive animals co-evolves with the animals' increase in adequacies. In any case, Shirley Strum saw things among the baboons that others before her certainly did not see. In her own words:

> Smart baboons. Everywhere I looked I saw socially smart animals. As social diplomats, they employed finesse—social strategies, sophisticated maneuvers and reciprocity—for their very survival. I had discovered extraordinary intelligence, planning and insight in their interactions with one another, both as individuals and as members of real or constructed families. (Strum, 1987, p. 128)

In the same way that in our own affairs, diplomacy enables us to avoid conflict, so too do the baboons possess diplomatic skills and these skills are the best insurance they have to avoid damaging overt aggression. As Strum indicated, it is the "social strategies" that give the male baboons "effective ways to counter the risks of real aggression" (Strum, 1987, p. 151).

Most female baboons, on the other hand, were without either political skills or power. The feminine care of the troop had its own ways. Female powers lay in a combination of raising young and political leadership. Again, Strum:

> The final point that the baboons made is perhaps the most striking: there is nothing inherently powerless or impotent in female roles, no matter how involved these are with raising young and being the stable core of the group. The old arguments assumed that these were the only roles and functions females had; but among female baboons, they formed the basis for a variety of other political and leadership positions. Real power resided with those who were "wise" rather than those who were "strong," those who could mobilize allies rather than those who try to push through with brute force. (Strum, 1987, p. 151)

Friendship alliances between males and females are the single best hope males have for successful mating strategies. There seems to be talk among the ladies. Information is passed about eligible bachelors. To fare well in this group is to fare well with the ladies. As Strum put it, "having female friends seemed critical to a male's ultimate reproductive success" (Strum, 1987, p. 120).

It is interesting to note the social structures and behaviors of many primate troops, the baboons in particular, from the vantage point of contemporary Western society with its rampant social dysfunctions, which are partly a result of gender and role confusion in family and other social groups. The focus of most, if not all, primate troops is the dominant males at the center. The females who are with child constitute the first circle outward from the dominant males. Beyond them are the remaining females, older youngsters, and less dominant males. At the outer edge are the most expendable adolescent males. The contours of this demographic clearly reveal the order of necessity and survival—a pattern for success.

There is a darker side of the foregoing demographic. It also reveals disturbing, yet all too familiar, patterns of making adolescent males expendable and the prevalent practice of rape. The former pattern is found throughout the animal kingdom, which suggests that the evolutionary judgment is that too many males create too much instability within a society. Apparently, this is a judgment with which human cultures agree, given the age-old practice of sending adolescent males off to war. Even contemporary commercial culture recognizes the problem of male teens, who constitute one of the highest liability categories in the auto insurance industry.

The latter pattern of rape is largely a result of the troop demographics, wherein the dominant males attract the females and the subordinate males do not, which may be linked to the pattern of male adolescent expendability. Male promiscuity and rape are well known among the primates. Rape even contributes to the overall mating strategy of various primate species. According to Robert Jay Russell, it is not dominant males who rape; rather, it is the subordinate males, those who find it difficult to create functioning consort bonds.

> Lemurs introduced the consort bond to primate evolution. In a sense, a consort bond represents the context in which a mating is supposed to take place. Successful consort pairings in a primate group serve to reduce the level of tension. A consort pair signifies to one and all that a couple is compatible and that mate selection has taken place. A dominant male defends this bond against other males, but sometimes less-dominant males cannot sustain their consort bonds. Many, perhaps even most matings take place outside the boundaries of consent and the consort bond. Nonconsensual sex works. Nature's way is ever pragmatic, not ideal. ...
>
> Since rape is common from lemurs to humans, then it can be argued that rape as a means of reproduction has been selected for by natural selection. It is equally likely that rape has been ignored by natural selection because it confers no reproductive advantage or disadvantage. Rape may be selectively neutral. For most primates, rape is a consequence of

the hormonal/behavioral complex that leads to male mating. This complex and its aberrations can be understood simply.

For males, successful mating entails two simultaneously successful behavioral acts. First, a male must be selected by a female; he must be able to form a consort bond. Second, he must assert and defend his dominance over other, competing males. If he fails in either of these behavioral acts, his mating success is in jeopardy.

Dominant males, especially those who pose no aggressive threat to females, are attractive to females. They have little difficulty forming a successful consort bond. Dominant males are successful in asserting their high rank over potential competitors. Their aggressive posturing toward potential competitors is sufficient. Dominant males have little need nor inclination to resort to rape.

Submissive males, on the other hand, have little or no success in forming either a consort bond or establishing a high rank among their peers. Submissive males are unattractive to females and are on the bottom of the pecking order. Their reproductive and dominance ambitions are frustrated. Their only real chance for mating success is rape. (Russell, 1993, pp. 141, 134)

Humans, however, are religious primates; therefore, the cultural, religious and moral components of human society work upon males to control their aggression and discourage rape. Without a functioning cultural pattern of religion and morals, however, that internal restraint on male sexual aggression weakens. When that happens, only the external control of law can control the urge to rape, but law is much less effective in this task than is religion.

At the opposite end of the primate social-political spectrum are the matriarchies. While no one has yet seen a female hierarchy form, they nonetheless exist. In other words, hierarchy is not an oppression designed and perpetrated by males. Females have and maintain clear and very stable hierarchies with very few reversals in dominance roles. Such behavior underscores an inherent conservatism in the females that provides an essential counterbalance to the seemingly unending turmoil of the male pack. However, these hierarchies are not always without their share of overt violence either! Robert Jay Russell:

> Thus, both the male and female infants of high-ranking females are privileged from birth, and from birth they learn how to exercise privilege. When they mature, these infants will most likely ascend to the top of their respective dominance hierarchies.
>
> The infants of low-ranking females lead a hellish life by comparison. Their mother is continually abused by higher-ranking colleagues. Under almost continual stress, she is ever-vigilant for the approach of a more dominant animal. Not infrequently, a higher-ranking female will swipe at her. Her infant may be injured in these attacks or it may be pulled from her body by overeager, higher-ranking juvenile females who aggressively solicit a chance to play aunt. (Russell, 1993, p. 130)

What females among primates (in this case, baboons) do have is an inner social cohesion that human females seem to be allowing to slip away. They have a shared social life that has little or no reference to the posturing and political obsession of the males. Once established in their hierarchy, they at least know who they are and what to expect from life. Strum:

> No matter how you viewed it, males were only temporary members of a group. The females were permanent. Moreover, females were predictable. Their first allegiance was to their family. (Strum, 1987, p. 79)

The males, on the other hand, are forced to continually defend themselves or to move on and go through the dominance struggle again and again. Having achieved primacy in one country, they have to do so again and again or die trying. Strum:

> The more I understood males, the clearer it seemed that they had a hard life. Where did their size, strength, and physical power get them? They were constantly reenacting their own expulsion from their Garden of Eden; they had to construct whole new lives for themselves after leaving behind all that was friendly, secure and familiar. Once in their new troop, they had to recapture all they had lost: their social closeness, allies, friends, experience and knowledge that ultimately constituted baboon wisdom. Despite great effort and enduring patience, they ended up with less than a female who had never left home could command simply with a look, gesture, or grunt. I felt sorry for males. (Strum, 1987, p. 127)

Humans are born social. Like all primates we are born into a web of relationships, into a context. That context in its immediate sense is our family. If the larger context is broken or pathological, then we are born into a broken or pathological context and are, to some extent, subsequently shaped by that context. In the same way, if we are born into an insane or disintegrated culture we will be shaped to one extent or another by that experience.

We are also all born of a female. Our first, most basic needs are met by that female. The most basic of our most basic needs is the willingness on the part of that female to provide us the in utero space to grow and develop. Our next need is to be welcomed into life by a father and mother who, through touch, food, support, and overall caretaking, provide us with a feeling of security and well being.

Beyond this closed circle of the family lie the extended family, the neighborhood, the town or city, the country, the continent, the planet, the solar system, galaxy, and universe. Our family and our religion are the vehicles that introduce us to these successive levels of relationship. The same contours mentioned earlier, which determine the shape of baboon social life are also evidenced in similar circles of experience in the human. In the end, the family introduces us to all subsequent circles of relatedness up to and including our relatedness to God.

If what Shirley Strum says about the female baboons is accepted as truth, then it makes us wonder about the relationship between women leaving the home to enter into the workplace as has happened since women's liberation in the sixties. Has the loss of the feminine core of our culture and society been the most significant factor contributing to the disintegration of our social fabric? Do our in utero young fear the choices of the "liberated" mother? Are they born frightened? Depressed? Angry? Have we abandoned the cultural foundation of our world by destroying the primates and denying the primate foundation of ourselves? If our primate nature, bound to the whole family of primates, is the foundation of our familial and cultural architecture, then the loss of functional contact with ourselves is the root cause of the despair we feel culturally and familiarly. The topic, though threatening, is necessary to face.

The Primal Root of Culture and Religion

Finally, we come to the question of culture among the other primates. Until recently, more of us have assumed that human culture has been the single defining adequacy that has clearly separated us from the chimps and other primates. What if this is not the case? What if, instead, as I have suggested, human culture is derived from primate culture? Shirley Strum has observed the presence of culture among baboons:

> Although I was committed to this new kind of approach, and did not want to reinstate a baboon model of human evolution, I was constantly struck by how much more like humans the baboons seemed now. They learned through insight and observation, passing new behaviors from one to another both within a single lifetime and across many lifetimes. This is social tradition, the beginnings of what eventually became "culture." (Strum, 1987, p. 153)

Others, such as Dudley Young, suggest that primates were the first animals to give expression to religious sensibilities:

> The story begins with the arboreal monkey evolving into the chimpanzee. Here is the animal base from which all man's higher activities arise. Many readers will be astonished to discover how much we knew of love and war before we learned to talk.
>
> When we stood up and moved from the forests onto the savannah, we became both more violent and, necessarily, more preoccupied with nurturing the young. To move simultaneously toward violence and domesticity put an obvious strain on the mind, and what we now know as the sex war was underway. Our desire to make both love and war were clarified on the dancing ground where divinity was discovered. (Young, 1991, p. xix)

Most of us can agree that cultures are born of religion. Could it be possible that humans owe even their religious impulse to the chimps? Again, the words of Young:

> In keeping with the tendency of the book thus far, the reader might expect me to suggest that the religious life was not a human invention but was in fact discovered by the chimpanzees; and so I shall. What I have in mind is the wonderful raindance described by Jane Goodall in her early book *In the Shadow of Man*. Astonishing as it may seem, she actually saw four males responding to the outbreak of a particularly heavy thunderstorm by charging up and down a hillside at Gombe, tearing off tree branches and hooting wildly. This continued through twenty minutes of thunder, lightning, and downpour, and was witnessed by a congregation of females and youngsters who had climbed into trees nearby to watch. The old joke that religion began with man shaking his fist at the heavens is thus not far wide of the mark.

The principal gods in historical cultures, such as Zeus and Yahweh, originated as weather gods, and the storm is an appropriate vehicle for divinity on several counts: it arises from nowhere and prevails everywhere, its source is invisible and yet its designated effects are palpable, and it manifests a quite astonishing power to move and disrupt the pattern of things as they are into a new arrangement—all in all, a plausible origin for the high winds of *pneuma*. (Young, 1991, p. 93)

Somehow it's less threatening to admit that we exhibit primate behavior such as grasping as a result of our primate heritage and memory. But when we begin to ask questions about culture, and about the source and support of culture, i.e., our relationships with God vis-à-vis religion, the temperature goes up. We have been reluctant to understand ourselves as animals and yet animals we are—divine animals, yes, but animals created by and loved by Divinity. If we are created as sacred primates, then it must be "good" to be a sacred primate, if we could only relax into it. What if our neurotic desires to be other than sacred animals is the root cause of the desiccated nature of our religious life and that desiccation the cause of our split with nature? Animals do not try to experience themselves as separate from the created order. Why, then, do we? Put native people on a reservation and their culture all but disappears. Place animals in a zoo and their niche behaviors atrophy similarly. We are cultural animals and our religions are our niche. They are designed to fit into a planetary habitat. To lose touch with our primate nature is to lose touch with nature. Nature is the source of our religions and our religions help us to live properly with nature. Another quotation from Dudley Young puts it well:

Returning to the raindance, what we can now see is a serious play devoted to the conjuring of increased power through contagion in the players in order to defy a formidable adversary both ubiquitous and not altogether perceivable. At once we notice something new; contagion is moving not only through the chimps but is coming to them from the sky. The storm is not only their adversary but their partner in a dance devoted to some extensive version of abandonment, what Yeats would call " the delirium of the brave." All it lacks in order really to justify the word "dance" is an element of rhythm and harmony.

This element, though never recorded at Gombe, was observed by Wolfgang Kohler in his pioneering chimp study of 1916: The whole group of chimpanzees sometimes combined in more elaborate motion-patterns. For instance, two would wrestle and tumble near a post; soon their movement would become more regular and tend to describe a circle round the post as a center. One after another, the rest of the group approach, joins the two, and finally marches in an orderly fashion round and round the post. The character of their movements changes; they no longer walk, they trot and as a rule with special emphasis on one foot, while the other steps lightly, thus a rough approximate rhythm develops, and they tend to "keep time" with one another. ...

It seems to be extraordinary," Kohler concludes, "that there should arise quite spontaneously, among chimpanzees, anything that so strongly suggested the dancing of some primitive tribes."

There is also a quiet prologue to the dance, and it emerges on those wonderful occasions, briefly described earlier, when the fading light of evening calls upon the whole chimpanzee troop, each sequestered in his tree, to drum in the darkness—the wood resounding each to each and all to the all-embracing night, as it isolates and enfolds them. To ponder this stirs us deeply, as if a door were opening to allow us back into our first world, something precious. And indeed brief reflection proves this to be actually so: not only do the African Bantu also drum in the darkness, but we can follow the line all the way down, through the Catholic Vespers and

Angelus to the Protestant Evensong and "Taps" on the army bugle, prayers at bedtime to "protect us from the perils and dangers of this night." It feels exactly right, and astonishing to think it comes from that far back.

Who would dare to suggest that animals pray? Might there be an instinct to appeal to some larger entity? Young continues:

> But surely the chimps can't be praying? No, but nor are they merely warning off predators, for the chorus of drumming and hooting sounds somewhat softly on the night: these animals, after all, are going to sleep. What they are addressing, as they lie in their nests, is above all the darkness descending; and the anxiety it arouses is consoled both by the sounds of self assertion—"Here I am in good heart"—and the sense of others not far; distant enough to inflict no presence, near enough to amplify and confirm my world. One can imagine a nascent interest in esthetics here, as pleasure is taken in shaping of hoots and drumbeats both to challenge and commingle with the general song.
>
> Of course the skeptics will urge that there is no question of addressing the sky at such moments, and the chimps are addressing only the predators, themselves, and each other. Such skepticism, as is so often the case, cannot be argued away but only invited to look again and consider that things may indeed be as they appear to be: the chimps *are* looking at the darkening sky, which has not only triggered this performance but is the medium through which their messages to predators, selves, and each other are mingled. What's more, one's ear tells one that this is indeed a chorus, and that the chimp is capable of perceiving this; and that for this to happen, the sounds must be addressing something sufficiently abstract and amorphous to reflect and engender the idea of "the troop as a whole"—to wit, the darkness descending. As with the raindance spectators in the trees, there is sufficient

leisure (i.e., release from the obligation to respond to signals given) to make room for the perception of a signal, both serious and playful, sent to everything and nothing, everywhere and nowhere—the sky in fact. (Young, 1991, p. 96)

The structure of stable social groups is essential to the creation of a culture that, once established, can endure and evolve. Hierarchy in both male and female primates is the way in which this is done. Wherever we look in human societies we see this same hierarchy. The Church, the corporation, the justice system, the political system, you name it. Pie-in-the-sky ideas of life without hierarchy are abstractions; they have no true objective reality. The fifty-plus million years of primate evolution reasserts itself over and over again and in every culture. Ken Wilber well notes the differences between healthy and pathological hierarchies. Actually, there are many examples of both. Still hierarchy seems to be the way of humans, of other primates and even of the biosphere generally.

So, am I claiming that human culture is dependent on the existence and functioning of the other primate cultures? No, I cannot make that claim with certainty. Instead I ask the question: What if it is? What if the primates are dependent on the mammals generally and the mammals on even earlier life forms? What if every level of life rests upon and is contingent upon those levels that precede it? In any case, it is a good thing to protect primate habitat from continual encroachment by human populations. We should do it for that reason only. But if we are in fact dependent on their healthy functioning for our own, then we certainly don't want to wait until it is too late!

CHAPTER EIGHT

The Trans-Mammalian Psyche

THE TRANS-MAMMALIAN PSYCHE is the psychic milieu shared by all mammals. The first mammals evolved 100 million years after the first reptiles. From that point on, though both shared a common core brain, the mammals evolved in a parallel but separate way from the reptiles. While the reptiles proliferated in span, their interior remained largely unchanged. Mammals, however, owing to a further evolution of their brain, emerged into a deeper interiority, which includes a deeper sensitivity than the reptiles. This amounted to a new adequacy, namely, emotion. The mammals allowed the creation to feel itself. This feeling life continued to evolve up through the primates and into the human.

The class Mammalia, which comprises nineteen orders and more than 15,000 species, is defined by any animal that feeds its young with milk secreted from special organs, called mammary glands, on the body of the mother. There are three types of mammals: the placentals (which include humans), marsupials (such as kangaroos), and mono-tremes (such as platypuses). The marsupials and monotremes differ reproductively from the placental mammals. Marsupials cannot feed their young in utero, due to their lack of a placenta. Their young are born the size of a bean and climb up and into a pouch that contains the much-needed nipples. On the other hand, like their reptilian ances-tors, the monotremes lay eggs. Still, following hatching, their young are fed at the nipples. While marsupials and monotremes do fit the strict definition of being mammals, only the placentals are mammals in the sense that humans and all primates are mammals.

Although there are differences in the ways the three types of mammals are brought into this world, they share a common characteristic: an infancy that is extremely physically tactile and shaped by a high degree of physical and emotional interdependency. The tactile connection in the womb, in the pouch, and/or to the mammary nipple has great importance in the development of emotion and the mammalian phenomenon of emotional bonding. Mammals have a need to bond both tactilely and emotionally with others. Is it any wonder?

Consider our own species. Humans are formed in a warm, sensual womb for the first nine months of existence. Then, once born, each of us craves the warm, soft touch of our mother, and we cry out for her nipple—the source of nourishment and comfort. Hour after hour, day after day, month after month, even year after year, human children are extraordinarily bonded to their mothers and, eventually, to their fathers. These bonds will last a lifetime, and they are the blueprints by which we will bond with others and the world at large.

This bond evolved over eons of time to ensure the survival of mammals. It was a necessary development because mammals, especially the higher mammals, do not have as many offspring over the course of a life as reptiles do. Consequently, the survival of mammalian offspring is very dependent upon parental attention and care. Physical and emotional bonding evolved to foster a level of affection and mutual interests between members of a species to ensure survival of the young and the group. Comparatively, reptile survival is dependent upon issuing hundreds to tens-of-thousands of offspring over a lifetime—a necessary prodigality, given the lack of parental care and the consequential high loss of life in the early florescence. A newly hatched reptile does not know its parents; in fact, there is a good chance that a parent may eat it. Conversely, imagine how warm and cozy the infantile experience of the world must be for a baby chimp who is patiently groomed by his protective, nurturing mother while he is suckling at her breast. This is a bond that endures over a lifetime, ensuring the survival of individuals within the continuity of family. It endures from generation to generation, ensuring the continuity and success of the species and the class Mammalia itself.

The organic structure that is responsible for the mammalian bonding capacity is the deep limbic system—a structure of the central nervous system that is unique to mammals. It plays an indispensable role in governing our mammalian bonding nature. Considering its relatively small size, it is power-packed with functions, all of which are critical for human behavior and survival. From an evolutionary standpoint, this is an older part of the mammalian brain that enabled mammals to experience and express emotions. It freed them from the stereotypical behavior and actions dictated by the brain stem, found in the older reptilian brain. The subsequent evolution of the surrounding cerebral cortex in higher animals, especially humans, gave the capacity for problem solving, planning, organization, and rational thought. Yet, in order for these functions to occur, one must have passion, emotion, and desire to make it happen.

This part of the brain is involved in setting a person's emotional tone. When the deep limbic system is less active, there is generally a positive, more hopeful state of mind. When it is heated up, or overactive, we experience negative and painful emotional shading. Due to this emotional shading, the deep limbic system provides the filter through which we interpret the events of the day. It tags or colors events depending on the emotional state of mind. When we are sad (with an overactive deep limbic system), then we are likely to interpret neutral events through a negative lens. For example, if I have a neutral or even positive conversation with someone whose deep limbic structure is overactive or "negatively set," then he or she is likely to interpret the conversation in a negative way. When this part of the brain is "cool" or functions properly, a neutral or positive interpretation of events is more likely to occur. Emotional tagging of events is critical to survival. The positive or negative charge we give to certain events in our lives drives us to act accordingly, such as approaching a desired mate or avoiding someone who has hurt us in the past.

The deep limbic system, along with the deep temporal lobes, has also been reported to store highly charged emotional memories, both positive and negative. If you have been traumatized by a dramatic event, such as being in a car accident or watching your house burn down, or if you have been abused by a parent or a spouse, the emotional component of the memory is stored in the deep limbic system of the brain. On the other hand, if you have won the lottery, graduated magna cum laude, or watched your child's birth, those emotional memories are stored here as well. The total experience of our emotional memories is responsible, in part, for the emotional tone of our mind. The more stable, positive experiences we have, the more positive we are likely to feel. The more trauma in our lives, the more emotionally set we become in a negative way. These emotional memories are intimately involved in the emotional tagging that occurs throughout our lives.

The deep limbic system is also intimately involved with bonding and social connectedness. When the deep limbic system of animals is damaged, they do not properly bond with their young. In one study of rats, mothers with damaged deep limbic structures would drag their offspring around the cage as if they were inanimate objects. They would not feed and nurture the young as they would normally do. This system affects the bonding mechanism that enables us to connect with other people on a social level; our ability to do this successfully in turn influences our moods. We are social animals. When we are bonded to people in a positive way, we feel better about our lives and ourselves. This capacity to bond then plays a significant role in the tone and quality of our moods.

The deep limbic system directly processes the sense of smell. The olfactory system is the only one of the five sensory systems that goes from the sensory organ to directly where it is processed in the brain. The messages from all the other senses (sight, hearing, touch, and taste) are sent to a "relay station," the thalamus, before they are sent to their final destination in different parts of the brain. Because our sense of smell goes directly to the deep limbic system, it is easy to see why smells can have such a powerful impact on our feeling states. The multibillion-dollar perfume and deodorant industries count on this fact: beautiful smells evoke pleasant feelings and draw people toward you, while unpleasant smells cause people to withdraw. Expensive perfumes and colognes can make you beautiful, sexy, and attractive to others, while a disagreeable body odor can make the other person want to rush to the far side of the room.

Bonding, smells, sexuality, and the deep limbic system are intimately connected. Napoleon once wrote to Josephine to ask her not to bathe for two weeks before he came home from a battle. He wanted her scent to be powerful, because it turned him on sexually. Likely, positive, sexual smells cool the limbic system and make us more in the mood for love. Sexuality is good for the bonded human brain. Whenever a person is sexually involved with another person, neurochemical changes occur in both their brains that encourage limbic, emotional bonding. Yet, limbic bonding is the reason casual sex doesn't really work for most people on a whole mind and body level. Two people may decide to have sex "just for the fun of it," yet something is occurring on another level they might not have decided on at all: Sex is enhancing an emotional bond between them, whether they want it or not. One person, often the woman, is bound to form an attachment and will get hurt when the affair ends. The reason it is usually the woman is that the size of a female's limbic system, in comparison to the rest of her brain, is larger than it is for a man. Consequently, she is more likely to get "limbically" connected.

The larger deep limbic system in females gives rise to several advantages and disadvantages. Due to the larger deep limbic brain, women are more in touch with their feelings—they are generally better able to express their feelings than men. They have an increased ability to bond and be connected to others (which is why women are the primary caretakers for children—there is no society on earth where men are primary caretakers for children). Females have a more acute sense of smell, which is likely to have developed from an evolutionary need for the mother to recognize her young. However, having a larger deep limbic system leaves a female somewhat more susceptible to depression, especially at times of significant hormonal changes such as the onset of puberty, before menses, after the birth of a child, and at menopause. Women attempt suicide three times more often than men.

The limbic system, through which mammals emotionally relate to and bond with each other and the world, has a huge psychic impact on us today because it is the divinely evolved gift that enables us to feel affection and love for one another and the world of nature—our Great Mother. For this reason, the central concern of this book comes to bear again: Since the mammalian deep limbic system is the link between the reptilian brain stem and the paleo-mammalian cortices, and since it is the functional link between the instinctual and affective psyches, what would it mean to drive nonhuman orders and species of mammals into extinction? Would it cause the link between the affective and instinctual mind in the primates to atrophy? Would it cause a similar effect in us? Has it already begun? Is our seemingly moronic ignorance of ecological wisdom the result of a functional reduction of bondedness between the mammalian and pre-mammalian psyches? Are the increasing phenomena of "bond-breaking" behaviors—divorce, abortion, eroding parenting skills—and "bond-substitution" behaviors—addictions—symptomatic of the loss of earthy spiritual rites and practices that honored our mammalian nature? Were functional, "nature-affirming" religious traditions our links to the deeper and broader life community? While we cannot answer these questions decisively, their contemplation is enough to make us "tune in" to the Trans-Mammalian Psyche in order to discover the truth about all mammals, especially ourselves.

One such truth that might be discovered is that humans can, in fact, know how animals feel and what they think, especially other mammals. Science, like religion, has often been dogmatic in the worst sense when it comes to this matter. From the perspective of science, a person who claims to know how an animal is feeling is guilty of the "sin" of anthropomorphism, and from the perspective of Western religions, if a person claims that animals have souls, then he is guilty of blasphemy. The great "sacrilege" is the projection of human feelings and thoughts onto animals that do not feel and think like we do. Descartes believed that animals felt nothing, arguing that animal squeals of pain were nothing more than mechanical noises—not physical and emotional expressions of severe distress. This misguided, even sociopathic, thinking has had a grim impact on animals used in scientific research to this day. Although most lab researchers today know that animals do feel pain and emotional distress, they continue to subject lab animals to painful, even atrocious, procedures, while absolving themselves of wrongdoing by hiding behind an appeal to the "sacrifices needed for the greater good." Using such an appeal to absolve personal responsibility and accusing animal sympathizers of misdirected sentimentality harkens back to the old dogmatism of Descartes. Unfortunately, such a lack of sympathy for others—animals included—has promoted, and continues to promote, the atrocities of slavery, genocide, and rampant habitat destruction.

What word could we use to describe our recognition of feelings and instincts in other animals? I suggest that we resurrect the ancient notion of *animism*, which claims that everything has a sentient life force that binds us all in relationship. In empathy we can actually identify with the feelings of animals. Horse whispering is an example of identification between mammalian minds. I suspect that "snake charming" is an "at-one-ment" with the reptilian mind.

Doctors Adele and Deborah Marlena McCormick, founders of the Institute of Conscious Awareness, point to this same reality in their lovely book *Horse Sense and the Human Heart.* Though they never used the word, I think they would agree that there is a *trans-equine* mind out of which the species is born and within which it has its governance. Horses can communicate nonlocally with other horses and, indeed, with other mammals through this trans-equine mind. In their words:

> In an animistic worldview, every material manifestation of the universe has a soul. Everything around us, animate and inanimate, is listening, seeing, feeling and thinking. Within this paradigm, animals occupy a central role in our lives and our interactions with them acquire greater significance. A one-sided or hierarchical dynamic gives way to reciprocity between ourselves and other species. (McCormick and McCormick, 1997, p. 17)

They go so far as to say outright that horses have nonlocal healing power:

> Since we can communicate with horses in a multitude of ways—mentally, physically, and through extrasensory perception, visualization and telepathy—these alternative avenues work. Other authors and experts agree that the keen extrasensory abilities of horses make their healing powers nonlocal. (McCormick and McCormick, 1997, p. 9)

The herd, then, is the subset of the trans-equine mind, which itself is a subset of the Trans-Mammalian Psyche; therefore, trans-equine mind is implicated in the functioning of the whole Trans-Mammalian Psyche, including the human. This is why the other animals figure into our myths; they are interior functions or organs of our psyche. Lose them and we lose our minds!

> It is also fascinating to note that a tendency to objectify horses throughout history has usually coincided with cultural periods when enlightenment and spirituality were at an ebb. By contrast, reverence, admiration, and deep appreciation for horses usually signals a reemerging cultural and spiritual renaissance. Like fine wine, art and music, a passion for horses has often ushered in a revival of the sacred esthetic traditions. (McCormick and McCormick, 1997, p. 20)

We inherit more than we know from our nonhuman animal forebears, and when we destroy them we lose the inheritance they bring us. We lose the genetic contribution they make and inherit a thinner, less complex gene pool. We also inherit a thinner, less complex mind, one that exhibits disintegration and therefore illness. Life is unbroken from the beginning until now. Even with the Cambrian extinction 570 million years ago, the Permian extinction 245 million years ago, the Cretaceous extinction some 67 million years ago, the Morine catastrophe 15 million years ago, and the Pleistocene catastrophe 730,000 years ago, life continued to complexify and become more conscious.

The present extinction rates can only represent a man-made catastrophe, one which E. O. Wilson has called the greatest setback to life since it emerged on the planet. We come from and embody the whole story of life. That story, along with the Earth and cosmic stories, comprise the architecture of our souls.

The first mammals appeared 216 million years ago, some 15 million years before the dinosaurs emerged from the reptiles. We were forced to stay small among the grand reptiles, but, following their extinction, we experienced an explosive complexification, proliferation, and overall evolutionary leap. Then, 114 million years ago, the placental mammals appeared, and 65 million years ago, the primates appeared. The apes evolved 36 million years ago; 5 million years ago, the chimpanzee emerged along with hominids such as Australopithecus afarensis. Roughly 2½ million years ago, the first humans walked the Earth. Modern humans were present 40,000 years ago. We have inherited a continuous transmission of mammalian emotional wisdom that should not be denied. In us, it is expressed as emotive consciousness in art, dance, song, and erotic rituals, as well as mothering, fathering, familying, and neighborliness.

The source of the human Affective Subpsyche is the Trans-Mammalian Psyche. Its experience in the human is called feeling, and its expression is called emotion. The Trans-Mammalian Psyche is not only present in the other mammals, but is embodied in the whole class Mammalia. The living mammals *are* the archetypes of the mammalian psyche. When we lose touch with the mammals, we lose touch with the sensitivity we share in common with them. We diminish in our ability to feel. When we lose the mammals themselves, we lose the archetypes of the Trans-Mammalian Psyche. When the mammal orders become extinct, the sensitivities they embody are extinguished in us. We not only lose our ability to feel, we lose our capacity to feel. Who hasn't had the experience of watching someone act out emotions that are not based on true feelings? They create behaviors based on what they think a feeling would look like when experienced. As T. S. Eliot put it, they are the hollow men, the stuffed men. When the mammals disappear, our feelings go with them. Affective disorders result and, worse, affective vacuums result.

Because we ourselves are mammals, we participate in the Trans-Mammalian Psyche. Our own experience of ourselves and other mammals is the most dependable evidence we can summon regarding the presence or absence of affective states in other living beings. We can see that a snake is alive, and we can have feelings for the snake, but we also feel that the snake does not have feelings for us. When we embrace a golden retriever, however, we have a very different experience indeed. The dog has powerful feelings that we don't feel from the snake. We sense that dogs love and that snakes do not. Snakes' adequacies are limited to instinct. Reptiles are the window to divine instinctual wisdom, while mammals are the window to love. Again, the McCormicks:

> Animals teach us how to love spiritually. Their feelings for one another are not only touching but enviable in their strength and depth. Through their example, we can learn to deepen our sensitivity and humanity. (McCormick and McCormick, 1997, p. 24)

The cosmos is like a divine prism. Different aspects of creation reveal different aspects of divine wisdom and love. The cosmos itself is a revelation of a stupendous creativity so profound as to stagger the imagination. Each quantum, particle, atom, molecule, cell, organism, and so on exhibits some spark of this creativity. The reptile exhibits instinctual wisdom as does the Instinctual Subpsyche of the human. The mammals reveal feeling, different sorts of thought, and so much beauty. I want to illustrate this with a story.

Once, some several years ago, I was in the waiting room of a doctor or dentist. I read a story that might have been in *Reader's Digest* but I can't even be sure of that. In any case, it was about a prisoner of war who had been held and tortured in a Korean POW camp. He was kept in a box just slightly shorter in any direction than he was tall. Thus, he was never able at any point to stretch out to his full length. He was fed a single bowl of rice each day. His torment was relieved only once a week when he was taken from his box to be tortured.

One day, a three-legged rat who was also blind and pregnant happened into his cell. His loneliness was such that even the rat was a relief in the boredom. When his bowl of rice arrived, he gave her a few grains and they both ate. She continued to arrive at mealtime for her rice and a trust developed between them. Each day, he shared a bit of his rice. One day, after being taken out to be tortured, he returned to his box to find his bowl of rice and the rat. She hadn't taken a grain of it. Instead, she waited for his return and their shared time. He fed her and himself; then they both slept. When her time came, she birthed and nursed her young in his box and was fed rice by him daily.

In time, her young grew and departed and so did she. He noted that the day he realized she was gone was the very worst day of his life. Further, he noted that the very best day of his life was the day she returned, still blind, still limping, and pregnant again! He said that he had never before, nor since, felt such joy! I was in my teens or twenties when I read that story. It moved me deeply. The rat and the prisoner had a profound commonality: the Trans-Mammalian Psyche and its voices of love, companionship, and emotional need.

Mammals are the window that open the world to the divine warmth of love. In Christianity, God actually becomes a mammal. Human mammals are the windows for culture, for thought, for technology. But when we distance ourselves from our mammalian depth, we become disordered. The harmonizing of thought, affect, and instinct is what wholeness, health, and holiness are made of. Anything less is shallow and trite.

Because milk is automatically given to mammalian young does not mean it is given without love. My wife had abundant milk for both daughters. I often sat with them during nursing time. I was clearly in the presence of love. I trust what I felt. Neither Descartes nor John Locke returned from the dead could convince me otherwise. I feel; therefore, I'm aware of being. I remember another time when one of the mares at the barn where my wife rides gave birth to a newborn colt. We arrived a few hours after the birth to find the newborn having difficulty nursing. My wife entered the stall and used her hands to gently manipulate the mare's nipples, drawing her milk into a cup. The colt looked on curiously, and as Carol squeezed the nipple, she sprayed the milk toward the colt's face. Gradually he came closer and was able to begin nursing. The mare gladly accepted this help from another mother, sensing the relief it brought her physically, and trusting the kindness offered by another mammal. United in the Trans-Mammalian Psyche, a primate assisted a horse in a mutually understood moment of mothering. This unity of understanding and appreciation belies an attunement that is spiritual in nature:

> Horses teach us to expand our consciousness by going beyond the human realm. They connect us with divine mind. Working with horses makes this experience tangible. To be in tune with a horse is to be in divine attunement, or at one with nature. (McCormick and McCormick, 1997, p. 110)

In reflecting on their own process of abandoning a too exclusively cognitive emphasis in their clinical practices and deepening to a more natural and spiritually grounded approach, the McCormicks speak about the natural, divine wisdom that unfolds when one honors our instinctual wisdom:

> Learning how to be oneself comfortably is among the most challenging tasks in life. To accomplish it, we must live life, not analyze it. This is a simple concept that is difficult to enact. In the beginning of our careers, we spent countless hours constructing a professional identity, only to discover to be truly effective we had to dismantle that professional persona and relearn how to be natural, how to live close to our God-given instincts. Instincts are our guide for behaving in a way that is appropriate for our species.
>
> Instincts and intuition are inseparably linked. They are the tools we're given to maneuver our way through the world. Each animal, each person is endowed with the resources

needed to have direct access to God's wisdom, if so desired. If cultivated and used properly, instinct and intuition can become the God within. If they are ignored, the individual simply exists, or worse, is destructive and careless.

Many recent books on spirituality discuss the concepts of "divine mind" and "interconnectedness." We made these constructs more real by journeying into the world of animal energy and instincts. We learned that the instinct within each of us is a reflection of the larger universe. (McCormick and McCormick, 1997, p. 117)

The Dreamers

Dreaming is a mammalian adequacy, not a reptilian one. It seems to emerge with the limbic lobe of the brain. Thus, all mammals are able to dream. My dogs dream nightly when we try to watch TV. They yelp and their legs half run in response to whatever landscape is projecting itself in their mindscape. One can feel and hear their fear, pleasure, even humor. One of my happiest memories is of the belly laughter of my daughters as they slept. Dreaming has many layers as well. Humans can dream primal dreams, mammalian dreams, instinctual (reptilian?) dreams (such as the DTs), and even Earth and cosmic dreams. My wife Carol reported a dream to me while I was working on the primate chapter of this book. She dreamed she was sitting on our porch watching several large gorillas swaying as they held onto the lace curtains at the window. She was enjoying watching them playing and felt no threat or fear from them. When she awoke she told me it was as if they appeared to her as guardians, providing the link between her being and the earth. Is this the same message that the Anthony Hopkins character received from the silver-back gorilla in the film *Instinct*? Do the animals in fact watch over us?

Dudley Young says that dreamtime is a time of learning:

What can we know of hominid dreaming? There can scarcely be a more important question for the origins of myth, since mytho-logic is dream logic but as with many important questions, much remains obscure. The simplest thing we know is that reptiles do not dream, whereas mammals do. This suggests that dreaming is concerned with the affective thinking and learning introduced by mammalian life and the limbic lobe of the brain. Babies do a great deal of dreaming, presumably to master the "blooming, buzzing confusion" (William James) of their experience. Animals, such as horse foals, that dream more than humans do in the womb, emerge more competent at birth as a result (quickly get to their feet to get a drink); which would suggest that "reality testing" in the playful space-time of dreamland not only sorts out what one has done today but prepares for, and even perhaps chooses, what one might do tomorrow. That such playfulness is serious business is indicated by the fact that both animals and humans deprived of dream-sleep tend to become forgetful and unhinged; and conversely, the unhinged tend to dream with urgent vividness. The demons of memory are significantly at work, not only choosing important material to be stored in the long-term memory, but also probably running some very old movies: even the tough minded Darwin thought that the disposition of children to dream of monsters involved archaic memories, of the time when we were much afflicted with reptiles. Perhaps the major point on this list is the first one; dreaming arises in mammals who, unlike the reptiles, nurture their young and thereby introduce emotion and learning to the world. (Young, 1991, p. 83)

I agree with Young that mythology is dream truth. Myths reveal our depth to us. They are not meant to be true in the sense that 1+1=2 is true. They are true in what they reveal to us about our depth nature—in other words, about who we are as people, as primates, as mammals, as bio-citizens, as geo-citizens, as cosmic citizens, and as citizens of heaven. The mythological dream structure maps out the layers and facets of experience and consciousness into an emotionally embedded, and often intuitively transcendent, terrain of sanity, where we can learn and grow. And more often than not, dreaming enables us to integrate emotions that might otherwise destroy us. Case in point: Jeffrey Masson notes the nightmares of a young elephant traumatized by the slaughter of his family.

> Animal behaviorists are unlikely to acknowledge that terror can return in the dreams of animals. And yet from a Kenyan "elephant orphanage" comes a report of baby African elephants who have seen their families killed by poachers, and witnessed the tusks being cut off the bodies. These young animals wake up screaming in the night. What else but the nightmare memories of a deep trauma could occasion these night terrors? (Masson and McCarthy, 1995, p. 45)

Is it any wonder that the animals that bond are the animals that dream? Living in an emotionally bonded world full of colorful nuance, ecstatic highs, and traumatizing lows would necessitate an organic mechanism that reconciles the incredibly diverse spectrum of emotional experiences delivered to us by our five senses. Otherwise, we would go insane. Dreaming, however, is not only a survival mechanism; it is a gift that enables mammals to learn in ways that other animals cannot. This has given us—the mammals—a definite advantage, namely culture.

The dreams of mammals are also the dreams of the cosmos, and in human cultures, the cosmos attempts to understand itself. Put another way, in living organisms, God comes to see and experience divine beauty, the radiance of the Divine Self. Humans have tended to flatter themselves with the belief that we are the only species in which beauty is appreciated. Not so. Again, that adequacy comes to us from earlier life forms than ourselves.

> One afternoon a student observing chimpanzees at the Gombe Reserve took a break and climbed to the top of a

ridge to watch the sun set over Lake Tanganyika. As the student, Geza Teleki watched, he noticed first one then a second chimpanzee climbing up toward him. The two adult males were not together and saw each other only when they reached the top of the ridge. They did not see Teleki. The apes greeted each other with pants, clasping hands and sat down together. In silence Teleki and the chimpanzees watched the sun set and twilight fall. (Masson and McCarthy, 1995, p. 192)

If the beauty that is being observed is the radiance of God, then beauty is observing beauty where any life form is hypnotized by the power, beauty, grandeur, or volatility of nature. The beauty of the creation is the radiance of its Source present to us. We are stunned because the same beauty is within us doing the observing. The dynamism of culture comes to us from the depths of the unfolding cosmic process itself. Our most immediate benefactors, of course, are the primates. However, there are less obvious benefactors that have given much to human cultures, such as horses. Again, the McCormicks:

> Through training in the form of disciplined play with the horses, clients learned to tap into their ancient "animal" mind and energies and apply them toward more creative and responsible living. (McCormick and McCormick, 1997, p. xxviii)

What the McCormicks are calling "ancient animal mind," I am calling the Trans-Mammalian Psyche. The transpersonal psyche of humans emerges out of and is supported by the Trans-Mammalian Psyche. In the exact same way that humans can be of one mind with one another and with the one mind of God, humans can also be of one mind with other mammals. The McCormicks hold that the accomplished riding of horses can only be done when this trans-mammalian mysticism becomes a reality. In their words:

> To ride properly and artistically, riders must get out of their intellects and only ride with their hearts and souls. We all

agree on the vital importance of interior riding and training. Riding with passion, with the interior self, is the path to
mysticism.

To become a centaur, we advance farther on the spiritual
road. We no longer experience distance. Two distinct and
separate beings join and become one. There is no differentiation between human and horse: we are the dancer and the
dance. (McCormick and McCormick, 1997, p. 195)

On a later page they explain in poetic detail the way in which this
mystical union becomes a reality. The process is to have the human
and the horse become one being, what they call a "centaur," a mythical
creature half human and half horse. While the following quotation is
admittedly lengthy, I wanted to allow the McCormicks' beautiful words
to speak for themselves:

On a horse, letting go must have a mental and spiritual component. Everything you do must be done with pure inten-
tions, free from malice, and in the spirit of complete love,
trust and confidence. This is when telepathic communication begins. The merging begins with an inner feeling of
complete peace. As we relax our human defenses, becoming less vigilant, our senses become more acute. Everything
around us becomes heightened. We become more sensitive
to the various aspects of the experience, such as the sound of
horses' hooves hitting the ground, their muscle movement,
their breathing. We begin to meditate on the inner energy
of the horse. We begin to meld with the horse by waves of
sensation.

Nonetheless, we can still find remnants of our intellectual processes as we feel our seat in the saddle and our legs
on the flanks of the animal. However, as we go deeper into
the unconscious we feel our seat, hipbones and legs being
absorbed into the body of the horse. Then our upper torso
and arms disappear as well. Interestingly, the last to go is

usually our hands because they are the human symbol of mastery control, conquest, domination and power. Finally, we are out of our body and we are the horse. Our mind is its mind, and we are one. The entity we have created explodes with creativity.

This leaves us in a state of pure feeling. The Greek word for this is *extasis*, meaning "to get outside of oneself," to free oneself from the shackles of rationality. (McCormick and McCormick, 1997, p. 196)

"To free oneself from the shackles of rationality" is the necessary prerequisite for integration of Tertiary Awareness—awareness characterized by a deep, soulful appreciation of the connectedness to the whole life community and to the whole of creation. Traditionally, it has been called nature mysticism. The integration of Tertiary Awareness on the part of the human species is the prerequisite for continued life on Earth and, if my thesis is correct, of human sanity and cultural functionality. Nor is the notion of a tertiary zone of mind without precedent. It has a firm basis in Jungian thought and some basis in Freudian thought.

Given our mammalian bodies and our mammalian natures and given our primate social needs, it should come as no surprise to us that we suffer neurosis when deprived of contact with other mammals, humans and pre-humans. Lack of touch is traumatizing for us. We develop exaggerated startle responses when our flesh becomes unused to touch. In the same way that when parched enough we cannot take in water, when touch deprived at an extreme enough depth we find it difficult to receive touch. If we in fact have a trans-mammalian dimension, then lack of trans-mammalian contact must lead to disorder. We know for certain that elderly folks do better emotionally and physically when they have cats and dogs as pets. By extension the same is true of horses and other mammals as well. Speaking of touch deprivation, the McCormicks say this:

We have learned this very lesson from horses whose owners have failed to handle them on a regular basis. For example, a deprived horse who is not used to being touched or groomed will jump or leap when brushed. Even though the handler is well intentioned, doing something very positive and comforting by our standards, the horse doesn't interpret it that way. Therefore, until the horse gets used to the sensory or tactile input, the handler must move deliberately and slowly. Lacking a former reference point and unaccustomed to human touch, the neglected horse experiences "care" as something endangering it. People who have had little emotional input are the same way. (McCormick and McCormick, 1997, p. 130)

The sad absence of emphasis on our own need to be in contact with the other life forms is a sad and destructive weakness in Western Christianity. When religion is grounded in the cognitive and affective experience of humans the result is, in the first instance, a dry dogmatism and, in the second, a syrupy sentimentality, what Carmelite William McNamara has called pretty poisons. Such religious experience never really satisfies our hunger for mystical union with God, nature, and each other. In fact, either approach, dogmatism or sentimentalism, is dangerous as well as trite. Dangerous because they help us to distance ourselves from the grotesque pain of the created order unleashed by the industrial assault upon the natural world, and trite because dogmatism and sentimentality are superficial. If our religious establishment does not speak for "God, the Father Almighty, maker of heaven and *earth*," then who will?

St. Francis was the prophet of the animals. This is a vocation that calls out to us all, and one that we must respond to with vision and urgency. St. Francis was awake to the whole chain of being. He believed that "animals are our connection to the divine on Earth—numinous messengers of God who perform a role similar to that of angels" (McCormick and McCormick, 1997, pp. 18–19). The animals are, in fact, messengers of God and, if the Gospel of Mark is to be believed, ministers of God.

That Jesus was related to the animal kingdom is shown in the Gospel of Mark, where we are told that after the temptations

in the wilderness by Satan, Jesus was ministered to by the
angels and the wild animals. (McCormick and McCormick,
1997, p. 19)

Those Christians who hate or fear any connection between themselves and the animals should contemplate the above quotation as well
as the following:

Jung saw the animals as the epitome of true devotion in
that they don't deviate from how God intended them to be.
(McCormick and McCormick, 1997, p. 19)

God intended us to be mammals or we would not be. God intended
us to be primates or we would not be. True spirituality is the willingness
to be the people God creates us to be. To stand against being a primate
is to stand against the will of God. To stand against the will of God is to
be not only sinful but also deluded. When we do so we become cruel to
ourselves as well as to others. I remember that, during a lecture, Brian
Swimme stated that the greatest cruelty is superficiality, and that the
cruelest people are those too shallow to feel what they do.

Mental health is about being in reality. To put it into rhyming form,
"Our animality is our reality." We've become too focused on our cognitive adequacies. If our families, religions, and cultures are to be healed,
we must begin to experience as mammals. What do our mammalian
children need—*as mammals?* What difference do their SAT scores
make if they commit suicide? What good is financial success if we cannot family properly? We must learn how to be cultural animals again.
We must open ourselves to the affective and instinctual dimensions of
our being. The McCormicks put it this way:

The mistrust we have in our intuitive ability leaves us, like
sheep, extremely vulnerable. Our culture's present emphasis
on the importance of intellect at the expense of instinctual
knowing has rendered us defenseless. We have crippled ourselves in our hesitation to mobilize our instincts, even when to
do so would save our lives. We treat our instincts like vestigial

appendages we no longer need, and instead we think, ponder, analyze and criticize. By the time we've thought things through and are ready to act, our enemy has cut us out of the flock as the next victim. Our hyperrationalism hurts us by limiting our spontaneity and ability to respond from instinct when necessary. Detached from our most valuable clues, we are becoming increasingly disoriented. As a result, our feelings of helplessness mount. (McCormick and McCormick, 1997, p. 30)

And our helplessness does indeed mount! I'm not the first person to point to the "culture of victims" we've created. And we are all, in fact, victims. All are victims of a pernicious information age in which we are overwhelmed by wave after wave of meaningless and disconnected data, devoid of feeling and unrelated to instinct. We are victims of a cognitive understanding of ourselves, the so-called "politically correct" frame of reference that is ideational and completely separated from our primate or mammalian natures. Thus, we forget how to form permanent bonds based on true goodness. Political correctness is about behaving. True spirituality is about goodness. Christ did not behave; so, he was subjected, though innocent, to capital punishment. Martin Luther King, Mahatma Gandhi, and Nelson Mandela were good—they did not behave!

Contact and bonding with animals reminds us that we are, in fact, animals. Animals bring Tertiary Awareness into focus, evoke bondedness with our environment, and expand not only the content but also the modalities of our consciousness. We remember our deeper selves and reconstellate the bonds that connect us to the larger Trans-Organic Psyche. Again, the McCormicks:

Working with horses would naturally bring instincts into play. Because of certain characteristics horses and people share—for instance, the need for strong bonding within a well-defined community—we felt that horses could strike a reparative chord in the human psyche. Horses represent what we hoped to achieve through therapy—an individual capable of establishing close bonds within a cohesive social group and a path toward restoring humanity, toward healthy membership within our human "herd." (McCormick and McCormick, 1997, p. 42)

I've written elsewhere that a woman's body is habitat for the person conceived within it. Life actually precedes conception in that the human egg and human sperm were both alive prior to joining in conception. Life is a continuum that reaches back through the four billion years since life flared forth on the planet, back to pre-life, pre-solar, and even pre-cosmic beginnings. Life is the presence of God in flesh. Our interactions with the soil, air, and water of earth precede conception to the extent that the sperm and egg require water, energy, and nourishment prior to conception. In conception, the newly emerging person gathers the nutrients, water, and energy present in the mother and, with these building blocks, self-organizes its body. The mother herself is embedded in the soil, air, and water of earth and is the interface between the planet that contains her and the child that she contains. At birth, this process continues as the child emerges into the life community of earth, into a specific culture, into a specific family, into a vast web of relationships that include the plants, animals, insects, the planet and the stars, the whole cosmos and its Source, God. While eco-author Theodore Roszak points out that this reality is from birth forward, he tends to avoid in utero discussions, due perhaps to a reticence regarding the culturally volatile abortion issue. You'll notice in the following quotation that Roszak says that we take the environment in with us at "first breath." Not true. We take in the environment from conception on through the breathing, eating, and drinking of our mothers. Nonetheless, the point is a good one:

Preserving an accessible trace of our innate animism is what Paul Shepard seems to have in mind when he speaks in praise of the way children in traditional societies are brought into the world. They take the environment in with their first breath. "The experience of such a world is initially that the mother is always there."

Along similar lines, the anthropologist and therapist Jean Liedloff concludes that the modern world's pathological suppression of our innate ecological connectedness begins from the moment of birth. It occurs in the commonplace practice of separating the infant from the mother. This act, routinely carried out in every hospital, violates the child's "evolved expectations" of the world, namely, to be held, to be made warm and secure against the mother's body. The traumatic separation breaks the physical "continuum" between mother and child, which ought to provide the newborn's transition from "the entirely alive surrounding inside the mother's body to a partly live one outside it."

And so the civilized baby enters life crying … as babies born into traditional societies and kept in-arm usually do not. The crying, which is a protest, is conveniently regarded as "normal" and allowed to continue until the baby learns it is useless to cry and resigns hope. At that point the civilizing process has begun. Liedloff defines the "appropriate environment" for the newborn as the bodily intimacy provided by anyone—father, siblings, grandparents, friends, neighbors—there to hold and care. "Mothering" can be done by all members of the family. (Roszak, 1992, p. 301)

He also points out that in this severing of relationship early on, we lose contact; there is a break between Tertiary Awareness and Primary Awareness. We are left with Secondary and Primary Awareness, which as I said earlier is the total topic of present-day psychology. In our time, psychology must rise to the healing of that break. Tertiary Awareness must be integrated with Secondary Awareness so that both can be integrated with Primary Awareness in the overall healing of our souls. For psychology to avoid this challenge is to fail. For eco-authors to avoid this challenge is to fail. Failure in this case can become absolute in that life on Earth dangles in the balance. This is no time for the cowardly, the faint-hearted, or the insincere.

CHAPTER NINE

The Trans-Organic Psyche

The collective unconscious ... as the ancestral heritage of possibilities of representation, is not individual but common to all men, and perhaps even to all animals, and is the true basis of the individual psyche. This whole psychic organism corresponds exactly to the body, which, though individually varied, is in all essential features the specifically human body which all men have. In its development and structure, it still preserves elements that connect it with the invertebrates and ultimately with the protozoa. Theoretically, it should be possible to "peel" the collective unconscious, layer by layer, until we come to the psychology of the worm, and even of the amoeba. (Jung, 1960, p. 152)

IN THIS CHAPTER, WE GO TO THE SOURCE of the Instinctual Subpsyche in the human. We are calling this deeper dimension of the human the Trans-Organic Psyche. What humans, primates, mammals, and reptiles have in common are the instincts. This adequacy the reptiles received from even earlier life forms, including amphibians, fish, insects, jellyfish, worms, and early multicellular and unicellular organisms. Instincts are the basic voices of life, the *basso profundo* of life itself. Instincts provide all life forms with the wisdom they need to survive and proliferate. In the human, instincts provide the voice of intuition, the deepest form of human knowing.

Following triune brain theory, I am saying:

- The cognitive function in humans is inherited from chimpanzees and developed to its present state.
- The affective function in humans is inherited from the mammals and is the voice of feeling.
- The instinctual function in the human is inherited from the reptiles and provides us with the voice of intuition.

To these three I am adding:

- The reptiles inherited instinct from all earlier life forms, reaching back to the prokaryotic cell, which represents the first flowing forth of life from the planet.
- Life inherits this wisdom from the self-organizing dynamics of the planet, which are derived from the cosmos itself. The cosmos comes from the mystery we often call God.

In a real way, Chapters Seven, Eight, and Nine are the "subconscious" mirrors of chapters One, Two, and Three. Let me explain. Chapter One is the Cognitive Subpsyche; its physical corollary is to be found in the primate brain with its rudimentary cognitive cortex. Thus, Chapter One mirrors Chapter Seven. Chapter Two is the Affective Subpsyche; its physical corollary is to be found in the mammalian brain with its ability to feel emotion. Thus, Chapter Two is mirrored "subconsciously" by Chapter Eight. Chapter Three is the Instinctual Subpsyche; its physical corollary is to be found in the reptilian brain, which includes evolution from the reptile back to the pre-biological earth. This chapter, then, mirrors Chapter Three.

Chapters One, Two, and Three comprise what I am calling Primary Awareness. Chapters Seven through Twelve comprise what I am calling Tertiary Awareness. Between them, Chapters Four, Five, and Six comprise Secondary Awareness, which includes the individual, familial, and cultural subpsyches. Secondary Awareness contains formatting structures that mediate Tertiary Awareness into Primary Awareness, unless repression intervenes. When it does so, a blockage is created between Primary and Tertiary Awareness, thus cutting us off from the depth and richness of our souls.

So, again, following Jung, I am saying that all depth (archetypal) functions of the human psyche are inherited from earlier life forms. Departing from Jung, I am saying that the archetypes in the human psyche are windows to adequacies that arrive in the human from the actual living community of life present at any one point in time on Earth. Extinction in the life community erodes adequacies in the human. The archetype might remain structurally in the human, but its living corollary is gone. The structure is only the window. It is the living counterpart of the archetype that possesses the actual living dynamic that is constellated in the infra-psychic symbol in the human. Thus, no reptiles, no instincts! No mammals, no feelings! No primates, no cognitive integrity! Disrupt the life community and you disrupt the structural dynamics of the psyche. The brain (to use a mechanistic modern metaphor) is the hardware; the life community is the software.

Imagine a single sponge afloat in the middle of the ocean. It is clear that the sponge is in the sea. What might not strike us as readily is that the sea is also in the sponge. The same sea that stretches endlessly on either side of the sponge also soaks the sponge to its center. In exactly this way, all of life around us and life within us is the same life. Call it Tao, Ku, Mind, Holy or Great Spirit, the trans-individual mind includes and suffuses every individual of every species from prokaryote to Pope.

> At the center of the difference between Whitehead's God and that of traditional theism is his Dictum that "God is not to be treated as an exception to all metaphysical principles," but as "their chief exemplification." … On the one hand, God enters into all other actualities: "The world lives by its incarnation of God in itself." … On the other hand, all other actualities enter into God: "It is as true to say that the World is immanent in God, as that God is immanent in the World."

... Because of this mutual influence, Whitehead's doctrine of God is sometimes called "panentheism." Unlike pantheism, God is not simply identical with the world; unlike traditional theism, God could not live apart from a world. God is essentially the soul of the world. (Tucker and Grim, 1994, p. 200)

Life remembers, individually and as a whole. In their book *What Is Life?*, Margulis and Sagan say:

... living matter is mnemonic, it remembers and embodies its own past. Life, according to Butler, is endowed with consciousness, memory, direction, goal-setting. In Butler's view all life, not just human life, is teleological; that is, it strives. Butler claimed that Darwinians missed the teleology, the goal-directedness of life acting for itself. (Margulis and Sagan, 1995, p. 182)

The process of memory occurs because life around us affects us profoundly on the inside, and our memory of that effect causes us to react to life on the "outside." In *The Biophilia Hypothesis*, E. O. Wilson and S. R. Kellert say:

Whenever a human being confronts a living creature, whether in actuality or by reflection, the "real-life" animal is an inseparable image of that animal's essence that is made up of, or influenced by, preexisting individual, cultural or societal conditioning. (Kellert and Wilson, 1993, p. 302)

Jung stated a similar understanding when describing the structure of the psyche:

The psychological conditions of the environment naturally leave similar mythical traces behind them. Dangerous situations, be they dangers to the body or to the soul, arouse affect-laden fantasies, and, in so far as such situations typically repeat themselves, they give rise to *archetypes*, as I have termed myth-motifs in general. (Jung, 1960, p. 155)

The point is that there is a psychic reciprocity between the interior of humans and what they experience as exterior to themselves. This reciprocity can be thought of as the ocean inside the sponge and the ocean outside the sponge. The sponge experiences a local version of the total experience of the sea—the tide, temperature, salinity level, and so on. Just so, the human participates in the whole life community and the whole life community is affected by the human individual, human culture, human economics, and the human species in all of its experiences. Further, the human is the invention of the whole community, and the whole community is included in and transcended by the human. Human intelligence is a product of the whole evolution event in its biological, geological, cosmological, and theological sequences. The human gathers evolution in itself and adds the adequacy of self-awareness to the event. The human includes (depends upon) all that went before and adds another level (i.e., self-awareness) to it. In the words of Jane Goodall:

> This theory enables us to trace the gradual evolution of intelligent behavior from invertebrates to humans. Thus, the cockroach, able to vary its escape reaction adaptively in proportion to the time it has had to explore the area (Barnett, 1958), shows an element of intelligent behavior. Its total capacity for intelligent behavior may not rate high (by human standards) but this should not prevent us from recognizing the component it has. Showing a more advanced level of abstraction and generalization, the pigeon can be trained to peck at representations of people in photographs (Herrnstein and Loveland, 1964). And the chimpanzee, as we have seen, can choose a photograph representing the solution to someone else's problem, in accordance with his like or dislike of the person represented. Stenhouse argues that it is the appearance and development of the fourth element, the withholding factor, that has played such a vital role in the evolution of human-like intelligent behavior. (Goodall, 1986, p. 38)

The human is derived from the same entity it transcends and awakens into self-reflection. While we bring the adequacy of self-awareness to the scene, we are nonetheless dependent on earlier psyches, biological, ecological, and theological adequacies. We are contingent; we are transcendent. This is in no place clearer than in our own embryogenesis. The human begins as a unicellular organism and then repeats the whole bio-ecological unfolding of life on planet Earth. We are the memory of the whole evolution event. Can it be any clearer that the whole evolution event is the database from which we emerge? Can it be any clearer that the biosphere in its total memory and functioning is the architecture of both our bodies and of our souls?

Elizabet Sahtouris says a similar thing in her book *Gaia: The Human Journey from Chaos to Cosmos*:

> One of the many remarkable things about life is its memory. The process of life creates and stores information—not just the kind of information needed to reproduce each new body from a single tiny cell, but remembered information about much of its evolution over aeons of time. The way each of us came into being shows us something of the whole dance of evolution since the time of the first protists. Before we are even born—in just a short nine months—we repeat many steps in a billion years or so of our evolution as earth creatures.
>
> Each of us began as a single cell, much like an ancient protist that began its life by sexual reproduction, as the offspring of two parents. This new creature cell divided again and again, cloning itself first into two cells, then into four, eight, sixteen, thirty-two, sixty-four cells, and so on until there was a simple, ball-like creature very much like a protist colony. This creature in its early stages lived very much like other protist colonies in a uterine sea—a special bag of salty liquid duplicating the real sea. (Sahtouris, 1989, p. 111)

As I mentioned in the Introduction, the developmental dynamic of humans is the same as the evolutionary development of the whole biosphere. Ken Wilber puts it into two words, "Transcend and Include." Clifford Grobstein says much the same thing in his little classic, *The Strategy of Life:* "Ecosystem, organism, cell, organelle, macromolecule, molecule, atom, proton—these are units at the successive levels of resolution at which we may examine life" (Grobstein, 1974, p. 63). His point is clear. Every level of living matter includes the level that precedes it; then, transcending those levels, it brings forth a further adequacy or function. The lower is included in and supports the higher. Kick out the lower and the higher disintegrates. But, unless the lower matter is called up into the higher, it can never live in the higher adequacy.

Yin and Yang

We are confronted with a profound truth of life: paradox. Each of us is a whole person, while at the same time, each of us is composed of parts and each of us is a part of something larger. This individual body that I call my own is a collection of organs that are a collection of cells that are a collection of atoms all the way down. The context for this individual body is the collective known as North American society, which populates the North American continent, which is one continent among many that comprise the crustal plates of this planet, Earth, which is one of nine planets found in our solar system, which is one solar system out of billions that comprise our galaxy, which is one galaxy out of trillions that populate the universe. We are individual and collective all the way down and all the way up.

Our paradoxical nature has always been known and made amply clear by our religions—Eastern, Western, and indigenous. Generally, it is referred to as *dualism*—the divided, and often contradictory, nature of existence. In human psychological experience, dualism manifests as the divided self, which is typically seen as the "good-self/bad-self" complex that is in a constant state of embattlement. Most of the world's religions and cultures have universalized this complex into mythical, theological, and philosophical stories, teachings, and doctrines that comprise the bedrock of most, if not all, cultures. Unfortunately, living in a constant war zone is not conducive to peace of mind and ultimate happiness; thus, the goal of all religion and philosophy has been to reconcile the divided camps into a unified kingdom. In other words, humankind has been trying to mend the crack in the cosmic egg for a very long time.

The problem with this approach, however, is that the cosmic egg is not cracked. It has never been cracked because of the unifying principle beyond dualism, called Tao, Mind, Spirit, God, or whatever. The cosmic crack, then, is a human projection of the division we feel within ourselves onto the world. Cosmic unity becomes dualistic in human beings because of our "higher" adequacies of choice—also known as free will. A human being is both an individual and a member of a vast collective, known as the cosmos, and when a human chooses to ignore the latter, a psychological isolation sets in. Our individuality and collectivity play out in a bonded relationship that exists between an individual and the environment that provides the context for the individual. However, when that relationship is ignored or denied, things fall apart. Daisaku Ikeda speaks to this matter: "Just as games must be played according to the rules, so there are rules human beings must follow if they are to survive on Earth" (Huyghe and Ikeda, 1991, p. 183). Bringing with him the full authority of the Roman Catholic prophetic and religious tradition, Pope John Paul II (recently deceased) addressed the moral and spiritual consequences of our failure to follow the rules:

> We seem to be increasingly aware of the fact that the exploitation of the Earth, the planet on which we are living demands rational and honest planning. At the same time, exploitation of the earth not only for industrial but also for military purposes and the uncontrolled development of technology outside the framework of a long-range authentically humanistic plan often bring with them a threat to man's natural environment, alienate him in his relations with nature and remove him from nature. Man often seems to see no other meaning

in his natural environment than what serves for immediate use and consumption. Yet it was the Creator's will that man should communicate with nature as an intelligent and noble "master" and "guardian" and not as a heedless "exploiter" and "destroyer." (Pope John Paul II, 1979, p. 29)

The denial of our fundamental relationship to the cosmos, both outside of ourselves as well as within ourselves, can be considered evil because it yields horrible amounts of unnecessary death, destruction, and waste. It is utterly necessary that we move out of denial and begin the work of remembering and repairing our relations to the cosmos. Parallel to the physical linkage via DNA, which goes "down" from the humans through the primates and earlier mammals, as well as through the reptiles all the way "down" through early life forms and through the cosmos to God, so too goes the psychic linkage. There is linkage in our depth to the first birds, the early mammals, the dinosaurs, to insects and amphibians, to jellyfish to worms to prokaryotic life forms, to coacervates, to the pre-living Earth, solar system, galaxy, universe, and God. Our interiors are an extension of God. Eliminate any layer of the structuring and you destabilize all succeeding levels. Examples abound both vertically and horizontally.

Vertically speaking, the most extreme example would be nuclear winter. If the basic photosynthetic relationship between earth and sun were severed for several months, what else would survive? Even if a human here or there were protected and supplied enough to survive, what could develop if the primary autotrophs were eliminated? Death would occur all the way up the chain of life.

Horizontally there are other questions. Could the monotremes, for example, be the psychic as well as material link between the reptiles and the higher mammals? If that were the case and if the monotremes were lost, would the psychic link between instinct and affect be severed? If so, we would no longer be able to experience our own instincts. The signal would be there from early life "up" to our own reptile brain, but the linkage between the reptile and mammal brains would be severed.

What if the frogs and other amphibians are the psychic link between the "terrestrial" left-brain and the "aquatic" right-brain functioning in the human? Could their loss represent a severing in the bi-hemispherical functioning of our own brains? We cannot know if either of the above is in fact true, but what if it were so? Amphibians would suddenly look more princely than froggish to us!

In ecopsychological thought, the destruction of species and habitat are not something that happens "outside" of us. Because we are dependent psychophysically on the whole life event, eco-destruction's effect is in the "inside" as well. It's as though we are gouging out areas of our own psyches when we destroy the life community in any way. As Daisaku Ikeda states it: "'Foolish' is an apt word for the self that is so immersed in instinctive pleasure that it happily eats away at the bases of its own existence" (Ikeda, 1982, p. 102). Certainly, it is foolish for humans to unravel the very web that supports their bodies and minds. However, another word comes to mind that better describes this behavior: *suicidal.* Ken Wilber addresses this matter:

> Yes, the point of a genuine environmental ethics is that we are supposed to transcend and include all holons in a genuine embrace. Because human beings contain matter and life and mind, as components in their own makeup, then of course we must honor all of these holons, not only for their own *intrinsic worth,* which is the most important, but also because they are components in our own being, and destroying them is *literally* suicidal for us. It's not that harming the biosphere will eventually catch up with us and hurt us from the outside. It's that the biosphere is literally internal to us, is a part of our very being, our compound individuality—harming the biosphere is internal suicide, not just some sort of external problem. (Wilber, 1996, p. 38)

We cannot overlook Wilber's point. Humans do transcend the whole evolutionary event, and we do gather it all up into self-awareness. As the pinnacle of evolutionary progress, we have greater adequacies than any other species on Earth. However, our profundity is fundamentally dependent on the health and integrity of the whole pyramid of life that supports us. To forget our contingency is to place ourselves in peril. Gregory Bateson addresses this peril from the perspective of systems dynamics:

> When you narrow down your epistemology and act on the premise "What interests me is me, or my organization, or my species," you chop off consideration of other loops of the loop structure. You decide that you want to get rid of the by-products of human life and that Lake Erie will be a good place to put them. You forget that the eco-mental system called Lake Erie is a part of *your* wider eco-mental system—and that if Lake Erie is driven insane, its insanity is incorporated in the larger system of *your* thought and experience. (Bateson, 1972, p. 492)

Psychic linkage is, in fact, nothing more than relationships. These relationships exist throughout the biosphere. The biosphere, the sphere of living things, is a vast, complex web of relationships. The goal of the relationship is unity that leads to stability. The more strands in the web, the stronger the web. The environment, the web, is the context for our linkage with all other life forms. In a very real way, we are our environment risen to self-conscious experiences of itself. The whole living community is linked physically and psychically all the way up and down. The linkage from being to being creates a trans-being web of relationships that I have called trans-primate, trans-mammalian, trans-organic, pre-organic, and cosmic. It is critically important that we broaden and deepen our understanding of ourselves in relation to the rest of the life community. As Roszak said, "How can so ancient and intimate a part of our organic development not have a role to play in determining our psychic balance?" (Roszak, 1992, p. 86).

The whole biosphere is trans-organic, self-making, self-maintaining, and profoundly present in each of its parts. The trans-organic mind is the linkage formed in relationships throughout the biosphere between countless billions of organisms great and small, simple and complex. In the words of microbiologists Lynn Margulis and her son Dorian Sagan:

> [In] our view, autopoiesis of the planet is the aggregate, emergent property of the many gas-trading, gene-exchanging, growing, and evolving organisms in it. As human body regulation of temperature and blood chemistry emerges from relations among the body's component cells, so planetary regulation evolved from eons of interactions among Earth's living inhabitants. (Margulis and Sagan, 1995, p. 28)

The diversity and fluidity of biotic relationships creates the stability of the whole trans-organic body and mind. Reptiles, mammals, primates, and humans are fluctuating expressions of the larger living community that works in concert to maintain environmental conditions suitable to sustaining life on this planet. This work is not strictly biological and ecological. It is psychological as well. The ecology of mind arises simultaneously with the ecology of the biological community. This is why the world is understandable to our senses. It is not possible to separate the biological from the ecological, the ecological from the psychological, and the psychological from the biological. It is an unbroken circle as it should be, as it needs to be, and any disruption of the circle results in stress and disease in every part of the circle.

Extinction and the Trans-Organic Self

Biodiversity is the measure of health of the whole trans-organic community. If the whole body is well, it can withstand even massive injury and recover. The same is true of the biosphere. What, then, is a biospheric injury? Extinctions are biospheric injuries or wounds. There have been five such wounds in the last half-billion years: Ordovician, 440 million years ago; Devonian, 365 million years ago; Permian, 245 million years ago; Triassic, 210 million years ago; and Cretaceous, 66 million years ago.

Presently, we are causing a sixth extinction event. This sixth extinction has been called life's greatest setback because we are losing more habitat and species across the spectrum of the five kingdoms than at any other time in natural history. Rebound from these losses will take millions of years. As I write this book, my fellow planetary citizens and I find out that the planet has warmed each and every year for the past twenty years. This warming trend could lead to catastrophic macrophase changes in the biosphere. The 200 years since the industrial revolution, during which so much damage has been done, is a blink in Earth's history; however, as Wilson reports, recovery will not be so brief:

> How long did it take for evolution to restore the losses after the first-order spasms? The number of families of animals living in the sea is as reliable a measure as we have been able to obtain from the existing fossil evidence. In general, five million years were enough only for a strong start. A complete recovery from each of the five major extinctions required tens of millions of years. In particular the Ordovician dip needed 25 million years, the Devonian 30 million years, the Permian and Triassic (combined because they were so close together in time) 100 million years. These figures should give pause to anyone who believes that what *Homo Sapiens* destroy, Nature will redeem. Maybe so, but not within any length of time that has meaning for contemporary humanity. (Wilson, 1992, p. 31)

Our instincts for survival arise out of the billions of years of life's memory on this planet. We know how to live in the life systems of Earth. Allowing that memory to resurface in Primary Awareness is presently needed if we are to live richly in the garden of plenty, rather than merely survive in a biologically, ecologically, and psychologically impoverished desert. Our lethargy, however, is leading us into peril. I am asking the reader to view the breakdown in culture, in the respect for life, in the collapse of biodiversity, and, especially, the growing sense of meaninglessness as indicators of the psychological breakdown that will necessarily occur with the breakdown in life systems around the planet.

It's my guess as well that the famous experience of Delirium Tremens, in which alcoholics in withdrawal from alcohol experience insects coming out of the walls, can also be traced to this Trans-Organic Psyche. In chronic addiction, the psyche of the individual becomes so disordered that functioning subpsyches below Primary and Secondary Awareness rupture upward into Primary Awareness and are seen by the individual. Following detoxification the subpsyches begin again to find their natural order and function again below the threshold of consciousness. So the question is begged, "Are the insects seen in DTs really there?" Yes and no. Yes, the disordered psyche is presenting its real depth in the form of an insect subpsyche. No, the ants are not crawling on that wall. The DTs are a projection from the person's disordered depth onto the wall.

The following idea is purely speculative on my part. It springs from my thinking about the Trans-Organic Psyche and has no basis in fact. Nonetheless, I think it can be of interest. I've often wondered about the connection between black leather clothing and juvenile delinquency. I have this image in my mind of a group of kids in their early teens hanging around on a street corner smoking, swearing, and acting tough. Beneath the hard exterior of each of these kids, I suspect a history of child abuse, abandonment, and addicted families. It's almost as though the black leather and chains and so forth are an attempt at a psychic exoskeleton. We'd associate the black exoskeleton with many kinds of insects. My speculation is this: Do our defense mechanisms, or at least some of them, arise from earlier zones of our own psyches? Do we remember earlier forms of bio-defense such as turtles and their shell-helmets, insects and their exoskeletons? I ask the reader to have patience! I recognize the rudimentary nature of these questions, but they are new ways to think about old realities. Unitive psychology is a new way to think about old ideas generally.

Ritual, Recovery,
and Remembering the Way Forward

It's one thing to know that we must bring Tertiary Awareness into Primary Awareness. But how do we do it? A big part of the answer lies in the transformation of culture and ourselves through ritual. Dudley Young understood the necessity of ritual very well:

> For the magic of representation to do its work, the ritual setting is important. As we have already observed, the practice of ritual is not an invention of irrational primitives, but is as old as the reptiles, which may mean not only that it is supremely useful but that we are more or less stuck with it. Throughout the animal kingdom, the moments of "sacred" encounter, of love and war, tend to be ritualized; that is, they proceed on "automatic pilot" along set lines instinctually programmed. The evolutionary function of these rituals is to make dangerous communications absolutely clear and to minimize bloodshed. It is surely not surprising that primitive man, seeking to put his technology of the sacred on a firm scientific footing, should have agreed with the rest of the animal kingdom that when approaching dangerous powers, ritual is a most important tool. (Young, 1991, p. 169)

Ritual is a series of behaviors that open the Cultural Subpsyche to signals from the tertiary zone. Ritual, properly done, conducts the bio-energies from the whole evolutionary event from primates to coacervates, from planet to God, into the cultural zone of the human. The Roman Catholic Eucharist puts this well in its consecration words: "Fruit of the earth and the work of human hands, it will become our spiritual food." In gathering for religious ritual, families (and thus the familial zone of the psyche) are given that same psychic food that is then received by the individual as food for the whole Primary Awareness zone of his or her psyche. Without a developed symbol system to shape the individual psyche, the individual is cut off from the deeper energies of life itself, the energies of God. Such a person will live life estranged from people, animals, the planet, and from God. This idea that we will not prejudice our children by giving them a religious tradition in childhood is a tragedy, a decision based on ignorance of the real needs and structures of the psyche. To further understand the importance of ritual in the work of cultural recovery and transformation, and its role in the human psyche, we must turn to a consideration of animism.

Animism is the collective name given to intuitive perception of God through nature. Nature speaks to us at an intuitive level through instinct, revealing wisdom and divinity. The voice of the instinct is heard in the ancient structures of the brain, the reptilian brain or brain stem, as well as within the cellular and atomic structures themselves. So, in view of the architecture of the soul, animism is the voice of the Trans-Primate Psyche, Trans-Mammalian Psyche, and the Trans-Organic Psyche, all of which are included in Tertiary Awareness.

Animism transcends the physical dimension. Consider the love that is shared between a woman and her horse, a man and his dog; as the relationship deepens, strong feelings of affection arise that can lead to self-sacrificing behaviors on the part of the dog for the man, or vice versa, that are clearly heroic. This relationship reaches into the atomic and sub-atomic levels, evidenced by the release of energy through strong emotions. In fact, the psychic bond can be so strong between the woman and horse that communication between the two can become extrasensory. "The magic of this chemistry opens the individual, allowing incorporation of the animal's spiritual essence. This pulsating interchange is our tie to the cosmos" (McCormick and McCormick, 1997, p. 21).

In this context I want to touch upon, albeit briefly, the relationship between humans and flowers via the Trans-Organic Psyche. It is easy to overlook the amazing role flowers play in human affairs. Wherever we meet them—in the wild, on a walk, in our gardens, on our tables, and at our weddings and funerals—flowers evoke in us feelings of joy, comfort, amazement, and a host of other feelings. They speak to us in beauty and we respond in joy. I'm not speaking metaphorically here.

I'm saying that the ascent of joy, the felt experience of joy, is an inner voice in us, which communicates with the flowers. The redwoods evoke the voice of awe in us. Farmers experience floods of quasi-religious elation when walking in cornfields or other fields of crops. We speak to humans in one way, to other mammals in another, and to plants in still another. We can love and communicate with any living thing. The experience felt in Primary Awareness comes through Secondary Awareness and has its source in Tertiary Awareness. The following quotation from *The Book of Tea* puts it poetically:

> In joy or sadness, flowers are our constant friends. We eat, drink, dance and flirt with them. We wed and christen with flowers. We dare not die without them. We have worshipped with the lily, we have meditated with the lotus, and have charged in battle array with the rose and the chrysanthemum. We have even attempted to speak in the language of flowers. How could we live without them? It frightens one to conceive of a world bereft of their presence. What solace do they not bring to the bedside of the sick, what a light of bliss to the darkness of weary spirits? Their serene tenderness restores to us our waning confidence in the universe even as the intent gaze of a beautiful child recalls our lost hopes. When we are laid low in the dust, it is they who linger in sorrow over our graves. (Okakura, 1991, pp. 109–110)

The same can be said of our experience of insects. Insects can evoke the voice of loathing and revulsion, or equally the feeling of delight. The former is associated with cockroaches and centipedes, the latter with butterflies and dragonflies. The point is not what particular feeling they evoke but that they do, in fact, inspire a response from us toward them. We fear wasps and resent mosquitoes. We can tolerate houseflies to some extent, but their presence in our soup inspires other feelings! If we are organic farmers, we feel friendship toward worms and ladybugs, but hostility toward potato beetles. We are nearly hypnotized by spider webs and delight in bumblebees.

Bees have even found their way into our religions, they have been symbolic of instinct and inspiration. When I was a boy, I had a recurrent dream that a huge bumblebee the size of a loaf of bread was flying around my bedroom light. I'd scream and my father would come to my rescue, scaring the bee away. As I grew up, the dream stopped. At thirty-two years old, I had a massive confessional experience. The very night of that confession, I had the dream of that very same bee. This time, as an adult, I could see that the bee was friendly and even goofy. The pleasure I felt in recalling the dream cannot even be described. The bee was and is a benign presence in my psyche.

Rituals, then, whether insectile, reptilian, mammalian, primal, Neolithic, or classically religious, provide structures through which evolutionary wisdom and knowledge can speak to Primary Awareness, and animism is the experience of that communication. Together, ritual and animism can heal human culture by reunifying the human psyche through reconciling the divorce between Primary Awareness and Tertiary Awareness.

Many, if not most, rituals involve remembering—things that have happened, where you came from, ancestors, motherland, fatherland, homeland, and so on. This is necessary for understanding who you are in relation to the world and cosmos, and, consequently, for understanding how to proceed in life. So, in honor of the Trans-Organic Psyche, I think it necessary to follow our life-psyche "down" to its anchoring and linkage with the planet Earth.

The most recent of the three earliest stages of life before we trace it back to its fiery beginnings, is the Proterozoic Aeon, a period stretching back from 1 billion years to 2.6 billion years ago. Before that came the Archaen period, stretching from 2.6 billion years to 3.8 billion years ago. Finally, the Hadean period that stretched back from 3.8 billion years ago to Earth's fiery cosmic birth 4.6 billion years ago. In its fiery beginnings, obviously no life could exist. Fire in our earliest ancestors, the fires of the planet, the fire of the supernova that preceded it, and the fire of the fireball are all, we might say, the fire of God.

Scientists will usually name the periods beginning with the oldest and ending with the most recent. But because we are looking "down" the "tube" of our souls, we should do just the opposite. So as above I've named them from the most recent to the oldest. For our purposes, then, it would go something like this:

- The first biologically modern human remains of Homo sapiens appears in the fossil record only about 50–60,000 years ago
- Before them came the mammals, birds, reptiles, fish, insects, and flowering plants
- Before them came marine plants and animals along all of the world's seashores
- Before them came isolated spheres of bacteria
- Before 3.5 billion years ago, the crust of the planet was too unstable to support life

No one really knows what happened during the first billion years of the planet's existence, save for the coalescence of rock and out-gassing. There was no possibility of life forming at that time; however, if there was life, the record in the rocks is silent because the rocks themselves were molten and unstable.

So, the cosmos begins as fire, Earth begins as fire, and we are that fire cooled into matter and evolved to a point that the fire can think about itself. From the cooling fire, pre-biotics formed that led to the first prokaryotic cells. Later came the eukaryotic cells, plants, animals, and so on.

The point is a simple one and one that we have emphasized over and over in this book: Humans are contingent! We are all inventions of the life community, which in its totality is an invention of the mind of God. We are an experience of the whole and are thus dependent on the whole. In self-reflection we draw the whole into awareness. It's not difficult to see how a primate or mammalian psyche might affect us. It's not too great a point to grasp this notion of a reptilian level of consciousness. Next, we are confronted with the idea that invertebrate psyches are wholes in themselves, subsumed and contained in greater wholes all the way up to the humans. Going deeper still, we encounter unicellular organisms.

How powerful is the mind of a unicellular organism? Human sperm and human eggs are unicellular. Consider the power they exert over the individual in whom they are contained. How loud is the voice of a single egg each month? How loud is the collective voice of sperm each day? When we're honest, we can admit that much of our lives are spent dealing with unicellular voices. If I think of my own body as a galaxy of unicellular organisms caught up in a marvel of levels to become a chordate, a mammal, a primate, and a human, I can see this ordering of these psyches as the real work of the ego.

If we accept this as true, then a "mental disorder" can be thought of as a *dis-ordering* of the subpsyches in their larger holons as we go up the ladder. There's nothing terribly difficult in this. If any level of these psyches that go back to the *anima mundi,* the galaxy, the cosmos, and even the pre-temporal mind of God becomes dis-ordered in its relationship to the hierarchical order, a mental or mood disorder would result.

Interestingly as well, the further "down" we go in the psyche, down the well of memory and heading toward the pre-biological Earth, the closer we approach eternal life. Microbial life does not have death programmed into its structures. Lynn Margulis explains:

> By trading genes and acquiring new heritable traits, bacteria expand their genetic capacities—in minutes, or at most hours. A huge planetary gene pool gives rise to temporarily classifiable bacteria "types" or "strains" which radically and quickly change, keeping up with environmental conditions. Bacteria in the water, soil, and air are like the cells of a growing global being. Whereas your genes are inside a body with a discrete lifetime, a bacterium takes and gives out its body's genes in and from the surroundings. Although, of course, like all life, bacteria can be killed by starvation, heat, salt, and desiccation, these microbes do not normally die. As long as the ambiance permits, bacteria grow and divide, free of aging. Unlike the mammalian body, which matures and dies, a bacterial body has no limits. A disequilibrium structure thrown up by an

evolving universe, it is, in principle, immortal. Sequestering order in a disordering universe, the silent bacterial biosphere preceded all plants, animals, fungi, and even the protist progenitors of all these forms of larger life. Without the bacterial biosphere no other life would ever have evolved, nor would it live today. (Margulis and Sagan, 1995, p. 76)

It's almost as though our depth reflects our Source. As most mystics from all traditions report, our depth and our Source identify. We discover the pre-temporal in the depth of the temporal. We can discover our Source because we remember our Source in our depth. When a human is conceived, the primal, mammalian, and trans-organic psyches are remembered in the anima mundi, and the mind of God.

So, as we arrive at the earliest sign of life on the planet, we also arrive at the base of our own Trans-Organic Psyche. The earliest relics of these early days of the life event are called stromatolites, which were bacterial colonies. It is assumed that microbial mats preceded stromatolites, but there are no surviving relics in the fossil record. Preceding these mats scientists speculate that pre-living matter self-organized and was sparked into life by the forces of the planet herself. Lynn Margulis speculates that it happened in this way:

Although the picture still lacks many details, there is broad agreement on certain general assumptions. One is that life arose by the self-assembly of small organic molecules into larger, more complex molecules. According to one hypothesis, the assembly took place on the surface of clays or other crystals. Such ordered surfaces could have attracted small molecules and held them in arrays that promoted the formation of small polymers—short chains of amino acids or nucleotides. The existence of these short chains would have made it possible for larger structures—primitive proteins and nucleic acids—to form spontaneously. The building blocks themselves, the small organic compounds, would have been formed by the action of lightning, solar ultraviolet radiation, and other forms of energy on the gases of the secondary atmosphere. (Margulis, 1982, p. 26)

Prior to this point, the barrier of fire, called the Hadean period of Earth, is encountered. Life disappears from view in the fossil records because the early Earth was a coalescing mass of fiery molten rock and boiling seas of organic and inorganic matter.

However, there is speculative data that suggests that organic matter itself began to self-organize through the formation of coacervates, which were differently concentrated regions, or points, within an aqueous medium that were "membrane bound" and that tended to resist dissolution within the surrounding aqueous environment of the early seas, which were far more soupy than they are today. In the following passage, A. I. Oparin opens a small, but intriguing, view of how coacervates may have made life possible:

> In the process of coazervate formation, organic substance not only became concentrated at definite points in space but, to a certain degree, it also acquired structure. Where previously there was only a helter-skelter accumulation of moving particles, in the coazervates these particles are already to a certain extent oriented with regard to each other. True, this orientation is not yet stable and is preserved only so long as the directive forces within the coazervate are operating, nevertheless we witness here the origin of some, though still very labile, elementary organization. Thus, in coazervates the behavior is subject not only to the simplest laws of organic chemistry but also to the newly superimposed colloid-chemical order. However, even this higher order of relationship is still insufficient to secure the origin of primary living things. To initiate life, it was necessary for coazervates and similar colloidal systems to acquire, in the course of their evolution, properties of yet a higher order, properties subject to biological laws. (Oparin, 1953, pp. 160–162)

Life literally rose from the planetary dust or, in this case, planetary mud. The natural laws of attraction between particles yielded new physical possibilities that promoted self-organization. From the psychic perspective, one could reasonably speculate that the early phenomenon of self-organization demonstrated in coacervates could be the seed of psychic self-organization, otherwise known as ego.

What, then, is the Trans-Organic Psyche? It is the visible life community that emerged from the planet in the earliest life forms and evolved into the history of life. It is memory—memory in action. As the chemical repetition of the past, life is a single tissue that reaches back beyond visible life into the invisible mind of God. Indeed, mind is present as the Source of the Trans-Organic Psyche. At this depth, the place where our psychic tissue is one with the pre-biological Earth, we find our "mother." Life, human life included, literally births "up" from the Earth. We *are* Earth!

Chapter Ten

The Pre-Organic Psyche

Once again, we are cognitive beings. We are affective beings. We are instinctual beings. We are cultural beings. We are primates as well as mammals, chordates as well as galaxies of unicellular beings. We are part of the flux of life through the biosphere. We are light, soil, and water drawn up into instinct, feeling, and thought. We are also beings of the Earth, of the cosmos, and of eternity. In this chapter we shall examine ourselves in light of the self-organizing mind or dynamic of Earth.

So, first I would like to make an assertion regarding the four forces of physics. We are able to say what gravity *does,* but we cannot say what gravity *is.* We know that it functions throughout the cosmos, but we don't know why. It's the same with electromagnetism, as well as with the strong and weak nuclear forces. We measure what they do, but we cannot say what they are. In the end, they remain mysteries. To say that gravity, electromagnetism, the strong and weak forces, sub-atomic and atomic structurization, molecular and mega-molecular structurization, cellular and multicellular structurization, chordate evolution, reptilian evolution, mammalian evolution, and primate and human evolution are all phases of the evolution of divine Mind in matter can be scoffed at. But this assertion cannot be disproved. In fact, it is what human religions have always held to be true and is, in my opinion, the only logical final means for describing the universe. It sounds very clever to say that the universe "just showed up," but our minds beg the question, "From what, from where?" Our physics cannot yet penetrate the earliest moments of the beginning, but our minds are coextensive with pre-time and pre-space—whether or not physics gives us permission to say so. Mysticism says so! In time, physics will find the mathematical language to do the same.

So, I am proceeding with these final chapters where we continue our plunge into our depth on the above premise. Earth's ability to "self-organize" is a function of Earth's mind-soul-field-*spiritus mundi*. Earth and cosmos form the foundation and context for life on Earth as well as the evolutionary dynamics of life. Both Earth and cosmos arise from the pre-temporal psyche, the mind of God—Paradise.

All living beings are subsets of Earth. Earth is a subset of this solar system, which in turn is a subset of this Milky Way galaxy, which itself is a tiny subset of the expanding cosmos. The cosmos is perhaps one of many subsets of the Mind of God. Incredibly, then, we are able to think with the Mind of each subset. True religious practice from shamanism to Tibetan Buddhism, from Confucius to Christ, is the training to "think" with each of those minds until we realize that they are all one Mind. In my opinion, any other goal of religion is a trivialization of its purpose.

Human-mind includes and transcends primate-mind. Primate-mind includes and transcends mammal-mind; mammal-mind includes and transcends reptile-mind; reptile-mind includes and transcends multicellular-mind, which includes and transcends unicellular-mind, which includes and transcends pre-organic-mind and Earth. The Pre-Organic Psyche remains, nonetheless, the source and context for all the minds above. Destroy the macro phase structures and dynamics of Earth, and you must disturb all the minds subsequent to Earth. Ruin the land, sea, and air, and you must in doing so, ruin the functioning of all beings of the land, sea, and air. Disrupt the planet-mind and you disrupt the deep structures of the human-mind.

So, to borrow an idea from Stephen Covey, we will look at Earth from the inside out. The core of Earth has a solid inner core of nickel and iron and a liquid outer core of iron. A mantle composed of olivine rock contains the core. The upper 350 km of the 2,900-km-thick mantle is soft and molten, and is called the asthenosphere. The mantle is surrounded by and contained in the crust, which is between 5 and 50 km thick. When it bends and/or breaks, earthquakes and volcanoes occur. The surface of the Earth consists of water, rock, soil, and atmosphere. The troposphere, where clouds and weather are created, rises from the surface to 11 km. Above the troposphere, the stratosphere and then the ozone layer stretch up another 47 km. Above this, the mesosphere marks the place where the circulation of air ceases. Beyond the mesosphere stretches the thermosphere from 90 to 550 km. Temperatures, due to radiation, rise to 1,200 degrees C. Above 550 km, there is the exosphere, which contains only the simplest elements of helium and hydrogen. Beyond 2,500 km, we reach the magnetosphere, which contains only hydrogen.

The atmosphere in its totality is the "envelope" in which life and evolution event take place. The atmosphere is the breath of life. The crust of Earth is the context for life, is the home, if you will, of the biosphere. Life and the crust co-evolve. The life-crust has four major periods:

- Precambrian
- Paleozoic
- Mesozoic
- Cenozoic

Between 4.6 billion years ago and 4 billion years ago, in what is called the Precambrian period, the major features of the Earth's crust took shape. This period is called azoic because there was not yet a suitable environment for life, or if there was some form of life, no traces of it remain. By 4 billion years ago to 3.5 billion years ago, the oceans had formed. Between 3.5 billion years ago and 2 billion years ago, during the Proterozoic period, oxygen was becoming present in the atmosphere due to the presence of single-celled algae. During this period animal life also appeared in the oceans in the form of sponges and protozoa.

During the Paleozoic period of life and the geological period called the Cambrian, the seas became shallower and the trilobites, cephalopods, and slugs appeared. This was all underway by 570 million years ago. Around this time, during what is called the Ordovician period, what are now Northern land masses were then close to the equator. Fish and corals emerged. During the Silurian period, about 430 million years ago, leafless plants appeared and so did scorpions. At this time there were only two massive continents. By the Devonian period, about 395 million years ago, the lakes and marshes were breeding ferns; bony fish and insects made their appearance. During the Carboniferous period of the Paleozoic, about 345 million years ago, bog plants, amphibians, and the reptiles appeared. This was also the first Ice Age. By 280 million years ago, during the Permian, the formation of the supercontinent Pangaea took place, climates became extreme, and a mass extinction took place.

By the Mesozoic period, life began a recovery. By 225 million years ago, in the Triassic period, there were shallow warm seas and a dry climate. The conifers and taxus palms appeared. So also did the mammals and the huge reptiles called dinosaurs. By 190 million years ago, during the Jurassic period, the separation of the supercontinent Pangaea took place. Climates became more temperate and the birds appeared. By about 136 million years ago, there were seasons of Earth and the flowering plants appeared. Sometime during this period a catastrophe took place and another mass extinction resulted. This catastrophe provides the dividing line into the Cenozoic period of life, the recent period of life.

Beginning about 65 million years ago, the climates cooled and the horses, whales, and monkeys appeared. The age of the dinosaurs was over and the mammals were in ascendancy. About 1 million years ago, during the Second Ice Age, the human appeared. I am indebted to the book *Gaiasophy* by Kees Zoeteman (1991, pp. 52–66) for the above sequence.

Earth's crust is divided into several plates, not unlike the plates of a human skull. Each of these plates "float" on the mantle below. The movement of these plates is characterized by two processes. The first is spreading and the second is subduction. Spreading occurs when two plates separate and new crust is formed by upwelling magma from below. Subduction occurs when two plates collide and the edge of one is forced beneath the other and "recycled" in the mantle below. There is also frictional transverse motion at plate boundaries, such as in the famous San Andreas fault in California. There are presently six major plates: the North American Plate, the South American Plate, the Antarctic Plate, the Indian Australian Plate, the Nazea Plate, and the Pacific Plate. There are also twenty or so smaller plates. During the writing of this book, we saw the level of natural and human disaster that resulted in Turkey due to the slippage of two plates.

So, Earth is in a constant state of flux. The atmosphere is in constant motion, with storms erupting here and there, sometimes very destructive storms. The seas constantly grind against the continents. The plates move and grind against each other and dive down into the Earth's interior to be recycled as magma. Catastrophes happen, extinctions and rebounds take place; all is in continual motion, continual conflict. All of this motion, this conflict, goes on in such a way and in such a time scale that life is able to endure, fluoresce, and evolve in the midst of it all.

If we look at the planet as a series of concentric envelopes beginning at the lightest outer edge, the magnetosphere, growing in density as we move through the exosphere, thermosphere, mesosphere, stratosphere, troposphere, crust, mantle, and core, we can ask ourselves important questions about what we humans are doing to our context. The upper atmosphere has been and is being seriously damaged by aircraft exhaust. The protective ozone layer is being frayed; the troposphere has huge and serious areas of damage above every industrialized city. The waters of Earth are nearly all degraded. The soils are as much as 50 percent depleted. The subsurface waters are depleted and often polluted. We have drastically altered the planet in all of its major life systems. None of this is new to the reader. But what has not been thought about in any adequate way is the effect or impact all this abiotic degradation has on our invisible selves, our souls. In the same way that our bodies are subsets of the body of Earth, our souls are subsets of the *anima mundi* (world soul).

Animism is the experience of synchronization between the human soul and the larger soul of the Earth. This can occur in two ways: unconsciously and consciously. Unconscious animistic experience can be described as uncritical acceptance of sentience in all things. For example, aboriginal people around the world "know" that everything "speaks." All one need do to hear what a tree or elk or rock or the wind is saying is to be quiet and listen. Among such people, the principle of universal sentience is unquestioned because they experience their soul as one with the larger anima mundi. In that state, the individual experiences no individuation. Unitive psychology could be called a conscious animism, in which the individual drives up into his or her self-awareness the infinite depth of being. In other words, the individual is conscious and aware of being in "participation mystique" with the holarchy of souls. His or her own soul, the world soul, the cosmic soul, the Source soul (i.e., God) are all consciously experienced. Thomas Moore addresses the point:

> The soul exists beyond our personal circumstances and conceptions. The Renaissance magus understood that our soul, the mystery we glimpse when we look deeply into ourselves, is part of a larger soul, the soul of the world, anima mundi. This world soul affects each individual thing, whether natural or human-made. You have a soul, the tree in front of your house has a soul, but so too does the car parked under that tree. (Moore, 1992, p. 267)

In this model of the architecture of the soul, the universe is once again seen as an intelligent, self-organizing phenomenon through the agency of conscious animism. Over the last 1,500 years, science has endeavored to open our eyes to the nature of reality. And it has done so with remarkable results, unveiling vistas great and small that boggle the mind. However, in its passion to dispel superstitious thinking, modern science stripped us of a meaningful cosmos, and left us with an impersonal, mechanistic worldview that was accidental, indifferent, and not sentient. Such a view did not sit well with our animistic souls that knew better even if our egotistical selves did not. In time, though, with the discovery of quantum mechanics in the twentieth century, scientific researchers began to glimpse phenomena that intimated that the universe is sentient rather than not sentient. Now, as we progress into the twenty-first century, science has begun to unveil realms of reality that reveal an innate intelligence pervading all of reality. This new view is both spectacular and subtle. We begin to understand that everything is related through a vast cosmic field of energy particles that seem to apprehend change nonlocally. Chaos mathematics, quantum fields, Gaian autopoeisis, and Rupert Sheldrake's *morphogenetic fields* all reveal patterns in nature of self-governance. As Sheldrake puts it, "Nature is now once again seen to be self-organizing. ... the basis of this self-organization is now seen as the universal field of gravitation and all the other kinds of fields within it" (Sheldrake, 1991, p. 95). Whether we call the self-organizing phenomena "souls" or "fields," the phenomena itself remains what it is. Souls or fields—what we are referring to is the "mind" of energy-matter. Such a view is wholly in accord with our innate and intuitive animistic knowledge.

Consciously orienting ourselves and our cultures to the knowledge and wisdom inherent to the anima mundi is the only way we will overcome the mess we are in. In our day, we can observe the ageless dualism of good and evil in opposition. On the one hand, there is the anima mundi, the soul of Earth, the Great Mother Spirit. On the other is the "Spirit of the World" in the present day, a spirit of destructiveness on a scale unparalleled in memory. The threat of nuclear holocaust is only the most obvious manifestation of this Spirit of the World. The destruction of the atmosphere, hydrosphere, and biosphere, due to pollution, habitat destruction, and species extinction, are equally violent manifestations of the same Spirit. Pope John Paul II cautions that "against the spirit of the world, the Church takes up anew each day a struggle that is none other than the *struggle for the world's soul*" (Pope John Paul II, 1994, p. 112). Elsewhere he comments on the same duality by comparing the present First-World/Third-World dichotomy to the Gospel story of the rich banqueter and poor Lazarus. What the

Pope recognizes is that the greedy Spirit of the World thrives at such an order of magnitude today that our contemporary social, political, economic, commercial, and industrial institutions that are responsible for creating it will not suffice to control it. The Pope recognizes that we are literally transforming Eden into Hell:

> This pattern, which is familiar to all ... represent[s], as it were, the gigantic development of the parable in the Bible of the rich banqueter and the poor man Lazarus. So widespread is the phenomenon that it brings into question the financial, monetary, production and commercial mechanisms that, resting on various political pressures, support the world economy. These are proving incapable either of remedying the unjust social situations inherited from the past or of dealing with the urgent challenges and ethical demands of the present. By submitting man to tensions created by himself, dilapidating at an accelerated pace material and energy resources, and compromising the geophysical environment, these structures unceasingly make the areas of misery spread, accompanied by anguish, frustration and bitterness. (Pope John Paul II, 1994, pp. 32–33)

This message cannot be overstated. The culture of commercialism that is engulfing the world is impoverishing much of the world for the benefit of a few wealthy nations. This pattern of consumption honors neither the Earth nor her poor and disenfranchised children. Our animistic souls know better. We must honor the Earth, our Great Mother.

Rupert Sheldrake, writing in admiration of Pope John Paul II, points to the Pope's honoring of Earth by kissing her: "The pope's honoring of the earth as mother is expressed through his custom of kissing the ground as soon as he alights from planes. It seems a shame that this is usually tarmac" (Sheldrake, 1991, p. 190). This Pope is unique in modern Western religion for his recognition of the eco-moral questions brought to the forefront presently. It's a pity that the Church is so slow in following his lead in this matter. I speak as a Roman Catholic mystic when I say that the great institutional sin of the Church in modern times is her lethargy with respect to the fate of the Earth. Her continual focus on egopieties as opposed to *eco*pieties represents a truly mortal sin, one that is killing the planet made by the God we worship.

Eastern religions, though, have been and still are a treasury of ecological wisdom and cosmological mysticism. The ancient Wang Yang Ming frequently pointed to the triunity of heaven, earth, and mankind: "Men ought to follow the pattern of heaven and earth, which leads them by the brightness of the heavens and the benefits of the Earth to harmonize all under heaven" (Makra, 1961, p. 15). Elsewhere in the same text, the kings and leaders are used as examples of this triune wisdom:

> The Master said: "Anciently the illustrious kings served heaven intelligently because they were filial in the service of their fathers. They served earth discreetly because they were filial in the service of their mothers. Superiors governed inferiors with ease because the young obeyed their elders. Hence, because heaven was well served and earth honored, the spirits manifested themselves brilliantly." (Makra, 1961, p. 35)

Modern-day Buddhist Daisaku Ikeda builds upon these ancient themes of China and Japan. What he calls the Mystic Law (Nam Myoho Renge Kyo) roughly identifies with the Chinese concept, Tao, which means "way" or "path." As Huston Smith points out in his classic, *The Religions of Man,* there are three Taos in one Tao. Smith is asserting that the Great Way is composed of three Paths: first, the Tao of Origin; second, the Tao of the how things emerge and evolve; third, the Tao of the how humans should live in order to be one with the first two. We could describe the same thing as a holarchy of self-organizing fields. In whatever way we describe it, "it" remains the same: the Mind of Origin, the Mind of cosmos, and the Mind of Earth. At our depth we are Earth, cosmos, and Spirit. From Ikeda:

The more we probe into our inner lives, the more we see the past and the future inherent in the present. As we look from the surface to some point deeper within ourselves, we see the stream of life broaden, become more abundant, and swell into a great tide. The ultimate source of this stream embraces the lives of all mankind, the formation of the earth, and the endless pulsations of the universe. It is the source of universal life. As the stream of life flows from this source, it divides itself into our individual lives. The Mystic Law is identical with the source of all life-flow. (Ikeda, 1982, p. 72)

There is no permanent healing or happiness unless we come to realize (make real) our true identity. "Happiness means the joy of living on an unshakable foundation rooted in the life-force of the cosmos" (Ikeda, 1982, p. 128). Neither psychology nor religion is bringing us to this realization in sufficient numbers to reverse the trend of horrendous damage we are inflicting on the created order and, therefore, upon ourselves. Nevertheless, it is possible to reverse this trend. The life-force is there for everyone to access because Earth and every being of Earth is contained in the Mind, the anima mundi of Earth. Those who are rooted to their depth are rooted to the Mind of Earth. When this is realized in our lives we become what Ikeda calls "Bodhisattvas of the Earth." In his words:

We can be Bodhisattvas of the Earth, confident of ourselves, full of the infinite life-force, and dedicated to helping others. The life of a Bodhisattva of the Earth is a truly humane, compassionate, and joyful life. The Bodhisattvas of Earth are described in the sutra as "welling up" out of the ground. "Ground" here is figurative for the ultimate foundation of life, which is the Mystic Law. The Mystic Law, which is the cosmic life-force, is identical with the life of Buddhahood. (Ikeda, 1982, p. 128)

We urgently need Bodhisattvas of the Earth from every creed— Jews, Christians, Moslems, Wiccans, Buddhists, Hindus, atheists, humanists, whatever. We must become primates of Earth, mammals of Earth. We belong to Earth, even while we are able to experience eternity. As we become so, we shall become happier and healthier and so will the rest of the life community that we are presently destroying. Joy will be our lot. Joy, the zest for living. Joy, the missing meaning in most of our lives and relationships. Joy, the presence of God in our souls. This is possible *now!*

The path of the Bodhisattva of the Earth starts where you are. You do not need to be highly educated. You do not need to be a millionaire, nor even a member of the middle class. You do not need to wear robes or shave your head. You simply need to start living the truth that is deep within you—the Mind of Earth, the Mind of cosmos, the Mind of Source incarnate. Open your self to the depths of your soul, and you will find the way to fulfillment and joy in the realization of the divinity in which you already participate. Then you will become a conscious vessel of the life-force—a Bodhisattva of the Earth. Ikeda speaks to the point:

> People in the state of Buddhahood may not seem very exceptional at first glance. Their activities are those of the Bodhisattvas of the Earth, who are able to lead benevolent lives because they are supported by the life-force of the Buddha, by the Earth that is identical with the Mystic Law. The Bodhisattvas of the Earth understand all aspects of life in the universe and the principles underlying them. They understand too the society around them and the trends of the times. By drawing on the cosmic life-force, they find their own life-force increasing limitlessly. And their freedom extends throughout the universe. Their joy is the joy of joys: an indescribable ecstasy welling up freely and spontaneously from the innermost essence of life. (Ikeda, 1982, p. 130)

The prayer of St. Francis of Assisi, "Make me a channel of thy peace," is about aligning our will with the way of Heaven and the soul of the Earth as she has evolved over time. The history of evolution can be thought of as a grand river down which Mind has moved toward more complex and more conscious awareness of itself through a multitude of river channels. This river that flows from pre-time to time to galaxy to Earth to life to reptile to mammal to primate to culture *is* the architecture of the soul. The history of life is contained in the present as the planet, the biosphere, and ourselves. Drastically alter the channels, and the course of the river is altered. Alter the course of the river, and our souls are altered. That alteration results in instinctual, affective, and cognitive pathologies. If we too drastically alter the present, then we are destroying the architecture of the past, as well as miscreating the future. We would do well to trust larger minds than our own. We need to open our minds, our Primary Awareness, to the older mind of Tertiary Awareness and honor the wisdom that is found there.

The planet mirrors our most fundamental attitudes toward life. Once again, Daisaku Ikeda:

> When changes in the environment seem to be a threat to human existence, it should not be overlooked that the cause of the evil is often within human beings themselves. Those who have allowed themselves to become slaves of greed, ignorance, and egoism, and who have thereby lost their essential humanity, are tearing away at the soil of the earth, provoking untimely seasons, disturbing the normal movements of the seas, and thus gradually destroying the basis for life on our planet. This, I think, is what Nichiren Daishonin meant when he said, "if the five sense organs of the sentient beings are about to be destroyed, everything in the surroundings cries out with vexation." (Ikeda, 1982, p. 39)

So, as we destabilize the architecture, we destabilize mind and society. While science and technology can help to limit the damage we inflict upon the created order, the real healing of the deep architecture of our souls can only come from a change in values. The realm of values is a spiritual realm. Our problem is a spiritual problem. The answer must be a spiritual answer, as Jung observed:

We are all agreed that it would be quite impossible to understand the living organism apart from its relation to the environment. There are countless biological facts that can only be explained as reactions to environmental conditions, i.e., the blindness of *Proteus anguinus*, the peculiarities of intestinal parasites, the anatomy of vertebrates that have reverted to aquatic life.

The same is true of the psyche. Its peculiar organization must be intimately connected with environmental conditions. We should expect consciousness to react and adapt itself to the present, because it is that part of the psyche which is concerned chiefly with events of the moment. But from the collective unconscious, as a timeless and universal psyche, we should expect reactions to universal and constant conditions, whether psychological, physiological, or physical. (Jung, 1960, p. 152)

One could say more, but more need not be said. It comes down to this: I am asserting that the planet provides not only the deep material substructures for all that exists on Earth, but that the soul of the Earth provides the deep psychic substructures for them as well. To alter one is to alter both and to alter either is to alter ourselves. Earth has a destiny and our destinies individually are subsets of that larger destiny. The destruction of Earth's destiny represents the certain destruction of our own.

CHAPTER ELEVEN

The Temporal Cosmological Psyche

WE ARE ALL CITIZENS OF THE EARTH, of the solar system, of the Milky Way galaxy, and of the cosmos. In the last chapter we dealt with the soul of Earth—the anima mundi, in which each of us derives our soulful context. The anima mundi, in turn, emerges from an even more fundamental sentience. About five billion years ago, the Earth and solar system formed out of an immense nebula. Fifteen billion years prior to the formation of our solar system, the universe was created *ex nihilo* by an unimaginable event called the big bang. The energy released in this miraculous event set the universe into an expansion that continues to this day. We are a product, as well as an extension, of this expansion. In a very real sense, from the infinitely large to the infinitesimally small, the universe is the primordial depth dimension of ourselves, which I call the Temporal Cosmological Psyche. The deep architecture of our souls *is* the cosmos.

Unfortunately, the majority of people in the modern and post-modern worlds are ignorant of our cosmic depth. We got into this mess because of failures on the part of Western religions and a mixed blessing in the scientific discipline of psychology. Western religions failed to effectively integrate the modern world into their spiritual vision in a timely fashion. This failure weakened their *raison d'être*, which is to guide people along the spiritual path while fostering enlightened culture. How could they serve as guides and cultural leaders when they did not understand the modern world? They could not; consequently, they were largely relegated to the back-seat driver positions of bully-pulpit moralists. While on the other hand, psychology, which could have bridged the gap between religion and science, especially through the early works of Carl Jung and the philosopher William James, largely abandoned the cosmic view of life for scientific materialism because the scientific model of inquiry has been extraordinarily successful in exploring, explaining, and exploiting reality. While the direction psychology has taken has proven quite valuable in understanding and treating the organic, behavioral, and developmental characteristics of psychic illness, it has done so by reducing the human soul to chemical, behavioral, and developmental formulas. Reduction of the human soul, however helpful it may be in laboratory studies and classroom lectures, does not yield an acceptable portrait of human health and happiness. The materialistic view of the human psyche simply does not do justice to the richness and complexity of human psychic experience.

In the materialistic worldview, everything is just stuff, and the kingdoms of life are kingdoms of animated stuff. In such a worldview, everything and everybody is essentially alienated because there is no underlying structure of soul that ties everything and everybody together; consequently, morality becomes highly relativistic. With the exception of the Jungian school of depth psychology and of the new schools of ecopsychology and transpersonal psychology, the mainstream clinical establishments opted for a shallow self-portrait that has left modern people everywhere gasping for meaning. Thinking of ourselves as separate from the cosmos is a misguided and dangerous abstraction of the dualistic mind—the ego—and we are paying the price.

The main problem with this trend is the erosion of the sense of the sacredness of life. In religion, the loss of a sense of the sacred has given rise to spiritual materialism—a commercial form of pseudo-religious behavior that panders to self-absorbed sentimentality. In psychology, the loss of the sense of the sacred has given free reign to the materialistic school of psychological thought that sees people as biochemical entities whose happiness and well-being are found in the right drug, prescription or otherwise. The result of these trends is the commodification of religion, the human psyche, and, consequently, human culture.

Increasing cultural triteness is the necessary condition for the globalization of a culture predicated upon the consumption of commodities, namely *commercialism*, which is making a wasteland of us all. Consider, for example, the ubiquitous presence of prescription drugs in contemporary societies, especially American society. We are inundated with information telling us that health, happiness, vitality, and virility are on sale at the local pharmacy. We are losing the time to live in a manner that fosters health, happiness, vitality, and virility naturally because we are increasingly preoccupied with the need to afford a living due to an economy that ensures that the costs of living continually rise. Living in post-modern, commercial societies with their plethora of expenses, time constraints, and stress-inducing personal and professional demands that foster dependencies upon drugs and other quick fixes, such as fast food, leaves us increasingly bereft of soul food, known as tender, loving, caring, joyful attention. Everybody is suffering the impact of this deficit, especially our children.

Millions of American parents do not have the time to raise their own children in a healthy manner. The social impact of this neglect is horrendous: children who are increasingly exhibiting symptoms of attention deficiency, hyperactivity, and depression, and who are increasingly dependent upon prescriptions of Ritalin, Prozac, or Zoloft to feel relatively normal and functional. Furthermore, American society has seen an increase in both suicidal and homicidal behaviors in children and adolescents. The two trends are definitely related. A society that is overly dependent upon drugs and other quick fixes as a means to psychological and emotional health for its children is in deep denial of basic social dysfunctions and teetering on the brink of insanity and self-destruction. This is not a path we should continue walking; commercialism is not a fit cultural model.

Mainstream religious and psychological institutions can correct themselves by embracing a more holistic view of spiritual and psychic life. A single Spirit informs humans, all animals, all plants, Earth, and cosmos, and that Spirit precedes and is coextensive with the cosmos. We are that Spirit. Until we accept the truth of this teaching, we have not accepted the truth about our deepest selves and the responsibility we have to honor all life. Until we accept ourselves in depth, we cannot solve our problems. As I said in the beginning, we must admit to being lost if we are to be found. We need a yielded will.

At first it seems strange and unfamiliar to talk about the cosmos as a dimension of the human self. But as we come to understand the whole story of evolution in its cosmological, geological, biological, and cultural or theological levels, we come to see that until we do, we remain shallow in our understanding of ourselves, others, and of God. Buddhism is a great help to us because nowhere but in Buddhism is there such a clear and ever-present understanding of these different levels of our being. Consider the following by S. N. Goenka from the Vipassana School of Buddhism:

> Let us begin with the physical aspect. This is the most obvious, the most apparent portion of ourselves, readily perceived by all the senses. And yet how little we really know about it. Superficially one can control the body: it moves and acts according to the conscious will. But on another level, all the internal organs function beyond our control, without our knowledge. At a subtler level, we know nothing, experientially, of the incessant biochemical reactions occurring within each cell of the body. But this is still not the ultimate reality of the material phenomenon. Ultimately, the seemingly solid body is composed of subatomic particles and empty space. What is more, even these subatomic particles have no real solidity. The existence span of one of them is much less than a trillionth of a second. Particles continuously arise and vanish, passing into and out of existence, like a flow of vibrations. This is the ultimate reality of the body, of all matter, discovered by the Buddha 2,500 years ago. (Hart, 1982, p. 26)

The emergence of our souls from eternity into time at conception is comparable to the light at the inception of the universe becoming galaxies and galaxy clusters. Religions and schools of psychology that ignore these deepest structures are counterproductive and ought to be reformed, transformed, or utterly abandoned. As we open ourselves to our depth, upon depth we grow. Ikeda speaks very eloquently to this point:

> The closer we approach the source of our life-force, the larger our subjective space grows, until eventually, it encompasses all human beings, all life, the earth and the stars, and all physical space, becoming one with the limitless cosmos. At that point there cease to be any physical distinctions. Human life, elementary particles, animals, plants, the sun, the stars—all things animate or inanimate fuse into the infinite pulsations of the cosmic life-force. (Ikeda, 1982, p. 85)

Where there is no joy, there is no depth of truth. True joy emerges spontaneously out of the depths of our own being when we open to the unimaginable beauty that is the source of the architecture of our souls as well as the architecture itself. Buddhism dwells in this place of understanding. Once again, Ikeda:

> The self, seeing more and more, rejoices in the wider scope opening up around it and in the new meanings and dimensions being added to the realm of life. With joy and lightness of heart, it seeks its own way to self-perfection.
>
> Encompassed in an ever-expanding life-space is a well-lighted future, one which can be contemplated with hope and confidence. This space spreads beyond the self to enrich the lives of others, to inspire familiar love, to create a richer social environment. It grows into a love for mankind, sympathy for all living things, and oneness with the cosmos. (Ikeda, 1982, p. 82)

Our world is a world of many cultures. Our understanding must be the same. Our world is a world of many species, and our understanding must be the same. We must understand that we emerge from the Spirit of God, and therefore we have the ability through that Spirit, which is also our own, to embrace the whole Earth and cosmos. Buddha-mind, which is Christ-mind, which is Krishna-mind, and so on, are all included in cosmic-mind, which enables us to include all worlds. When we realize that we are this cosmic-mind, we can begin to think with that mind. To be of one mind with the cosmos and its Source is to be enlightened. To be enlightened is to be fully human, fully well. Until we do so, we cannot become fully human. The goal of unitive psychology is to become fully human.

The significance for psychology is that we all have the same infinite depth as a resource for healing and wholeness. What good, however, is knowing that if we have no way to access the depth? Unitive psychology provides a model to be used for exactly that purpose. A key tenet of this model is that *there is no such thing as **objective**.* Thinking themselves contemporary or even avant garde, many psychiatrists, psychologists, and counselors of all stripes continue to hold to the shabby and even worn-out concept that "objectivity" is the preferred approach to the counselor-client relationship. If objectivity is the goal, real relationship is impossible. Objectivity is an abstraction! It is not borne out by the reality in which we live. Only by real relationship, i.e., subject to subject, can counseling work at all. In an article called "Chaos and Compassion," counselor H. B. Gelatt points to this interpenetration of phenomena:

> This article is about connections, ignorance, and compassion. And it is about chaos. One of the most powerful lessons from the new science, called Chaos, is the concept that everything is totally connected to everything else in an unbroken wholeness.
>
> It is the notion of *everything* being *totally* connected to *everything* else and *unbroken* wholeness that is new and powerful—and at first seems to be too bizarre or too incomprehensible to

be readily adapted to personal and social phenomena by the counseling profession. For example, the concept of "seamlessness" ... emerges from chaos theory, and yet we continue to separate personal and social, right brain and left brain, client and counselor and other items. Chaos theory shows that there is no such thing as objectivity, and yet we continue to "be objective." (Gelatt,1995, p. 108)

In this universe everyone and everything has an interior dimension that is subject. As Thomas Berry puts it, the universe is not a collection of objects, but a community of subjects. That subjectivity is the presence of God throughout space and time. That presence *is* the Temporal Cosmological Psyche. It is the context and unity of all galaxies, all solar systems, all planets, all species, all cultures, and all individuals. If we wish to penetrate its mystery, and our own, then we must approach all beings as subject and learn their language. Stars speak the language of stars, horses speak the language of horses, humans speak the language of humans, and so on, and all these languages are dialects in the language of God. In God as God, we are able to understand all of the myriad tongues of the cosmos as our own. Such a profound level of subjectivity reveals the architecture of the soul for what it is—the self-organizing evolution of God. Turning to the Buddhist mystic, Ikeda, once again, I delight in sharing his thought on the matter:

> The Mystic Law is the force and wisdom inherent in the entire cosmos, which is itself the source of all physical and spiritual phenomena. From the innermost depths of the cosmos, the Law gradually becomes manifest in definite form, and as this happens, human lives take on individuality. Simultaneously, the individual environment takes form as objective environment, or shadow. The subjective existence and the objective environment make up a single existence, which takes form as the life-force residing in cosmic life becomes manifest. That this existence can be divided into two is unthinkable. The formation of a human life as a subjective existence is identical

with the formation of that life's environment. They can no more be separated than can the growth and development of animals and plants be separated from the world in which they live. Each human life, together with its environment, partakes of the fundamental life-force of the entire cosmos. (Ikeda, 1982, p. 41)

Ultimately, our environment is the whole cosmos! Our first environment is the womb. Our second environment is the family and home. When we open and grow, our environment becomes the neighborhood and then the state and nation. Then we become aware of our continent, our planet, our solar system, our galaxy, and our universe. In the end, our home is the cosmos, the Mystic Law, the Temporal Cosmological Psyche, God. Throughout this growth, the inner cosmos of understanding is coextensive with the outer cosmos of perceptual fields, and they are unified as the mind is one with the body. Beyond this conscious expansion, however, is an even greater engine of cosmological expansion, as Jacobi points out:

The collective unconscious as suprapersonal matrix, as the unlimited sum of fundamental psychic conditions accumulated over millions of years, is a realm of immeasurable breadth and depth. From the very beginning of its development it is the inner equivalent of Creation, an inner cosmos as infinite as the cosmos outside us. (Jacobi, 1959, p. 59)

So, how do we access the Temporal Cosmological Psyche? Carl Jung spoke of the dream as the opening window to the depth psyche. Certainly, dreaming is one way. There are others, though. A living spiritual master, for instance, can be a very effective guide and catalyst. One reason why the whole Judeo-Christian spiritual enterprise has been such a failure is that the priests, bishops, and even popes, excepting John Paul II, are seldom spiritual masters. The West needs real teachers, real windows into the "cosmic night" of wisdom. Unitive psychology can be used as an instrument for cultivating such people. We must open to the whole well of the cosmic night, open to the major religions, to the earlier tribal religions, to the primate psyche, to the mammalian psyche, to the trans-organic psyche, to the planetary psyche, to the cosmic psyche, and to God. Only then, in the fullness of understanding and experience, can we don the robes of the spiritual master and healer with authority.

We can only heal the world as we heal ourselves. We can only heal ourselves if we heal the world inside us. It is all one. We know that the most fundamental healing can only come from understanding our-selves and our place in the cosmos. We can only understand the cosmos if we understand its context in God. Maslow comments on this same insight in the following:

> For instance, it is quite characteristic in peak experiences that the whole universe is perceived as an integrated and unified whole. This is not as simple a happening as one might imag-ine from the bare words themselves. To have a clear percep-tion (rather than a purely abstract and verbal philosophical acceptance) that the universe is all of a piece and that one has his place in it—one is a part of it, one belongs in it—can be so profound and shaking an experience that it can change the person's character and his Weltanschauung forever after. In my own experience I have two subjects, who, because of an experience, were totally, immediately, and permanently cured of (in one case) chronic anxiety neurosis and (in the other case) of strong obsessional thoughts of suicide. (Maslow, 1964, p. 59)

We need only awaken to the wisdom that is our own depth, a wis-dom that precedes both space and time, the wisdom that is God, to be healed. To be in touch with that wisdom is to have integrated the Temporal Cosmological Psyche with Primary Awareness. In doing so, we experience ourselves as one with the very fabric of space and time. Having experienced this unity, we can begin to experience the unity that precedes it.

CHAPTER TWELVE

The Pre-Temporal Cosmological Psyche

WHAT CAME BEFORE THE EXPLOSION of the singularity that set the cosmos into its amazing expansion, ushering in time and space? From where do the most elusive sub-atomic particles arise and to where do they go? The answer to these questions is called by many names: Paradise, Eternity, Heaven, Pure Land, Ocean of Luminosity, Pure Mind, God, Great Spirit, Light, Absolute, Source, and so on. Whatever the name, the supernatural state of being to which it refers is unimaginably powerful, sentient, creative, omnipresent, joyous, and perfect. As Paradise, it is the pre-spatial and nonlocal common origin of us all. As Eternity, it is the pre-temporal and timeless *now* that enables the cosmos—the very architecture of our souls—to exist. This eternal *now* is not the "now, now, now" of an infinite span of moments in time, known as "forever"; rather, it is a timeless, dimensionless state of being that precedes and is concurrent with the entire cosmos. By the grace of God, the cosmos burst forth in a fiery genesis twenty billion years ago, and it is still flaring now. The entire created order of the cosmos is recreating itself every moment. Now is the moment of our death, and now is equally the moment of our birth. By whatever name, we have arrived at the wellspring of the architecture of our souls.

The holy of holies is an elusive mystery. This is not to say that it is impossible to know; however, it is impossible for us to know it through the usual channel of discursive thinking. Great Mystery seems to elude our every attempt to grasp it rationally. What we know about it has come to us through nontemporal and nonspatial methods of knowing, such as intuition, "spiritual sight," and contemplation, because Spirit is expressed throughout the cosmos as nontemporal and nonspatial awareness. The tools must fit the job. Physical science has historically failed in its attempts to substantiate, let alone understand, God because its tools and paradigm are temporal and spatial in nature; however, recent developments in quantum mechanics may have provided science with its first proof of the divine. In the words of physicist Jean Staune: "Quantum phenomena prove the existence of another level of reality—one which lies outside space and time since nonlocality is its principal characteristic" (Staune, 1999, p. 15). Mysticism, on the other hand, has known about this other level of "nonlocal" reality for millennia because the tools and paradigm of mysticism are congruent with the eternal now.

Awareness, then, is the window to the divine, and like a window, the cleaner it is, the more we see. Those who are pure of mind and heart know God by living in the eternal now, which is Paradise. Our ignorance of this fact causes us to miss out on what could arguably be called the lion's portion of our being, which is the Pre-Temporal Cosmological Psyche—a substrate of the human soul from which fundamental notions of moral order and God emerge. The loss of Paradise occurs when the Pre-Temporal Cosmological Psyche—our window of awareness—becomes obscured by the temporal and spatial distortions of the discursive mind that is temporally and spatially preoccupied. Regaining Paradise requires the reconciliation of time with eternity by understanding and experiencing their interpenetration. This marriage of time and eternity can only be accomplished by walking the path of contemplative mysticism.

In my opinion, the reason why the Western world is in a collective identity crisis is that its religious traditions have abandoned the mystical path of knowing—contemplation, which Ken Wilber describes in the following excerpt:

For pre-rational Nature can be seen with the eye of flesh and rational Mind can be seen with the eye of reason, but transrational Spirit can be seen only with the eye of contemplation. And contemplation is definitely not feelings plus thought; it is the absence of both in formless intuition, which, being formless, can easily integrate the forms of Nature and Mind, something that either or both together could never do for themselves. (Wilber, 1998, p. 109)

I cannot think of a reason for the existence of a religion other than contemplation and the moral formation that it presumes. It is contemplation that provides us with a unitive vision in which God, nature, and the human are experienced as one. Hence, to disregard contemplation is to condemn oneself to live a paradigm that ignorance is regarded as knowledge and alienation is accepted as the norm. These are the mistakes that religion is supposed to correct, but how can it when the religious leaders and teachers themselves do not contemplate regularly? Ken Wilber addresses this point quite poignantly:

The conclusion seems obvious: when the eye of contemplation is abandoned, religion is left only with the eye of mind—where it is sliced to shreds by modern philosophy— and the eye of the flesh—where it is crucified by modern science. If religion possesses something that is uniquely its own, it is contemplation. Moreover, it is the eye of contemplation, adequately employed, that follows all three strands of valid knowing. Thus religion's great, enduring, and unique strength is that, at its core, *it is a science of spiritual experience* (using "science" in the broad sense as direct experience, in any domain, that submits to the three strands of injunction, data and falsifiability). (Wilber, 1998, p. 169)

Indeed, cognition and affect are not fit vehicles for religious experience. Without contemplation, religion is dogma and sentiment. Both are often shallow, boring, and sometimes even sickening. But when the eye of contemplation is opened, something new emerges—the earliest and most luminous dimension of the self, the Pre-Temporal Cosmological Psyche, the self we were before the universe began.

Paradise can neither be measured nor proved but we can sense it in the way we sense someone standing behind us whether or not we know they are there. Physics as a science cannot speak of anything before time. Language breaks down at that point because language depends on time ordering. "Before" means the time before this time. There is, however, no time before the beginning of time. Consequently, science is beset with a huge paradox. The physicist Sean Odenwald puts it this way:

> In terms of the theories available today, it may well be that the particular dimension we call Time had a definite zero point so that we can not even speak logically about what happened before time existed. The concept of "before" is based on the presumption of time ordering. A traveler standing on the North Pole can never move to a position on the earth that is one mile north of north! Nevertheless, out of ingrained habit, we speak of the time before the genesis of the universe when time didn't exist and ask "What happened before the Big Bang?" The list of physicists investigating this "state" has grown enormously over the last 15 years. The number of physicists, worldwide, that publish research on this topic is only slightly more than 200 out of a world population of 5 billion! (Odenwald, 1987, p. 3)

From the perspective of mysticism, however, the time paradox is a clue. What Odenwald is calling an "ingrained habit" of thought, I am calling a zone of the psyche that is intuitively nudging the mind. Our intuition that being itself or awareness itself pre-exists space and time is not some naive need on our parts, not the final frontier of the "opiate of the masses," but a functioning level of the architecture of our souls. It is the place of rebirth, of resurrection, of re-creation. It is existence prior to existents.

When one contemplates the scientific literature that grapples with the origin of the universe, one witnesses rational thought bending to the necessity of nontemporal and nonspatial ways of knowing. In another article Odenwald says this:

> During its earliest moments, the universe may have existed in a nearly incomprehensible state which may have had more than 4-dimensions, or perhaps none at all. Many of these theories of the earliest moments hypothesize a "mother space-time" that begat our own universe, but you cannot at the same time place our minds eye both inside this Mother Space-time to watch the Big Bang happen and inside our universe to see the matter flying around. [Nonetheless,] this is exactly what the fireworks display model demands that you do. (Odenwald, 1997, p. 2)

If we cannot talk about something without creating words such as "mother space-time," then perhaps that "mother" exists. Mother space-time isn't far removed from "Father God." If we cannot do physics without the use of such words, perhaps that is because a "Mother" does exist. I'm saying that because our minds have their Source in pre-time, we cannot think without a pre-time dimension to our thought. We know more than we can calculate mathematically. At time zero minus one second, we bump into God!

Apparently, the vacuum of space is not empty after all. In fact, it is brimming full with dynamic activity. Again, Odenwald:

> True, the cosmos consists overwhelmingly of vacuum. Yet vacuum itself is proving not to be empty at all. It is much more complex than most people would guess. "But surely," you might ask, "if you take a container and remove everything from inside it—every atom, every photon—there will be nothing left?" Not by a long shot. Since the 1920s physicists have recognized that on a microscopic scale, the vacuum itself is alive with activity. Moreover, this network

of activity may extend right down to include the very structure of space-time itself. The fine structure of the vacuum may ultimately hold the keys to some of the deepest questions facing physics—from why elementary particles have the properties they do, to the cause of the Big Bang and the likelihood of other universes outside our own. (Odenwald, 1996, p. 1)

"Nothing." "Emptiness." "Vacuum." These are all other words for God from the scientific perspective. Because we know in our own souls that awareness precedes anything to be aware of, we are forced to create substitute names for God. The reality of existence forces us to go there. Science is pushed to the mythological.

So, how should we think of the great, dark void that we gaze into at night? All clues point to the space-time being a kind of layer cake of busy phenomena on the submicroscopic scale. The topmost layer contains the quarks and electrons comprising ordinary matter, scattered here and there like raisins in the frosting. These raisins can be plucked away to make a region of space appear empty. The frosting itself consists of virtual particles, primarily those carrying the electromagnetic, weak, and strong forces, filling the vacuum with incessant activity that can never be switched off. Their quantum comings and going may completely fill space-time so that no points are ever really missing. This layer of the cake of "empty space" seems pretty well established by laboratory experiment. Beneath this layer we have the domain of the putative Higgs field. No matter where the electron and quark "raisins" go, in this view, there is always a piece of the Higgs field nearby to effect them and give them mass. Below the Higgs layer there may exist other layers, representing fields we have yet to discover. But eventually we arrive at the lowest stratum, that of the gravitational field. There is more of this field wherever mass is present in the layers above it, but there is no place where it is entirely absent. This layer recalls the Babylonian Great Turtle that carried the universe on its back. Without it, all the other layers would vanish into nothingness. (Odenwald, 1996, pp. 3–4)

Whatever "nothing" is, there's a lot of it everywhere. Again and again, we are forced to the same question: "Could there be some mysterious field 'outside' our universe that determines its probability?" (Odenwald, 1996, pp. 3–4).

In a little known but brilliant book called *Dawn After Dark,* Rene Huyghe and Daisaku Ikeda discuss the cultural malaise of the Western world. Their dialogue brings them into mysticism, theology, psychology, physics, and just about every discipline one can think of. In one of the many supreme moments of their dialogue, Ikeda explains the Buddhist term Shunyata, or Ku. Both are similar if not identical to what I am calling the Pre-Temporal Cosmological Psyche. First, Ikeda:

> The fifth element, Ku, or Shunyata is simultaneously the universal space that includes and encloses the other four elements and the place that serves as the source of energy generating the other four. While itself lacking form and color and incomprehensible in space-time terms, it is the original and true existence from which earth, water, fire and wind manifest themselves in the space-time world. The four elements that form the phenomenal world arise from the infinite energy sea of Shunyata, to which they must ultimately return. (Huyghe and Ikeda, 1991, p. 188)

Ikeda is pointing to a pre-spatial, pre-temporal intelligence without which we cannot think about space or time or a beginning. Huyghe responds:

> If I understand the term correctly, I should prefer to regard Ku not as a fifth element, but as something apart from, and antedating, the formation of the other four elements. You yourself point out how different it is from the others because

it is " a concept of spiritual order." I consider *void* too negative a definition. But, then, how are we to be expected to understand something that can exist outside space and time? Perhaps *original reality* is not the most adequate expression. By it, I mean Being in its primordial detachment, before it has assumed form or appearance. In other words, it is energy in its pure state before it has been embodied and materialized in the elements of the physical world. (Huyghe and Ikeda, 1991, p. 191)

Huyghe again struggles to find language to say God without saying God. He comes up with "original reality," which is very similar to my own "Originating Mystery" that I use in another book, *Cultural Addiction: The Greenspirit Guide to Recovery.* How different is any of this from Odenwald's "void"?

In the meantime, physicists and astronomers do the best they can to fashion a cosmology that will satisfy the intellectual needs of our age. Today, as we contemplate the origin of the universe we find ourselves looking out over a dark, empty void not unlike the one that our Egyptian predecessors might have imagined. This void is a state of exquisite perfection and symmetry that seems to defy description in any linguistic terms we can imagine. Through our theories we launch mathematical voyages of exploration, and watch the void as it trembles with the quantum possibilities of universes unimaginable. (Odenwald, 1987, p. 5)

I would like to suggest that we drop the circumlocution and just say "God"! We trust, as Alcoholics Anonymous does, that each person will understand the word God according to his or her understanding. We all participate in this pre-temporal aspect of being, although we understand or imagine it differently. Herein lies the common ground between religion and science: both seek to understand the nature of reality but through different means. In an issue of the magazine *Science and Spirit,*

Charles Townes, a Nobel Laureate and inventor of the laser and maser, speaks to the inevitable confluence between science and religion:

> [W]e come to the similarity of science and religion. The goal of science is to discover the order in the universe and to understand through it the things we sense around us, including humanity. This order we express as scientific principles or laws, striving to state them in the simplest and yet most inclusive ways. The goal of religion may be stated, I believe as an understanding (and hence acceptance) of the purpose and meaning of our universe and how we fit into it. Most religions see a unifying and inclusive origin of meaning and this supreme purposeful force we call God. Understanding the order in the universe and understanding the purpose in the universe are identical, but they are also not very far apart. Finally, if science and religion are so broadly similar, and not arbitrarily limited in their domains, they should at some time clearly converge. I believe this confluence is inevitable. For both represent humanity's effort to understand our universe and must ultimately be dealing with the same substance. (Townes, 1999, p. 19)

I truly love science. This book and all my work spring from a foundation in world religions and mythology compiled with cosmology, ecology, geology, biology, and psychology among others. The deepest and most comprehensive authors I've come across are Daisaku Ikeda, Thomas Berry, and Ken Wilber. What they all have in common is this great mystical synthesis of science and spirit. Religion without science becomes trite and corny. Science without spirit becomes dry and brittle. It isn't that the discussions of either are not stunning in and of themselves. The problem is that each is a half-truth without the other. "Half-truth" is the real meaning of the word *heresy*. Body and soul are each half-truths. Knowledge and spirit are each half-truths. The real leaders of scientific discovery, such as Einstein, insist on unitive truth. Consider this by T. Magnin, priest and physicist:

> The reality of being cannot be fully comprehended through science. Einstein urged us to acknowledge that scientific inquiry is ultimately based on a conviction closely akin to the religious feeling that the world has meaning and can't be understood. (Magnin, 1999, p. 28)

We are thinking, feeling, and intuitive beings. We have individual familial and cultural histories. We are primates and mammals. We include reptilian, amphibian, and early life forms. We are products of earth and sun. We are products of the cosmos and, along with the cosmos, products of God. We exist with one foot in time and one in pre-time. We come from pre-time, dwell in time, and are destined to post-time. They interpenetrate. Our depth opens to eternity. In a somewhat angry and defensive explanation of this, C. G. Jung speaks of the substitute of the soul:

> Critics have sometimes accused me outright of "philosophical" or even "theological" tendencies, in the belief that I want to explain everything "philosophically" and that my psychological views are "metaphysical." But I use certain philosophical, religious, and historical material for the exclusive purpose of *illustrating* the psychological facts. If, for instance, I make use of a God-concept, or an equally metaphysical concept of energy, I do so because they are images which have been found in the human psyche from the beginning. I find I must emphasize over and over again that neither the moral order, nor the idea of God, nor any religion has dropped into man's lap from outside, straight down from heaven, as it were, but that he contains all this *in nuce* within himself, and for this reason can produce it all out of himself. It is therefore idle to think that nothing but enlightenment is needed to dispel these phantoms. The ideas of the moral order and of God belong to the ineradicable substrate of the human soul. That is why any honest psychology, which is not blinded by the garish conceits of enlightenment, must

come to terms with these facts. They cannot be explained away and killed with irony. (Jung, 1960, pp. 64–65)

This "substrate" that Jung refers to is what I'm calling the Pre-Temporal Cosmological Psyche. We don't doubt the existence of cosmos. It is all around us. It can be known, studied, measured, and quantified with the senses. This is the work of science. Things are different, more subtle with eternity. It must be felt, intuited. But it can be known, if we are willing to repeat the experiment in mysticism that allows us to know. In knowing eternity we break free of time past and its absolute barrier at the beginning. Because Spirit is the Source of both time and space, it precedes and transcends it. To know eternity is to know God. The presence of God in space and time is the Temporal Cosmological Psyche. The presence of God as the Source of space and time is the Pre-Temporal Cosmological Psyche. Wilber puts it this way:

> … the source of these spiritual feelings is not nature itself. You might stare for hours at a sunset, and suddenly disappear into the World Soul, and feel yourself at one with all intuition. Worms and rats and foxes and weasels do not stare for hours at the sunset, and marvel at its beauty, and transcend themselves in that release—even though their senses are in many cases much sharper than ours, even though they see nature more clearly than we! No, nature is not the *source* of this Beauty; nature it its destination. The *source* is transcendental Spirit, of which nature is a radiant expression. (Wilber, 1996, p. 291)

Moment by moment, God thinks the cosmos into being! Stars, planets, moon, simple and complex life forms, the bedraggled being that is dragging this pen across this loose-leaf pad—all are expressions of the Pre-Temporal Cosmological Psyche!

It's a peculiar quirk in the human that we can know that Spirit supports us and still feel the need to deny Spirit. Alcoholics Anonymous confronts that peculiar fact of our nature in its "Big Book":

> When, however, the perfectly logical assumption is sug-
> gested that underneath the material world and life as we see
> it, there is an All Powerful, Guiding, Creative Intelligence,
> right there our perverse streak comes to the surface and we
> laboriously set out to convince ourselves it isn't so. (AA, Big
> Book, 1976, p. 49)

"Perverse" is the right word. When we deny that God is both Source
and sustainer of our world, we claim ownership of that world for ourselves. We then claim the "right to choose" to destroy it and in doing so
destroy ourselves!

There is presently a new understanding dawning among most disciplines. That understanding began in physics and is spreading throughout most systems of human knowing. It represents a shattering of this
sense that humans own the created order and have the right to choose
to destroy it should that destruction appear to be an advantage at the
time. What we are beginning to see is that we don't have the right to
choose, the right to ownership, the right to exploit, the right to destroy.
We are beginning to see that we come from elsewhere, and that we
arrive in space and time along with everything and everyone else. We
are a common citizen of the cosmos, not its lord and ruler.

We come from the other side of a mirror, and the mirror, in the end,
is the self. On the frontal surface of this self we see the created order,
space, time, cosmos, animals, and so on. On the back surface of this
mirror we see pre-space, pre-time, pre-Creation, the Mind of Buddha,
the Mind of Mysticism, of God. This rear surface of ourselves is the
Pre-Temporal Cosmological Psyche. The Promised Land—paradise,
whatever we call it—is the radiant presence of God.

We cannot escape that which is the basis of our own psychic and
spiritual assumptions. This "pre-time" shows up as the religious stories. Dance therapist Joan Chodorow puts it this way:

> The *abyss, the void, chaos* and *alienation* are prominent
> images in the world's creation myths (Campbell 1949, pg.
> 271–2; Eliade 1967, pg. 83–131; Schaya 1971, pg. 61–73 and

pg. 101–15). The first three (the void, the abyss, chaos) tend to be used interchangeably to describe the pre-existing state out of which the world was created. (Chodorow, 1991, p. 83)

In his amazing book *The Rebirth of Nature,* biologist Rupert Sheldrake points to this pre-existent state and how physics cannot do without it and still create believable theories of cosmogenesis. However we try, and by whatever names we choose, we cannot shake God out of the equation. We might talk about "eternal ideas," "laws," "vacuums," or whatever else we come up with. Still, the "nothing" from which the cosmos emerges might be *no-thing* but it is not nothing. This following excerpt from Sheldrake's book is a lengthy one but it goes to the heart of the matter:

> The nothingness "before" the creation of the universe is the most complete void that we can imagine—no space or time or matter existed. It is a world without place, without duration or eternity, without number. It is what mathematicians call "the empty set." Yet this unthinkable void converts itself into a plenum of existence—a necessary consequence of physical laws. Where are these laws written into that void? What "tells" the void that it is pregnant with a possible universe? It would seem that even the void is subject to law, a logic that exists prior to time and space.
>
> This way of thinking bears a strong resemblance to the traditional Christian theology of creation by the word, or *logos* of God. The mother principle is the primal chaos, or the pregnant void. The theological notion of God-given eternal laws of nature was built into the foundations of mechanistic science, and it pre-exists as the implicit metaphysical basis for modern cosmology. If the mind of God is dissolved away, we are left with free-floating mathematical laws playing the same role as laws in the mind of God. Stephen Hawking, for example, takes for granted this assumption of eternal laws and believes that if physicists understood "the basic laws of the creation and subsequent evolution of the universe,"

theoretical physics would reach its end, an end he thinks is already in sight.

However, in order to entertain this ambitious idea, Hawking has to make a number of other gigantic assumptions, still shared by most physicists. One is the old reductionist doctrine that everything can ultimately be explained in terms of the physics of the smallest particles of matter: Since the structure of molecules and their reactions with each other underlie all chemistry and biology, quantum mechanics enables us in principle to predict nearly everything we see around us, within the limits set by the uncertainty principle. (In practice, however, the calculations required for systems containing more than a few electrons are so complicated that we cannot do them.) ...

Modern mathematical cosmology is in fact a strange theoretical hybrid between the paradigms of eternity and evolution. It retains the Pythagorean or Platonic assumption so beloved of mathematicians—the notion that everything is governed by an eternal realm of mathematical order, transcending space and time. Yet it opens up a great evolutionary vision of all nature and in doing so throws its own foundations into question. If all nature evolves, why should the laws of nature not evolve as well? Why should we go on assuming that they are eternally fixed? (Sheldrake, 1991, pp. 125–127)

Because God is the source, we simply cannot write the story without His presence. Because we are derived from God's being, we cannot think God out of our equations. As Dionne Warwick sings it, "There's always something there to remind us." We might strip God of all story, all context, all personhood, and reduce our stories to a vestigial, mathematical law, but we cannot get rid of this last trace. Let's state it clearly: "Nothing comes from nothing." There is indeed an uncaused cause even if we choose to give God a mathematical rather than mythological name. But name God we must: Raven, Phan Ku, Mawa-Lisa, Buddha Mind, Holy Spirit, Spirit of Allah, Jahweh, Braman, Tao, Vacuum, Plenary Emptiness, Originating Mystery.

There is memory in nature, and this memory has instilled in us the intuitive knowing that God is. God the Source becomes God the Evolver becoming God Incarnate. The God who creates is present throughout the creation and remembers the whole creation event. The Divine Memory is the Pre-Temporal Cosmological Psyche and all that flows from it. We remember who we are through, with, and in God; in so doing, we are healed. I'm a thinking being, a feeling being, and an instinctual being. I come from a history, a family, and a culture. I'm a primate, a mammal, and a reptile. I'm a member of Earth's life community, a citizen of the stars, an expression of the cosmos. I am the awareness of God in time and space and, as such, I pre-exist both time and space. This is who I really am.

If we are to be well and if we are to understand our context and ourselves, then we must do what Ken Wilber suggests:

> What if you inquire within, pushing deeper and deeper into the source of awareness itself? What if you push beyond or behind the mind, into a depth of consciousness that is not confined to the ego or the individual self? What do you find? As a repeatable, reproducible experiment in awareness, what do you find?
>
> "There is a subtle essence that pervades all reality," begins one of the most famous answers to that question. "It is the reality of all that is, and the foundation of all that is. That essence is all. That essence is the real. And thou, thou art that."
>
> In other words, this observing Self eventually discloses its own source, which is Spirit itself, Emptiness itself. And that is why the mystics maintain that this observing Self is a ray of the Sun that is the radiant Abyss and the ultimate Ground upon which the entire manifest Kosmos depends. Your very Self intersects the Self of the Kosmos at large—a supreme

> identity that outshines the entire manifest world, a supreme
> identity that undoes the knot of the separate self and buries
> it in splendor. (Wilber, 1996, p. 199)

I am Earth and her animals and plants. I am this splendid evolving universe. I am an expression of the very spirit of God. And so are you. Our problem is that so few of us really know the truth. So few really know who we are. Our religious, mental health, and educational establishments have failed to the extent that they do not support our journeys into self-knowledge. The horrifying truth is that most often they impede it. Unitive psychology seeks to remedy this pathological ignorance by unifying our understanding of ourselves. The architecture of the soul is the model of that unification. As each of us comes into focus in that architecture, our respective souls will be healed, and that health will be experienced as wholeness, and that wholeness will be known as holiness. T. S. Eliot said that the end of all our exploring brings us to the place we started, but now knowing the place for the first time. Thomas Berry once told me that the order of Creation, the order of Salvation, and the order of Beatification must identify. Our Source, our present existence, and our destiny are one. In honor of Ken Wilber's influence upon *The Architecture of the Soul*, I will give him the last words:

> [Y]ou are exactly where you were prior to the beginning of
> the whole show. With a sudden shock of the utterly obvious, you recognize your own Original Face, the face you had
> prior to the Big Bang, and the face of utter Emptiness that
> smiles as all creation and sings as the entire Kosmos—and it
> is all undone in that primal glance, and all that is left is the
> smile, and the reflection of the moon on a quiet pond, late
> on a crystal clear night. (Wilber, 1996, p. 43)

Bibliography

Listed works shown with an asterisk (*) are those from which I have excerpted or quoted in this book. The publisher and I express gratitude for permission to include quoted passages from those works.

*Alcoholics Anonymous (1976). *Alcoholics Anonymous.* New York: Alcoholics Anonymous World Services, Inc.

*Alcoholics Anonymous (1978). *Twelve Steps and Twelve Traditions of Alcoholics Anonymous.* New York: Alcoholics Anonymous World Services, Inc.

*Albon, S. L., Brown, D., Khantzian, E. J., and Mack, J. E. (eds.). (1993). *Human Feelings.* Allendale, NY: The Analytic Press.

Amen, M.D., D. G. http://www.brainplace.com/bp/brainsystem/limbic.asp.

American Psychiatric Association (1987). *Diagnostic and Statistical Manual of Mental Disorders* (3rd ed.). Washington, D.C.

American Psychiatric Association (n.d.). *Diagnostic and Statistical Manual of Mental Disorders* (4th ed.). Washington, D.C.

Baker, R. A. (1992). *Hidden Memories.* Buffalo, NY: Prometheus Books.

*Bateson, G. (1972). *Steps to an Ecology of Mind.* London: Jason Aronson.

Bateson, G. (1979). *Mind and Nature: A Necessary Unity.* New York: Bantam Books.

*Bateson, G. (1991). *A Sacred Unity.* New York: Collins.

Butz, M. R. (1995). "Chaos Theory: Philosophically Old, Scientifically New," *Counseling and Values* (Vol. 39, No. 2, p. 84).

Bowers, K. S. (1987). "Intuition and Discovery," in *Theories of the Unconscious and Theories of the Self*, R. Stem (ed.). New York: The Analytic Press.

Brack, C. J., Brack, G., and Zucker, A. (1995). "How Chaos and Complexity Theory Can Help Counselors to Be More Effective," *Counseling and Values* (Vol. 39, No. 2).

Briggs, J. and Peat, F. D. (1989). *Turbulent Mirror*. New York: Harper & Row.

Campbell, J. (ed.). (1976). *The Portable Jung*. New York: Penguin Books.

Caws, P. (1987). "How the Body Becomes a Self: A Response to Kemberg," in *Theories of the Unconscious and Theories of the Self*, R. Stem (ed.). New York: The Analytic Press.

*Chamberlain, L. (1995). "Chaos and Change in a Suicidal Family," *Counseling and Values* (Vol. 39, No. 2, p. 117).

*Chang, C. (1962). *Wang Yang-Ming*. New York: St. John's University Press.

*Chodorow, J. (1991). *Dance Therapy and Depth Psychology*. New York and London; Routledge.

Cloos, H. (1954). *Conversation with the Earth*. New York: Alfred A. Knopf.

Cohen, M. J. (1993). "Integrated Ecology: The Process of Counseling with Nature," in *The Humanistic Psychologist*, pp. 277–295. World Peace University.

Colbert, E. H. (1955). *Evolution of the Vertebrates*. Science Edition. New York: Wiley Liss.

Colbert, E. H. (1965). *The Age of Reptiles*. New York: W. W. Norton.

Creature Features (n.d.). National Geographic Explorer, Special Edition. Discovery Channel.

DeCaussade, J. P. (1966). *Abandonment to Divine Providence*. New York: Doubleday.

*Edelman, G. M. (1989). *The Remembered Present: A Biological Theory of Consciousness.* New York: Basic Books.

Etkin, W. (ed.). (1964). *Social Behavior from Fish to Man.* Chicago: University of Chicago Press.

*Feinstein, D. and Krippner, S. (1988). "Personal Myths—In the Family Way," in *Family Myths,* S. A. Anderson and D. A. Bargarozzi (eds.). New York: The Haworth Press.

Fortune, D. (1935). *The Mystical Qabalah.* London: Ernest Benn.

Fox, W. (1995). *Toward a Transpersonal Ecology.* Albany: State University of New York Press.

*Gelatt, H. B. (1995). "Chaos and Compassion," *Counseling and Values* (Vol. 39, No. 2, p. 108).

Gleick, J. (1987). *Chaos: Making a New Science.* New York: Penguin Books.

*Goldsmith, E. (1993). *The Way: An Ecological World View.* Boston: Shambhala.

*Goodall, J. (1986). *The Chimpanzees of Gombe.* Cambridge: Belknap Press, Harvard University Press.

Gould, S. J. (1989). *Wonderful Life.* New York: W. W. Norton.

*Grobstein, C. (1974). *The Strategy of Life.* San Francisco: W. H. Freeman.

Grof, S. (1985). *Beyond the Brain.* Albany: State University of New York Press.

Hamilton, V. and Moses, B. (1988). *In the Beginning: Creation Stories from around the World.* San Diego, New York, London: Harcourt, Brace, Jovanovich.

*Hart, W. (1982). *The Art of Living: Vipassana Meditation as Taught by S. N. Goenka.* Singapore: Vipassana.

The Hatherleigh Guide to Psychiatric Disorders (1996). New York: Hatherleigh Press.

*Huyghe, R. and Ikeda, D. (1991). *Dawn After Dark.* New York and Tokyo: Weatherhill.

*Ikeda, D. (1982). *Life: An Enigma, a Precious Jewel.* Tokyo: Kodansha International.

Ikeda, D. (1985). *Buddhism and the Cosmos*. London: MacDonald.

Ivey, A. E., Ivey, M. B., and Simek-Morgan, L. (1993). *Counseling Psychotherapy: A Multicultural Perspective* (3rd ed.). New York: Allyn & Bacon.

*Jacobi, J. (1959). *Complex Archetype Symbol*. New York: Princeton University Press, Bollingen Series.

Jaynes, J. (1976). *The Origin of Consciousness in the Breakdown of the Bicameral Mind*. Boston: Houghton Mifflin Co.

*Jung, C. G. (1960). *The Structure and Dynamics of the Psyche* (Vol. 8). New York: Princeton University Press.

Jung, C. G. (1961). *Collected Works* (Vol. 4). New York: Bollingen Foundation.

Jung, C. G. (1966). *Two Essays on Analytical Psychology*. New York: Princeton University Press.

Keating, T. (1986). *Open Mind, Open Heart*. Warwick, NY: Amity House.

*Kellert, S. R. and Wilson, E. O. (eds.). (1993). *The Biophilia Hypothesis*, Washington, D.C.: Island Press. See especially Atwood, L. E. "The Sacred Bee, the Filthy Pig, and the Bat out of Hell: Animal Symbolism as Cognitive Biophilia."

Kelly, K. (1992). "Deep Evolution: The Emergence of Post Darwinism," *Whole Earth Review* (Vol. 4, p. 20).

Lectures on the Sutra: The Hoben and Jurvo Chapters (1978). Tokyo: Nichiren Shoshu International Center.

LeDo, J. (1996). *The Emotional Brain*. New York: Simon & Schuster.

*McCormick, A. and McCormick, M. D. (1997). *Horse Sense and the Human Heart*. Deerfield Beach, Fla.: Health Communications.

*McGoldrick, M. (1995). *You Can Go Home Again*. New York: W. W. Norton.

Macy, J. (1991). *World As Lover, World As Self*. Berkeley: Parallax Press.

*Magnin, T. (1999). "Meeting At the Crossroads," *Science and Spirit* (April/May, Vol. 10, No. 1).

*Makra, M. L. (1961). *The Hsiao Ching*. New York: St. John's University Press.

Manheim, R. (1969). *Kabbalah and Its Symbolism*. New York: Schocker Books.

*Margulis, L. (1982). *Early Life*. Boston: Science Books International.

Margulis, L. and Guerten, R. (1991). "Two Plus Three Equals One," in *Gaia 2: Emergence*, W. I. Thompson (ed.). Hudson, NY: Lindisfarme Press.

Margulis, L. and Sagan, D. (1986). *Microcosmos: 4 Billion Years of Microbial Evolution*. New York: Simon &.Schuster.

*Margulis, L. and Sagan, D. (1995). *What Is Life?* New York, London, Toronto: Simon & Schuster.

Margulis, L. and Schwartz, K. (1982). *Five Kingdoms*. San Francisco: W. H. Freeman.

*Masson, J. M. and McCarthy, S. (1995). *When Elephants Weep*. Delta Books.

*Maslow, A. H. (1964). *Religions, Values and Peak-Experiences*. New York: Penguin Press.

May, R. (1988). *Physician of the Soul*. Amity, NY: Amity House.

Moms, D. (1965). *The Mammals*. New York: Harper & Row.

Moms, D. (1969). *The Human Zoo*. New York: McGraw-Hill.

*Moore, T. (1992). *Care of the Soul*. New York: Harper Collins.

*Morris, D. (1967). *The Naked Ape*. New York: Dell.

Myers, G. E. (1987). "Introspection and the Unconscious," in *Theories of the Unconscious and Theories of the Self*, R. Stem (ed.). New York: The Analytic Press.

Neumann, E. (1954). *The Origins and History of Consciousness*. New York: Princeton University Press.

The New Jerusalem Bible (1985). New York: Doubleday.

Odenwald, S. (1983). "The Decay of the False Vacuum," *Astronomy* (Nov. 1983, p. 66, on-line).

Odenwald, S. (1984). "The Planck Era," *Astronomy* (March 1984, p. 66, on-line).

*Odenwald, S. (1987). "Beyond the Big Bang," *Astronomy* (May 1987, p. 90, on-line).

Odenwald, S. (1991). "Einstein's Cosmic Fudge Factor," *Sky & Telescope* (April 1991, pp. 362–366, on-line).

Odenwald, S. (1993). "Galaxy Redshifts Explained," *Sky & Telescope* (Feb. 1993, on-line).

*Odenwald, S. (1996). "Space-Time: The Final Frontier," *Sky & Telescope* (Feb. 1996, pp. 24–29, on-line).

*Odenwald, S. (1997). "The Big Bang Was Not an Explosion!," Washington Post, Horizon section, May 16, 1997 (on-line).

*Okakura, K. (1991). *The Book of Tea*. Tokyo, New York, London: Kodansha International.

*Oparin, A. I. (1953). *Origin of Life*. New York: Dover Books.

Page, G. (n.d.). *Monkey in the Mirror*. PBS.

Peck, M. S. (1983). *People of the Lie*. New York: Simon & Schuster, Inc.

*Peterson, D. and Goodall, J. (1993). *Visions of Caliban*. New York: Houghton Mifflin.

Pope, C. H. (1955). *The Reptile World*. New York: Borzoi Books, Alfred A. Knopf.

*Pope John Paul II (1979). *The Redeemer of Man: Redemptor hominis*. Boston: St. Paul Books.

Pope John Paul II (1987). *On Social Concern*. Boston: St. Paul Books.

*Pope John Paul II (1994). *Crossing the Threshold of Hope*. New York: Alfred A Knopf.

Pope John Paul II (1995). *Lift Up Your Hearts*. Ann Arbor, Mich.: Servant.

People of the Forest: The Chimps of Gombe (1991). Discovery Channel.

*Roszak, T. (1992). *The Voice of the Earth*. New York: Simon & Schuster.

Roszak, T., Gomes, M. E., and Kanner, A. D. (eds.). (1995). *Ecopsychology: Restoring the Earth, Healing the Mind*. San Francisco: Sierra Club Books.

Rothberg, D. and Kelly, S. (1998). *Ken Wilber in Dialogue*. Wheaton, Ill.: Quest Books.

Russell, P. (1979). *The Brain Book*. New York: Penguin Books.

*Russell, Robert Jay. (1993). *The Lemur's Legacy*. New York: G. P. Putnam's Sons.

*Sagan, C. (1977). *The Dragons of Eden: Speculations on the Evolution of Human Intelligence*. New York: Ballantine Books.

*Sahtouris, E. (1989). *Gaia: The Human Journey from Chaos to Cosmos*. New York: New Age Pocket Books.

Satir, V. (1988). *The New People Making*. Mountain View, Calif.: Science & Behavior Books.

Seltzer, W. J. (1988). "Myths of Destruction: A Cultural Approach to Families in Therapy," in *Family Myths*, S. A. Anderson and D. A. Bargarozzi (eds.). New York: The Haworth Press.

Sessions, G. (1985). *Deep Ecology*. Salt Lake City: Peregrine Smith Books.

Sharpe, K. (1997). "The Creative and Purposeful God in a Big Bang Universe," *Journal of Ultimate Reality and Meaning*.

*Sheldrake, R. (1991). *The Rebirth of Nature: The Greening of Science and God*. New York: Bantam Books.

*Smith, H. (1958). *The Religions of Man*. New York: Harper & Row.

*Spezzano, C. (1993). *Affect in Psychoanalysis*. Hillsdale, NY: The Analytic Press.

*Staune, J. (1999). "Beyond the Horizon: On the Edge of Physics," *Science and Spirit* (April/May, Vol. 10, No. 1).

*Stevens, A. (1993). *The Two Million Year Old Self*. College Station: Texas A&M University Press.

*Strum, S. C. (1987). *Almost Human: A Journey into the World of Baboons*. New York: W. W. Norton.

Thomas, L. (1992). *The Fragile Species*. New York: Charles Scribner's Sons.

*Townes, C. (1999). "Gathering of the Realm: The Convergence of Science and Religion," *Science and Spirit* (April/May, Vol. 10, No. 1).

*Tucker, M. E. and Grim, J. A. (eds.). (1994). *Worldviews and Ecology: Religion, Philosophy and the Environment*. Cranbury, NJ: Associated University Press.

Tzu, L. (1961). *Tao Te Ching*. New York: St. John's University Press.

Wertheim, M. (1999). "Lonely Planet: An Interview with Steven Weinberg," *Science and Spirit* (April/May, Vol. 10, No. 1).

White, C. (ed.). (1990). "Social Justice and Family Therapy," *Dulwich Center Newsletter* (No. 1). Lower Hutt, New Zealand.

Wilber, K. (1995). *Sex, Ecology, Spirituality: The Spirit of Evolution.* Boston: Shambhala.

*Wilber, K. (1996). *A Brief History of Everything.* Boston: Shambhala.

*Wilber, K. (1997). *The Eye of Spirit.* Boston: Shambhala.

*Wilber, K. (1998). *The Marriage of Sense and Soul.* New York: Random House.

Wilber, K., Engler, J., and Brown, D. (1986). *Transformations of Consciousness.* Boston: Shambhala.

Wilbur, M., Kulikowith, J. M., Robetts-Wilbur, J., and Torres-Rivera, E. (1995). "Chaos Theory and Counselor Training," *Counseling and Values* (Vol. 39, No. 2, p. 129).

*Wilson, E. O. (1992). *The Diversity of Life.* Cambridge: The Belknap Press of Harvard University.

*Young, D. (1991). *Origins of the Sacred: The Ecstasies of Love and War;* New York: St. Martin's Press.

Zeller, M. (1975). *The Dream.* Boston: Sigo Press.

*Zoeteman, K. (1991). *Gaiasophy.* Hudson, NY: Lindisfarme Press.

Index

About the Author

ALBERT J. LaCHANCE, PH.D., LADC, CAS, DAPA, has written and spoken widely on the subjects of psychology, addiction, spirituality, and ecology. Since 1991, he has run Greenspirit: The Center for Counseling and Consciousness, in Manchester, New Hampshire, where he has counseled individuals, families, and groups, and has consulted organizations regarding interpersonal dynamics. Prior to this, he worked with Thomas Berry for five years at his Riverdale Center for Religious Research. Dr. LaChance is an American Academy certified Addiction Specialist in the areas of sex addiction and chemical dependency. He is a clinical associate of Dr. Patrick Carnes, and a member of the National Council of Sexual Addiction and Compulsivity, the American Psychotherapy Association, and the National Association of Alcohol and Drug Counselors. He is also a licensed Addictions Counselor in the state of New Hampshire.

Dr. LaChance has authored several books, including *Embracing Earth: Catholic Approaches to Ecology* (co-authored with John E. Carroll) and *Jonah: A Prophecy at the Millennium,* a fourteen-hundred-line mystical poem springing from the work of T. S. Eliot. His book *Greenspirit: Twelve Steps in Ecological Spirituality* represented a major contribution to the fields of psychology, spirituality, and ecology when first published in 1991. A revised and updated edition of this book, titled *Cultural Addiction: The Greenspirit Guide to Recovery,* will be published by North Atlantic Books in 2006. Dr. LaChance has also contributed chapters to a number of books, including *The Other Half of My Soul: Bede Griffiths and the Hindu-Christian Dialogue* (edited by Beatrice Bruteau), *The Greening of Faith: God, the Environment, and the Good Life* (edited by John E. Carroll, Paul Brockelman, and Mary Westfall), and *Sister Earth: Ecology and the Spirit* (by Dom Helder Camara), to which he contributed the introduction.

Dr. LaChance has taught world religions from high school through to the graduate level, at several colleges, including the University of New Hampshire, New England College, and the College for Lifelong Learning. He has spoken nationally for Cross Country University on the topics of sex addiction, and psychology and spirituality, and has conducted numerous local workshops. He has also been interviewed widely on television and radio, in newspapers, and in magazines. Dr. LaChance continues to write, counsel, teach, and speak on all the above topics.